Getting Through The Day

Getting Through The Day

Strategies for Adults

Hurt as Children

NANCY J. NAPIER

W. W. Norton & Company • New York • London

First published as a

Norton paperback 1994

The text of this book is composed in 11½|13½ Fournier 285,
with display set in Ellington.
Composition and manufacturing by the Haddon Craftsmen, Inc.
Book design by Ruth Mandel.

Library of Congress Cataloging-in-Publication Data

Napier, Nancy J.
Getting through the day : strategies for adults hurt as children | Nancy J. Napier.
p.   cm.
Includes bibliographical references and index.
ISBN 0-393-31242-9
1. Adult child abuse victims—Rehabilitation.   I. Title.
RC569.5.C55N38   1993
616.85'822390651—dc20   92-38849

W. W. Norton & Company, Inc.
500 Fifth Avenue, New York, N.Y. 10110
www.wwnorton.com

W. W. Norton & Company Ltd.
Castle House, 75/76 Wells Street, London W1T 3QT

2 3 4 5 6 7 8 9 0

To the memory of Fran, a survivor of childhood abuse, who lived her life the best she could, long before anyone knew how to help her . . .

and

To the Healing Spirit that pervades our shared emotional world.

Contents

8   *Contents*

Acknowledgments

It is impossible to name individually, and acknowledge adequately, the therapists who have inspired, taught, and guided me in ways that have influenced the writing of this book. All have added immeasurably to my understanding and skill as a clinician. For those specialists who work with the effects of dissociation, in particular, my gratitude is immense. In one-to-one discussions, and through their books, conference presentations, and tapes, they have helped me develop a greater sense of competency and mastery when treating abuse survivors who may be in the throes of chaotic dissociative events.

I would also like to thank my friends and colleagues, who are continuing sources of inspiration and support. They have encouraged me to keep going each time my own healing has demanded deepening and applauded each time I've taken a new step, both personally and professionally. Without their presence, it would have been an impossible journey. In particular, my gratitude goes to Beverly Decker, whose clinical acumen and caring friendship have supported me through many challenging moments. Karen Peoples continues to be an important companion along the way of spiritual and personal development, and our many long talks—about the shared unconscious and the urgent need for all of us to open our hearts more than we ever imagined possible—have supported and nourished me deeply. Maxine Stein provides the jolts I need, now and then, to wake up and take another step, and I am grateful for that. Pat Jobling continues to be, as has been true for many years now, a special muse who both triggers my thinking and creativity and forces me to go ever deeper into understanding of unconscious and dissociative processes. And, to Garrett Oppenheim, continuing thanks for an openness and willingness to help me explore states of consciousness that have contributed greatly to what I am able to share with others.

To the many workshop participants with whom I have had the privilege of interacting over the years, and to my clients especially, go thanks for your willingness to share your hope, creativity, pain, fears, shame, and anger so openly. Your demands that I be *real* have encouraged me to deepen my own healing, and your courage in facing the effects of childhood trauma has been an inspiration. Without you, there would be no book.

I am pleased to have this opportunity to continue my collaboration with Susan Barrows Munro. Her support and feedback are a constant source of renewal. My agent, Jim Levine, has provided the gentle prodding and encouragement that proved essential in getting this book written. Without his efforts, I doubt the work would have been completed.

Getting Through the Day

1

Introduction

I KNOW I'VE BEEN HURT, BUT NOW WHAT?

This book emerged from a deep feeling of necessity, from my response to workshop participants, clients, and people I've never met personally who have called me for help in dealing with what sometimes seems to be the overwhelming challenge of just getting through the day as a survivor of childhood abuse. It is for those of you who may have experienced any kind of childhood hurts, for your therapists, and for others who are close to you. It is meant to provide information and exercises that will help make the days, the nights, and the relationships easier to manage. It's hard to be someone who was hurt badly as a child. It's challenging to be your therapist. It can be confusing to be someone who loves you.

As a therapist, I didn't intend to specialize in treating adults who were abused as children. This focus emerged organically, both from my interest in hypnosis and altered states of consciousness and from my experiences in dealing with my own childhood pain. As a psychotherapist, I have spent a number of years helping abuse survivors deepen their healing process. Along the way I have had to deepen my own healing. I have had to learn to acknowledge, tolerate, and deal with my own hurts more profoundly than I ever would have imagined possible. Only in this way have I been able to accompany others into the dark, hidden places of childhood with any sense of comfort, safety, and confidence.

Healing from childhood hurts is a powerfully involving process. It can be so even when the hurts you experienced weren't extreme. In fact, you may be someone who grew up in a home where the adults were overwhelmed with responsibility and simply ignored you. You may have lived in a home where a relative was ill and the family focused all its energy on caretaking, with little left over for your needs. Or you may be someone who was adopted at birth and subsequently has struggled with abandonment issues at the very core of your being. Perhaps you are one of many people for whom the psychological abuse of being ongoingly devalued as a child was so pervasively devastating that it felt as if you were being beaten regularly. Or, you may, in fact, have been brutally attacked, sexually assaulted, and psychologically battered.

Whatever your experience, it is your own and it is unique to you. It can't be compared to anyone else's. As you read the following chapters, please be gentle with yourself and find your *own* truth in the ideas shared here. Whatever your truth may be, it is your key to freedom. It will tell you how you came to be the person you are and what you need to resolve and change in order to become the person you want to be.

Sometimes abuse survivors need to know "nuts and bolts" kinds of things other people take for granted, such as "How do I give myself permission to say, 'No'?" Others have an urgent need to learn to handle intense feelings that may sweep over them from out of the blue. Still others want to know how to manage the urge to let themselves become numb whenever difficult feelings begin to emerge.

Underlying all the work that adults who were hurt as children must do to reclaim their lives is the following premise: Even as you work on resolving wounds that occurred in the past, you also need to be able to deal with your world in the present. I've heard many people say, "I can't stand to live like this! What will make me feel better, safer, more competent *today?* I know I have to look at the past in order to heal, but how do I get through the next hour?"

It matters how you live today. If you can't get through this moment, then what happened to you in the past can seem pretty removed and unimportant. Some days may be easier to handle than others. Yet childhood hurts affect how you experience yourself and the world and can make it difficult to maintain a sense of internal equilibrium when life presents you with its inevitable challenges. Knowing some strategies that will help make today an easier place to live can be of real value.

You may be more than familiar with those times when it's hard just to get out of bed in the morning or to care about the fact that your boss wants that project tomorrow. So what if there's a house to clean or groceries to buy? What can any of that really matter, you might think, when deep inside you are dealing with the experiences of a child—you—who was traumatized and whose feelings are flooding your awareness?

Reclaiming and processing your unacknowledged or unremembered past is one of the fundamental tasks of healing. Another is healing the wounds that exist in your relationships with other people. Equally important to the process of becoming a healthy adult in the present is learning to cope effectively with your current day-to-day life. It's important to be safe in the present, to be able to take care of yourself adequately, and to know what to do if you begin to feel overwhelmed by the demand that you act like an adult when you really feel like a three-year-old.

Childhood Trauma and Dissociation

In recent years, many books have been written for abuse survivors. What few of them emphasize, though, are the special issues that arise when a traumatized child uses *dissociative* strategies to deal with hurtful experiences. In Chapter 2, we'll explore the effects of trauma-based dissociation in some detail. For now, I want to emphasize that, while this book will be helpful to *anyone* dealing with the effects of childhood hurts, it will also offer information and strategies for those who are struggling with the special challenges that arise when a child dissociates herself from her body, her feelings, her thoughts or urges.

It's hard enough to deal with having been hurt by people who had more power than you. It's especially challenging when you may not even remember that you were hurt and yet find yourself terrified of certain kinds of people and situations for no apparent reason, or feel like a little kid when a moment ago you felt just fine as the grownup you are.

Dissociation exists along a continuum, ranging from normal, non-traumatic dissociative moments to the profound dissociation that often occurs with extreme abuse and results in multiple personalities.[1] We'll look at this kind of dissociation in detail in the next chapter. At one end of the continuum are the natural dissociative moments we all experience, whether we've been hurt as children or not. Some of the most common include staring off into space while riding in a train or bus; becoming so absorbed in music or reading that we don't hear someone enter or leave the room; losing track of time—time flies when we're having fun and drags when we're bored; focusing so intently on something that we don't realize we've hurt ourselves—later, when a bruise appears, we're sometimes baffled about how it got there until we remember that we walked into a table while having a heated conversation with a friend.

As we move along the dissociative continuum, we begin to find people who used dissociative strategies in protective ways when they were children. In order to deal with a difficult experience, for example, we use dissociation to forget certain aspects of what happened even as we remember others. Many adults abused as children use this kind of dissociation. Perhaps you can think of a time in your own childhood when you remember certain events, but you know there are gaps in your memory.

An example from my own life comes to mind. I vividly recall the day my sister came home from the hospital as a newborn. I ran home from kindergarten, thrilled that I would finally get to meet the new member of the family. I recall what the day looked like. I remember how I felt. I have vivid images of seeing my sister for the first time.

What I didn't recall until many years later, in therapy, was how I felt when my father moved out of our house just weeks before my sister was born. In fact, I had no recall of how it felt to have him gone, or how we said goodbye, or even of the few visits he made after he left. It was only after working in therapy that these memories became available. As a young child, I just couldn't handle the deep hurt of losing my father, so I put all my conscious awareness and feelings into the arrival of my sister. I dissociated everything that had to do with him during that time.

Problems arising from trauma-based dissociation can be hard to understand and frightening for abuse survivors and those close to them. What many people have found is that information about dissociation and how it operates in adult life provides a sense of relief and mastery. A good portion of this book is dedicated to providing that information. Also, it helps to understand that trauma-based dissociation operates in such a way that there is a continuing potential for confusion and unanticipated reactions in adults who used this strategy as children.

The more you understand about dissociation, the more empowered you can feel in your day-to-day life. For example, it helps to know that it may be because of dissociation that your moods switch quickly and without warning. Knowing that dissociated feelings are as pure as the first time you felt them in childhood can help you get through some of those particularly difficult moments when intense feelings unexpectedly surface. Also, it helps to know that panic and nightmares often accompany the emergence of previously unremembered events from childhood. Realizing this can help if you suddenly find yourself awash in panic and can't identify any external, present-day source for your feelings. The more you know, the greater your ability to handle the present moment effectively.

Even if you didn't use dissociative processes to deal with life in a troubled family, chances are that, if you were abused physically, emotionally or sexually, your normal childhood development was affected. Most of us who grew up in a dysfunctional family of *whatever* kind struggle with how to be effective adults in the present. Whether experiences were traumatically dissociated or not, we all have inner child parts, some of which relate to unresolved childhood events. Whether emotions were traumatically dissociated or not, most of us need to learn better ways to deal with our feelings once they are triggered and we find ourselves reacting in ways that may not be good for us. Learning new strategies that help us live more consciously within ourselves, whatever our original strategies for dealing with childhood hurts, can make it easier to get through this moment, right now.

If you *did* use dissociation to get through an abusive childhood, you may already be working with a therapist who has helped you place yourself along the dissociative continuum. Or you may be reading about dissociation for the first time and be curious about how it may operate in the unconscious strategies you developed as a child to cope with hurtful experiences.

About Therapy

Everything that is offered here is meant to help you get through the many moments that make up the present day. What this book can't do is take the place of solid, ongoing psychotherapy with a professional who is trained in working with abuse survivors. Self-healing is a wonderful, natural process that is available to all of us, but it can't take us through the blind spots we don't even know how to recognize. For most people, it is too hard to do this work on their own. With a competent therapist, you have the help of an informed guide. Your therapist becomes a safe "container" for the powerful feelings that are part of healing and provides a secure context within which you can go deeper and with more certainty than you ever could on your own.

At this point, I'd like to share with you my bias: eventually, in order to heal fully from the effects of childhood abuse, you will benefit from going into therapy, if you haven't already. It's impossible to explore and resolve, by yourself, the interpersonal wounds that occur when childhood hurts are brought about by the very people you needed to trust, perhaps the very people on whom your survival depended.

If the idea of therapy frightens you, that's natural. Most of us feel uncertain and downright scared the first time we walk into a therapist's office. In Chapter 12, we'll explore what to expect, what to look for, and how to envision what a therapy process might involve.

In addition to therapy, it is important to have support from friends, and from others who are also healing from childhood hurts. You may find that you get a great deal of comfort from ongoing support groups. Or you may discover that groups are too much for you to handle and that you prefer to have a few close friends you can talk to about what is happening in your life. It's helpful to know that a therapist alone can't provide all the support you may need as you go through your process of healing. The same applies to your partner, if you're involved in a relationship. No one person can be enough.

What This Book Offers

This book draws upon many approaches and offers strategies geared especially to help you cope today, right now, with the parts of yourself that hold dissociated and unprocessed memories of hurtful experiences. For example, you can learn how to send child parts to safe places "inside" when you have something to do that is particularly scary for them. We'll explore ways in which you can soothe yourself when you get upset. Using self-hypnosis and guided imagery exercises, you can tap into future resource states and learn how it feels to be confident and to have a sense of safety that may have been lacking when you were a child. Tapping into these kinds of experiences can give you a boost, some hope, when things feel stuck and too big to handle. We'll also look at some ways to deal with compulsive behaviors that push you into action when sitting with your feelings could be more healing.

Some of the exercises and ideas in the book address the difficult journey into your memories. All are offered with the hope that you will keep in mind that whatever you experienced, then, happened a long time ago. You survived. You are here, now, and that is proof that you can get through the work of remembering and coming to terms with your past. Your early experiences didn't do you in then, and they won't now. Yes, it will be frightening and at times it will *seem* to be overwhelming. The key thing to keep in mind is that feeling over-whelmed, terrified, enraged, or filled with despair is just that: a feeling, a remembering. You can let it flow through your awareness without having to *do* anything with it. You can also learn to pace yourself gently, so that you aren't recreating the overwhelmed feelings of childhood by pushing yourself too hard.

You'll also learn how to remind yourself that *feelings are to be taken seriously but not literally*.[2] This is an important theme throughout the book. Your feelings need to be acknowledged and owned. That doesn't mean, however, that the feelings are literally related to what's happening in the present. Just because you feel that the noise in the hall is your father coming to rape you doesn't mean it's true. What may be true is that you hear something that *reminds* a part of you of your father's approach. As you understand better what's happening to you, you can choose to deal with it in new ways. You might decide to focus your awareness on the fear and listen to the child part that is experiencing it, rather than hide in a closet. When you are able to choose to listen and bring your adult awareness into the fear, your ability to stay focused in the present increases.

A word here about memories. Currently, there is a controversy brewing over the reliability of memories that come into conscious awareness during the process of healing from childhood abuse. While memory seems to be context-specific, being constructed and recon-structed over time, it is essential to keep in mind that memory content is but one element of a cluster of symptoms in abuse survivors. Taken together, body states, self-destructive behaviors, interpersonal diffi-culties, flashbacks, and memory content give a clearer picture of the origins of childhood abuse.[3]

There is also controversy over the use of hypnosis in the retrieval of dissociated memories. When misused, hypnosis may involve abuse and the potential retraumatization of survivors.[4] Many therapists using hypnosis have found that survivors are able to recall memories that previously were not readily accessible. While this may be true, some professionals fail to recognize that "forcing" clients to bring into awareness a memory that the unconscious has wisely pushed away from conscious recall may create a very real risk of retraumatization. Because of the aftereffects of abuse, which include a tendency to comply with the perceived demands of authority figures, survivors are vulnerable to potential revictimization.

Hypnosis is a proven and useful tool in the process of healing—when it is used wisely, and in conjunction with what is emerging naturally from a survivor's unconscious.[5] Then it can become a means for deepening work with memories that have begun to surface, increasing a sense of safety, promoting communication between and among parts of the self, and accessing profound states of comfort. Some of the chapters that follow contain exercises that draw on hypnotic techniques. These approaches are *self*-hypnotic in nature, and respect the slow and steady pace of remembering and healing that can convey empowerment rather than retraumatization. I want to encourage you *never* to use self-hypnosis to push yourself; instead, let it become a gentle support that can help you accomplish many of the tasks of healing.

Many clinicians who work with adults who were abused as children, and who move with these clients through the experience of bringing an unremembered event into consciousness and resolving it, support the view that—even if details of specific memories aren't accurate—working with them may bring relief, and that's what matters. Seeing the change that can occur when a memory surfaces and is resolved often creates a willingness to suspend judgment and work with whatever emerges. If you are willing to accept the fact that some of your memories may be more like metaphors than an accurate recall of actual events, then it doesn't matter how memory works. What matters is that you are able to tap into a way of representing past abuse that, when explored and resolved, brings relief. We'll explore issues around memory in more detail in Chapter 8.

For now it's enough to know that when you have strategies available that allow you to go into old feelings and memories with your *adult*, present-day awareness, you are on the road to freedom. As long as your childhood experiences remain unconscious and unprocessed, you risk falling into them at any moment, any time. Until your history is integrated into your adult consciousness, it holds the potential to pull you back to unremembered terror and pain, without your really knowing what you are feeling or why. We'll pay particular attention to dealing with unresolved pockets of childhood memories in the chapters on containing feelings, using mindfulness to reorient to the present moment, and understanding what things trigger you into these difficult feelings and responses.

Sometimes it may feel as though your whole day were lost in the past. For example, some abuse survivors have a hard time experiencing themselves as grownups. If this is true for you, even if you can't find a sense of yourself as an adult, you *can* increase your ability to observe your feelings and to deal with them. Over time, you'll discover that something has changed, that you feel more present and aware than you did before. It doesn't matter whether or not this developing state of mind feels "adult." What does matter is that its presence in your ongoing consciousness can make a big difference in how you handle your daily life.

If you are gentle with yourself and allow yourself to pace the healing process in small, slow steps, you can free yourself from the hold the past has had on you. We'll explore ways to slow yourself down, ways to pace your exploration and discovery that allow you to validate your right to be treated with respect, especially by yourself.

A theme that comes up often in therapy with survivors of childhood abuse is *the slower you go, the faster you get there.*[6] There is a great deal of wisdom in this simple statement. Because abuse creates feelings of being overwhelmed, it's not unusual for survivors to move into high gear and overwhelm themselves as part of their recovery process. While it's understandable that you want to be free of the pain and struggle that may characterize your present life, going slowly will allow you to learn how it feels to respect your needs for safety. You'll have a chance to experience mastery, to go through a natural process of absorbing new information at your own pace, a pace you can manage.

In fact, one of the things that survivors often don't learn is how to modulate their feelings. If this applies to you, you may be one of those people who experiences things as all-or-nothing, as profoundly intense or intensely boring. You may, at times, be swept along with whatever feeling happens to be triggered by some event, experiencing the chaos that can arise when things are out of control. Or you may have learned how to numb out, turn to stone or wood, and not feel anything at all. In Chapter 6 we'll look at some strategies for changing how you learned to cope with your emotional world.

Whether you work on your own or with a therapist, you will find that the capacity you have for dealing with the hurts of childhood fluctuates. For example, sometimes you'll feel strong and ready to plunge in deeper. Those are times when you may want to use some of the exercises in the book that allow you to discover more about what you feel. At other times, you may want to hide in a good book or stay in bed. At times like those, you are telling yourself that you have taken in enough for now. You need time to process things unconsciously. Listen to yourself. Be gentle. Remember that, as a child who was hurt, you had to shut down what you really felt. You had to handle more than you were equipped to manage. You had to learn not to know what you really needed or wanted. Part of healing is allowing yourself to reawaken to what feels right for you in the present moment. What a precious gift it is to be able to say, "Yes, I know what I want right now," and then be able to give it to yourself. Cherish that gift. It's important and you're worth it.

About Choice

An underlying theme of this book is *choice*. It's about the constant opportunities offered in daily life for you to choose to heal. As a child, you chose to survive—and you did! It was one of the few choices available to you. So, even if you feel your life isn't working the way you would like it to today, you *did* succeed at your most important decision—to get through it all. *Now, each moment of your adult life offers new choices.*

It can be hard, though, because now you know, ahead of time, that choosing awareness can mean that you will have to tolerate some pretty uncomfortable feelings. As we explore some ways to deal with the discomfort, keep in mind that this book is intended to be a bridge between where you are right now and your most fundamental, unconscious impulse to be whole. Deep in your psyche, outside conscious awareness, is the urge to heal, to reclaim your whole self—to be free of the confines of a troubled and unprocessed past.[7] The information and strategies offered here can help you connect with that place inside.

This is no fix-it manual, though. Rather, you might think of it as a *map*. You are the explorer of your own, unique internal terrain. No one knows you better than you know yourself, even though there will be times when you can't see yourself clearly and need the help of your therapist. All the exercises and strategies offered here are general suggestions. They tap into a vast store of creativity and wisdom we each carry inside: the unconscious.[8] Your unconscious can take in these strategies and make them specifically useful to you. Your own creativity can embrace what's meaningful to you and leave the rest. You may find that, as you work with some of the suggestions in the book, your own ability to come up with strategies that help you get through the day will increase.

The most basic choice any of us faces as we delve more deeply into childhood hurts is deciding that *we* are the source of our own healing. We must become the source of our own rescue, even as we allow an experienced guide, such as our therapist, to help us discover this truth about ourselves. No one outside us is going to come along and say, "Ah yes, I see. I can make it better for you now,"—not a friend, not a fellow traveler on the healing journey, not even a therapist.

Instead, each of us must take the journey *inside ourselves* and deal with what we find there. *We can have help, but no one can do it for us.* Each chapter offers ideas and tools that will help you to choose healing to connect to the present moment even as you continue to open up the hurts of a painful childhood.

Each time you choose to deal with your feelings in healthy ways, to remove yourself from abusive situations, or to take some time to get in touch with the memories, feelings, thoughts, or body sensations associated with some past hurt, your inner strength increases. You add to this foundation of strength every time you make the choice to reclaim your feelings, each time you acknowledge and own what happened to you and how it has affected your life.

It's also important to know that you can choose to have moments away from the healing process. Healing goes on even if you're having a good time doing something else, or a quiet time with a good book, or a blank time staring at the television set. That deep place in your psyche, the part of you that always seeks to heal, carries on the process no matter what you're doing. *It's your decision to heal that matters.* Once that is made, the process carries itself along.

Spirituality

We'll also touch on issues of spirituality. The world of meaning and the unknown become part of the healing process as abuse survivors ask themselves, "Why did this happen to me?" "How could there be a God if little children are allowed to be hurt?" Although such existential questions are inescapable, they can't really be answered in any final way. What they *can* do is open the door to your spiritual beliefs and how you explain your world.

Many times survivors report how important it was, and is, for them to have an awareness of parts of themselves that are spiritual in nature. These parts may be experienced as guides or as wise men or women who lead the way to brighter, happier places inside a hurt child's internal, imaginary world. Sometimes they were the only source of hope for a young child who had nowhere else to turn.

I do not limit the concept of spirituality to a belief in God or religion. Spirituality may be expressed in your connection to nature or in a belief that you are part of a larger organism of consciousness, even if you leave the nature of that organism undefined. Spirituality can refer to anything that gives you a sense of connection to something more than yourself, to something that brings meaning to your life. If you are interested in tapping into this aspect of your consciousness, some strategies are offered to help you do so.

The Collective Unconscious

Another aspect of the healing process that touches on things spiritual is the concept of the collective unconscious.[9] The existence of a collective unconscious was proposed by Carl Jung, the famed psychologist who originally was a student of Freud. According to Jung, within the collective unconscious are all the thoughts, feelings and accumulated experiences of humanity throughout time.[10]

All of those who have healed, who have led full and vital lives, have contributed their consciousness to this collective. While we are compelled to be aware of our shared pain as human beings, we can also tap into our collective potential to heal and be whole. Every person who has come before you, and who has healed and moved beyond the confines of a hurtful childhood, has blazed a trail you can follow unconsciously.[11] All the learnings and accomplishments of those who have healed already are available within your own unconscious and can guide you on your way. Also, it's important to realize that each time you make a choice to go deeper into your own healing you contribute something to the collective, as well. All who come after you draw unconsciously on *your* achievements.

An example of how the collective unconscious may be currently affecting those of us who were hurt as children is the recent emergence of people who willing to publicize their victimization on television and in other media. At the same time, therapists have made available information that previously would have been found only in professional publications or at professional conferences. All of the public revelations and books demonstrate an important message: *no matter what happened to you, or what strategies you used to get through those experiences, you are not alone.*

It's as though a tide of awareness were sweeping through our collective unconscious. The increasing understanding of dissociative processes in childhood, supported by public revelations from people who have recovered memories in adulthood, has been tremendously freeing for people who suffered child abuse. It is helpful to be reminded of the fact that there are people who have healed successfully. They demonstrate an important truth about what happens when there is abuse: the way you are today is the result of a reasonable response to an extraordinary and unreasonable situation, and there is a way to move out of an accommodation to trauma into new, more effective strategies.

Successfully facing a hurtful past isn't the only challenge where help from our shared, collective unconscious is useful. Those who have accomplished the journey of healing have faced the often frightening and uncomfortable experience of *change*. They have answered for themselves the difficult questions we all must confront when we choose to heal: What will I lose if I get better? What are the risks of becoming aware of my full self? What will change? Am I entitled to a different life? Will I know myself?

The thing to keep in mind as you ask yourself the many questions that must arise as you journey into healing is that you can draw on the wisdom others have found in their struggles with these important issues. Because of this collective wisdom, there is hope. Once any one person accomplishes something, it becomes possible for the rest of us.

SPECIAL ISSUES FOR MULTIPLES

Those of you who may have multiple personalities, something we'll explore in more detail in the next chapter, face challenges unique to your situation. In each chapter, I have made special comments you may wish to consider as you work with the material offered. For you, especially, it's important to have an ongoing dialogue with a therapist as you delve more deeply into your world of multiplicity. This sharing can create a greater sense of stability and equilibrium in the present, as you explore your inner process.

Some Technical Notes

The cases described throughout the book are all composites. None represents an actual person. They have been compiled from many different individuals I have met or heard about in workshops, as clients, on the telephone, at conferences, and in clinical discussions with colleagues. In fact, any resemblance between the people described in this book and actual living persons is purely coincidental. These composites have been created to describe general patterns found in the lives of people who used dissociation as their primary survival strategy in childhood.

If your story doesn't seem as dramatic as some of those described in the following chapters, fine. Allow yourself to remember that we each are the star of our own dramas. No one else's story can match your own for its immediacy and impact on your life.

As you explore the approaches offered in this book, please keep in mind that each of us is unique. What works for one person may not feel relevant for another. Your style of going inside and discovering what's bothering you, quieting an inner child's terror, or encouraging yourself to get out of bed and go to work will be unique to you. It's fine—even better than fine—to take these suggestions and change them to create what works best for you. Not all strategies are appropriate for every person. It's a good idea to read each one and see how it feels as you consider it. If it seems right, great! If it doesn't, that's fine, too.

Throughout the book I refer to "him" and "her" randomly. Girls and boys alike are hurt as children, and this book is for the women and men alike who are struggling to free themselves from a painful past.

There are notes for each chapter. They are at the back of the book and provide references and further details on ideas presented in the chapters.

The reference list at the back of the book includes titles on healing, abuse recovery, spirituality and related subjects. Inevitably, it will be out of date almost as soon as this manuscript takes final form. Thankfully, so many good books come on the market regularly that it's impossible to keep up with them all! It is certain that I will have missed some that are special to you and that you have found to be immeasurably helpful. I apologize for this and hope that you will pass along to your friends the names of books that have served you well in your journey of recovery.

In *Recreating Your Self*, I mentioned that I was certain my ideas would change and evolve from what I wrote there a number of years ago. I want to say the same thing here. This book contains what I understand to be helpful *at this point in time*. I am bemused to say that I have received calls about things I said in *Recreating Your Self* that I understand differently now. Such is the price of putting ideas in print. They get frozen in time when, in fact, the ideas presented in any book are really the seeds of new thoughts to come.

And so, I hope you will allow your *own* ideas to continue to evolve as you move through your healing process. There are no *right* answers. There are only the answers we have available now. It is certain that new and more effective ways to heal the hurts of childhood will emerge, and probably in the very near future. It's an exciting time to be in a healing profession, but it's also a time that requires all of us to have open minds and open hearts.

2

Dissociation and Childhood Hurts

WHEN YOU HAVE A NEED NOT TO KNOW

If you happen to be one of those people who used dissociation as a way of coping with a difficult childhood, you unconsciously chose a good survival strategy. Unfortunately, what works so well in childhood creates all kinds of problems in adult life, so the process of healing involves learning to use other kinds of psychological coping strategies when you're afraid or distressed. For example, instead of dissociating feelings of fear by unconsciously pushing them outside your awareness, you may begin to identify the feeling as fear. Then you can take steps to soothe yourself, which we'll explore in detail in later chapters. For now, it's helpful to know that there are options to dissociative strategies, now that you are grownup and can be more aware of what you feel as you move through your day-to-day activities.

If you find yourself saying, "Hey, I wasn't hurt *that* badly as a child. None of this applies to me," let yourself be curious about the following information anyway. What I will talk about in terms of multiple personalities represents an exaggerated version of how parts operate unconsciously in many of us who had difficult or unhappy childhoods. Also, if you have friends who were traumatically abused as children, this information may help you understand the unique challenges they face and what life is like for them on a daily basis.

In this chapter we'll consider the essential concept of *parts of the self*, especially as they operate within a context of *dissociation*. It's important to remember, here at the beginning, that dissociation is a normal part of human consciousness. Most of us dissociate at least some of the time: when we daydream; when we drive along and enter "highway hypnosis," where we don't realize how far we have gone or how we got there; when we become deeply engrossed in a task and seem to lose awareness of our surroundings; and at countless other times when our attention wanders or blanks out.

Parts of the Self

Central to the coping strategies presented in this book is the concept of *parts*. Instead of our each being a unified, one-dimensional being who is the same all the time, most of us have a rich world of shifting states of mind, moods, and behaviors within which we define ourselves. Different parts of us are activated in response to environmental and interpersonal events, as well as to internal fantasies, fears and memories.[1] These parts may represent or encompass mood states, performance states, talents, fears, unresolved hurts and unremembered experiences from childhood, as well as spiritual awareness.

For example, when you are at work and things are going well, it's likely that you are able to access certain skills and states of mind that are appropriate for the task at hand. Generally, the parts of you that support your present-day adult capacities are active when you are at work, unless something goes wrong. When this happens, you may access parts of your consciousness that encompass feelings of fear or vulnerability, instead of a sense of adult competence.

When you're not at work or engaged in other day-to-day responsibilities, you might naturally be in an entirely different mood, engaging in entirely different behaviors that, in turn, activate other parts of you. For instance, when you're at home you might experience parts that are more relaxed and casual than when you are at work—unless "home" was a place where you were hurt. If this were the case, you might find yourself accessing parts that are anything but relaxed. These are times when your present-day self seems to fade into the background and inner child parts emerge. It's when inner child parts come into the foreground of your experience that dealing effectively with day-to-day living can become a difficult challenge. We'll look at strategies for dealing with these parts in later chapters.

Parts of the Self and the Dissociative Continuum

It's important to keep in mind that, even if you didn't use dissociative strategies as a means of coping with a difficult childhood, you do have parts. Much of what will be described here will help you move towards a more *conscious* awareness of these aspects of your inner world.

As I mentioned in Chapter 1, dissociation happens along a continuum. At the nontraumatic end are the many experiences of daydreaming and floating off into reverie I have described above. Other kinds of normal dissociation include forgetting where you put your keys, momentarily forgetting why you got up to go across the room, or becoming so absorbed in a book that you don't hear what is going on around you. At the other end of the continuum are various trauma-based kinds of dissociation that sometimes result in multiple personalities.[2] If you live with this kind of dissociation operating in your consciousness, daydreams may become terrifying fantasies, experiences of reverie may become frightening flashbacks, and forgetting may be profound. Hours or whole days may be lost. The thread of a conversation with someone may disappear midstream, leaving you with embarrassing gaps in memory. Sometimes, at this traumatic end of the dissociative continuum, you may even discover yourself walking along a city street without knowing why you are there or even how you got there.

At this point, let me make a "therapy" comment. Throughout this chapter, I'll have lots to say about multiple personalities and all the variations of this kind of trauma-based dissociation. As you read, I would ask you to keep in mind the "medical school syndrome." This is a situation in which medical students become convinced they have every disease or condition they learn about as they go through their coursework. It's no different when you read about psychological responses to trauma. Some of you will decide, based on what you read here, that you must have multiple personalities.

Diagnosing this response to trauma requires a good deal of expertise and must be done by a mental health professional who specializes in the treatment of dissociative disorders. Self-diagnosis may *feel* right, but you really need an expert opinion (and, preferably more than one).[3] Much of what I say in this book will relate to many of you who were hurt as children and who used dissociative processes to protect yourselves *but who do not have multiple personalities*. With that caution in mind, let's continue our exploration of the dissociative continuum and its relationship to the many parts each of us has inside.

One area where you might think you have multiple personalities, and don't, concerns parts of the self of which you aren't consciously aware. Each of us has certain parts we aren't aware of at times. Think of a time when you have been asked to take on a specific role, such as teacher, boss, lover, or friend. When you step into one of these roles, chances are that you bring with you a particular state of mind, way of thinking, or way of feeling. When the situation changes, and you have to take on another role, such as when you go home from work or when you're shopping, your mood probably shifts and your way of thinking and behaving may be quite different. *The key thing that allows you to function within a context of constancy and predictability is your ongoing sense of I-ness, a continuous sense of self, that exists throughout your experience of your different parts.*

For a person with multiple personalities, this continuous sense of *I-ness* may be lacking. For example, at the extreme end of the dissociative continuum, the shifts from one part of the multiple's self to another may bring with them complete shifts in the sense of *I-ness*. Instead of a continuous sense of "being me even though I'm in a different mood now," the multiple's *sense of self* shifts as parts are activated and then replaced by other parts coming and going in and out of overt expression. When this happens, one part may experience itself as a young girl with her own name and qualities, while another part may feel it is a strong, aggressive teenage boy. This isn't true for all multiples, but does illustrate the classic form of multiple personalities, as described in *Sybil* and *The Three Faces of Eve*.[4]

Identifying multiple personalities is complicated by the fact that sometimes there *is* an ongoing sense of *I-ness*, even though the inner parts are as strongly defined as in the multiple where a continuous sense of self doesn't exist. It is because of these subtleties and complexities that anyone suspecting he or she may be a multiple needs to be diagnosed by a professional who is especially trained to do so.

Identifying Your Parts

Take a moment to identify some of the parts of yourself of which you are aware. For example, you might be aware of how you behave and feel when you are at work and things are going along well. When you are identified with this part of yourself, your body may feel a certain way, and you may be in a particular state of mind that feels solidly effective. On the other hand, there may be times when you are aware of a child part of you that is frightened or that keeps you from doing things you want and need to accomplish in your present-day life. If possible, let yourself notice which parts feel as though they have developed into resources in your current life, and which feel as though they hold old, unresolved feelings and behaviors from the past. Learning to identify and interact with the many parts of you that comprise your complex self is one of the major tasks of healing and of becoming more competent and empowered in the present.

If you are a multiple, your task is the same, but it is complicated by the way your parts may experience themselves as separate people. Because of this, communication with your parts may, at first, feel as though it is with individuals as well defined as yourself. The thing to keep in mind is that, in the long run, all the parts of you constitute *one* psychological being, no matter how powerful, individual, or separate they may feel at this point. As you heal, one of your goals is to work towards an ever-increasing, continuous sense of *I-ness*.

In nontraumatized people, most parts of the self operate unconsciously and automatically. They usually cause no difficulties as they shift in and out of our ongoing experience; in fact, they add to the richness of our capacities and the depth of our emotional lives. Things change in how we are affected by our inner parts, though, when they are characterized by unresolved, and perhaps unremembered, hurts we experienced as children. When this happens, a powerful dynamic is put in place where certain parts of the self are created to hold, encompass, or embody certain aspects of abuse. In time, they may become autonomous, to some degree or another, and exert a tremendous influence on daily life, for both multiples and non-multiples.

These dissociated parts are created so that the child who is being hurt doesn't realize the extent of the trauma she is experiencing. For instance, many adults who were traumatically abused as children describe floating up in the corner of the room, or on the ceiling above their bodies, during abuse experiences. It's not unusual to hear these trauma survivors talk about how they learned to shut out any sensations in their bodies while they were being beaten or otherwise abused. I've heard people describe a moment in childhood when they felt a knot of determination develop inside: They would stop feeling anything, and they absolutely would *not* let their abusers know they were hurt. At this point, it's important to emphasize that most of these individuals did *not* develop multiple personalities, even though they successfully used dissociative processes to protect themselves during childhood trauma.

The step from using dissociation to block out certain aspects of experience to developing multiple personalities is a seemingly small but powerfully meaningful one. For example, one of the pervasive—and tragic—responses to the extreme childhood abuse or neglect that result in multiple personalities is the relentless, if unconscious, presence of *terror*. Imagine, for a moment, what it would be like if you were frozen with terror *all the time*. For most multiples, somewhere inside there is a constant state of terror that affects every moment of every day, even if the multiple is totally unaware of it on a conscious level. For this reason, the multiple's extreme form of dissociation must accomplish a dissociation *of the self from itself,* rather than from aspects of a traumatic experience. In other words, it is a little girl pretending that the abuse is happening to someone else.[5]

Because they were able to draw on the dissociative process unconsciously, abused children who dissociated didn't realize, thankfully, that some part of them *did* know how the abuse felt. Some part of them *did* experience the hurt. Another part felt the rage. Yet another felt the despair of betrayal, even when the abused child believed he was completely numb in body and spirit. The underlying reality is that, even when these parts are outside a child's conscious awareness, they are present inside. Their pain, terror, and other unconscious, unresolved experiences can significantly affect life during adulthood, a subject we'll return to in later chapters.

Alters, Ego States, Subpersonalities, or Fragments?

There are many names for parts of the self, all of which represent states of consciousness encompassing feelings, thoughts, memories, beliefs, sensations, or impulses to act. There are *alters,* a term used early on to describe the parts that exist when there are multiple personalities arising from trauma.[6] Then there are *ego states,* those naturally occurring parts of the self that are somewhat autonomous and arise with or without trauma.[7] The term *subpersonalities* is similar to ego states. Subpersonalities exist in all people and embody all varieties of feelings, capacities, unresolved issues, spiritual orientations and consciousness, and wisdom.[8]

Alters, ego states, and subpersonalities are all theorized to exercise some degree of autonomy within the human psyche, but do not necessarily arise from trauma alone. Again, the underlying premise is that there is a natural multiplicity operating in all people, and these are some of the ways that natural multiplicity has been described.[9] Finally, there are *fragments,* the many partially developed parts of the self that contain certain aspects of your experience or feelings, but do not have autonomous power to affect your behavior the way more developed parts may have.[10] Again, you most assuredly do *not* have to be a multiple to have fragments of unprocessed childhood experience within your consciousness.

An illustration of how a fragment may operate might be helpful here. The process described is similar to one you might initiate with any parts that hold awareness from your childhood, however subtle or powerful they may be. With a fragment, you may be dealing with a part of you that encompasses a previously unremembered portion of a childhood experience. For example, you may consciously remember a time you went to the beach with your family. Your recollection is that it was a good day, that you enjoyed yourself, but you find that, even as an adult, you have an irrational fear of the ocean. You may discover, held within an unconscious portion of your awareness, a fragment encompassing an unremembered, unprocessed piece of the beach memory: your brother held you underwater that day until you were afraid you would drown. Once you connect with this unremembered piece of the memory, you may discover that the fragment disappears and that the content it held becomes part of your ongoing adult awareness.

Essentially, it doesn't matter what you call the many parts of yourself. What's important is that you develop a means of connecting and communicating with them. On a day-to-day basis, it's easier to deal with life's ongoing challenges when you have available the full array of your psychological capacities for doing so.

Trauma-Based Dissociation

One of the real benefits of learning how trauma-based dissociation operates in your life in the present is that this new information can affect how you interpret some pretty confusing or terrifying internal experiences. For example, it's not unusual for people who are dissociated as a result of childhood trauma to be convinced that they are crazy, which they most emphatically are *not*. Examples of experiences you may have if you used dissociation to cope with early childhood trauma include: unexpected mood shifts, as though suddenly you were "injected" with a feeling; hearing voices arguing in your head; and feeling unaccountably frightened by what seems to be nothing at all.

The symptoms resulting from trauma-based dissociation are more pronounced for multiples than for people who didn't take the extra, unconscious step of creating parts so well defined that they function as separate personalities. For all adults who used dissociation to cope with childhood hurts, multiple or not, understanding why certain things happen as they do, or why the mind works as it does, can be profoundly reassuring and freeing. The more you understand, the more mastery you may experience in the present.

It's important to know that, for many adults who were hurt traumatically as children, the effects of trauma-based dissociation can be healed.[11] New strategies for dealing with feelings and challenges in your present-day life can be learned, and in time you will feel less need to move *away* from a conscious awareness of what is going on inside you.

In general, some people are more naturally dissociative than others. Think back for a moment: Were you one of those kids who day-dreamed all the time when you were at school? Did you seem just to "go off"? Did people always have to "call you back" to the present? Did anybody else in your family go around with his "head in the clouds"? For those who are naturally dissociative, being abused or traumatized—even in a natural disaster, for example—is likely to produce greater dissociation.[12]

While we still don't completely understand how dissociation is created or how it works, we do think that it is a capacity that is passed along in a family.[13] It may be that some children learn to dissociate by observing parents who use this mechanism, or it may be that there is an inherited tendency to dissociate under stress. People who are excep-tionally talented at hypnosis are good dissociators.[14] So are people who have rich fantasy lives, as well as those who are able to go into altered states of consciousness with ease. For most people, some de-gree of dissociation is natural and normal.

Dissociative Barriers

Depending on the degree of trauma a child undergoes and the degree of overwhelming experience that must be kept out of conscious awareness, the "barriers" that separate parts of the self may be more or less "transparent" or "opaque."[15] You might imagine these barriers as blank screens that can be pulled down between parts of the self. The screens serve to keep the parts from being aware of one another, and especially from the "core" personality of the abused, or otherwise traumatized, child.[16]

As a symbol to represent degree of dissociation, you might imagine that the greater the amount of dissociation, the more opaque the screens will be. Conversely, the less powerful the dissociation required in childhood, the more transparent will be the screens between parts of the self.

Keep in mind that the screens are only a symbol to represent a dynamic process of consciousness. In fact, the whole idea of "barriers" is just that: an idea. It's a way of expressing activities in the unconscious that we don't really understand. What we do know is that some kind of dissociative process serves to keep certain awarenesses from becoming conscious. In this way, for example, a child can go to school and perform quite well, without any conscious awareness of the terror she experiences at home. Another child may fly into rages without any conscious knowledge of the helplessness that lies beneath the rage. Or the child may overeat, or become a compulsive reader, as a means of not knowing what he really feels inside. All of these strategies operate as barriers to *conscious* awareness.

An important part of the healing process is to move from a more to a less dissociated way of dealing with psychological reality. In other words, as healing progresses, the screens become more transparent, so that you are increasingly able to see what's behind them. As the strength of the dissociative barriers lessens, you'll know more about what you really think, feel, and want to do. The more transparent the screens, the more complete your awareness of what's going on inside. If you were severely abused as a child, chances are the screens that represent your dissociative barriers will tend to be quite opaque. Your conscious awareness probably contains what is on *this* side of the screen. To a greater or lesser degree, what exists on the other side of the dissociative barriers is unknown to you.

If you are a multiple, you may have more or less opaque barriers between your inner parts. Stepping over that line to create more defined personalities within you doesn't automatically mean that you have no recall of your childhood or of the feelings, thoughts, and urges your parts encompass. What you *will* find different in your process is that the separateness of various thoughts, feelings, and urges to behave in certain ways are more purely held within particular parts of you.

Non-multiples, as well as multiples, may have total amnesia for certain events, as dissociative barriers from childhood continue to operate in the present day. For example, you may remember the story of the former Miss America, Marilyn Van Derbur, who had a "day child" and a "night child" inside her.[17] During her childhood, and throughout much of her young adult life, Marilyn apparently had no knowledge that she was an incest victim. Her "night child," the part of her that experienced the abuse, was completely dissociated from her conscious awareness. It was as if the screen were pulled down and locked in place. In her ongoing, conscious awareness, she was the "day child," a bright, happy little girl. She had no hint of the presence of the night child until her memories began to return when she entered therapy well into midlife. All she knew before then was, as she got older, her life wasn't working and something was terribly wrong.

It's important to emphasize, again and again, that even this level of forgetting doesn't necessarily indicate that multiple personalities exist. Part of what makes dissociation so effective is that this level of forgetting or lack of awareness is quite possible, even when it doesn't go to the extreme of creating the underlying psychological response that results in multiple personalities.

Dissociative Barriers in Multiples

For some people who *do* have multiple personalities, the dissociative barriers may be so firmly locked into place that there is no awareness at all between the everyday self and other parts of the multiple. When the barriers are this complete, one part of a person might perform as a prostitute with a definite sense of "I-ness," or identity, and a particular way of being in the world. When this part is at work, her life is predictable, her personality consistent. People who know her in this role recognize her and can describe what she is like as a person. Later, when the "prostitute" goes inside and a "business self" comes out into the daytime world, a whole different mood state and personality are present. People who know the business self would be able to describe her. She, also, has a sense of "I-ness" and a predictable way of being. Then, at home, when a child part comes out and wanders around the house or curls up in a ball on the floor, this child part experiences her own sense of "I-ness" that is also consistent with her feelings, thoughts, and behaviors. If you were this multiple, with dissociative barriers so firmly in place, you might not even be aware of these different parts of yourself.

When the dissociative barriers are this impermeable, it's often impossible, at first, for the various parts to realize that they are different aspects of one person's consciousness. In fact, it is deeply upsetting to some multiples to think that there may be a time when the parts will become more "integrated" and less distinct as seemingly separate individuals. As far as the parts are concerned, the fact that they all exist within one body, and yet may have different and conflicting goals, isn't a problem and isn't something they want to change.[18]

As we move along the dissociative continuum, there are degrees of how defined, or separate, a multiple's personalities seem to be. While for some multiples the barriers are as complete as described above, for others the screens are locked in place and yet are somewhat transparent. When this is the case, certain parts may be aware of one another, and yet unaware of still others. The everyday self, also, may be conscious of the existence of some parts and not others. Because each multiple is unique, the dissociative barriers among parts will be unique, as well.

If you are a multiple, sometimes you may feel unable to prevent another part from being "out" in the world, even as you realize, consciously, what is happening. Even if you have this kind of awareness, you may have experiences of losing time, of not knowing what you've been doing for the last minutes or hours, and lapses in awareness during conversations with people. This can occur when still other parts, ones you don't know about, operate outside your conscious awareness altogether.

What is difficult is that knowing another part is "out" may not give you the power to control the behavior, thoughts, or feelings of that part. Once the healing process has begun, and you have developed some transparency within the dissociative barriers, you can more readily set up communication and collaboration among your parts. This is an important aspect of recovering from childhood trauma, whether you are a multiple or not, as internal communication and collaboration support the curtailing of self-destructive or dangerous activities in which parts may engage. It also supports the process of creating safety and bringing dissociated memories and feelings into conscious awareness.

For some individuals who are diagnosed as multiples, there may be an ongoing sense of "I-ness" most of the time. This "co-consciousness" indicates that the dissociative barriers among many of the parts are fairly transparent. For others, there are likely to be parts of the self that are outside conscious awareness and that function somewhat autonomously.

For some adults who were traumatized as children, it is painful, but relatively easy, to define and express early childhood experiences of which they have been vaguely aware all their lives. For others, it can be terrifying to bring into conscious awareness dissociated feelings, thoughts, and memories that have operated so naturally that they've never been defined consciously. When a therapist asks about dissociative phenomena such as losing time, the client may ask, "Well, doesn't everybody?" Dissociating is all the person has known. It's like asking a fish, "How's the water?" The fish is likely to answer, "What water?"

Whether you are a multiple or not, when you've lived your whole life using dissociation as a protection against feeling intolerable pain or anger or experiencing the effects of overwhelming physical abuse, it's easy to take for granted the switches from one mood state to another, the sometimes seemingly bizarre behaviors that are so unlike you, and the lost time. As healing proceeds, things settle down and it's not nearly as unnerving as it may be in the beginning.

For those of you who have multiple personalities, the process of beginning to make dissociative barriers more transparent can be truly harrowing. If you weren't aware before of the existence of parts of the self that may present themselves as separate entities, the process brings this into consciousness. Sometimes, at first, it can be pretty scary to discover that there are aspects of your personality that believe they aren't part of you at all. For example, there may be male parts in a woman, and vice versa. There may be children, animals, and other kinds of beings. Some of the parts may be extraordinarily enraged. Others may quiver with fear or curl up in a ball in an attempt to disappear. Some may hate you and want to hurt you. Others may be so young that they have no way to communicate their distress other than to cry.

For some multiples, then, the beginning of the healing process may create a feeling that everything is getting worse. The important thing to remember is that things settle down as healing proceeds. In fact, as you learn to experience your therapy process as a safe place in which you may explore your inner world, experiences of "switching" from part to part helter-skelter and generally feeling out of control lessen. As the dissociative barriers become increasingly transparent, communication among parts increases, with the result that a consensus of goals and behaviors may be reached that makes daily living more manageable.

In essence, the experience of multiplicity has as much variability and individuality as does any other aspect of human development. While there are general similarities in how dissociative barriers operate in multiples, the ways in which you will experience them and how your inner world will appear to your conscious mind will be uniquely your own. What is offered here is a general guideline; if your experience is different, trust yourself. An increase in co-consciousness will emerge within whatever metaphor, imagery or understanding works for you.

The Importance of Volition

Officially, dissociation is defined in Webster's as, ". . . a split in the conscious process in which a group of mental activities breaks away from the main stream of consciousness and functions as a separate unit, as if belonging to another person." It is, in a sense, a process that allows us to move in and out of different states of consciousness. When we do this voluntarily, as in meditation and self-hypnosis, dissociation can have wonderfully positive effects. For example, self-hypnosis—which represents a conscious, volitional use of dissociation from the body—can be an effective way to ease physical pain. In meditation, you can enter an altered state where you seem to be less connected to your thoughts and feelings; again, this is volitional. *Both of these processes are different from the unconscious, involuntary dissociation that takes a trauma victim outside her body so she won't feel the pain or away from her thoughts and feelings so she won't know how terrible her experience was.*

We can use dissociative processes voluntarily when we deliberately get in touch with inner child parts, or various subpersonalities, and discover new understandings and awarenesses. It's different, though, when the feelings embodied by a child part inside "come over us" involuntarily. This is what happens with the dissociative process operating in so many adults hurt as children: they shift unexpectedly into a part that knows about the abuse. At times like these, the dissociative process can be frightening, eliciting feelings of helplessness and confusion.

Perhaps the single most important distinction between parts whose origins are naturally occurring and nontraumatic and those that arise as a result of trauma is the presence, or lack, of a sense of *volition*.[19] As we'll see in Chapter 3 on therapeutic dissociation, there are many ways that parts of us operate unconsciously to convey positive and negative states of mind and feeling, and to prompt certain behaviors. Most of the time, though, we can shift away from these parts if we choose to do so or if we have something that needs our attention and we can't afford to be sidetracked by a child part.

Take a moment, now, to think of a time when you may have become aware of some upsetting feelings that came up during an interaction with a friend or family member. Maybe you decided to have a dialogue with an inner child part, or to go deeper into your feelings, or to come out of them so you could focus on another activity. Did you find that you were able to choose what you wanted to do? Did you succeed, at least enough to allow yourself to get some freedom from or resolution of the feelings?

For many people who were hurt as children, it's possible to make these choices with some degree of success. And so, even if you can't shift completely away from unpleasant or distressing feelings, you might at least be able to keep some sense of yourself and remember that you will feel better eventually. It's different if you are a multiple or a survivor of childhood trauma who has fairly well-defined inner parts. When this is the case, it may feel as though you have no control over your moods.

Let's consider how you automatically respond to distressing experiences that may come up in day-to-day living. For example, let's say someone hurts your feelings and you get in touch with a deep sense of shame. Are you able to talk to yourself, reassure yourself, and shift away from the shame after a while? Or do you find that you just can't seem to shift gears once you're into it, that you have to ride it through because nothing seems to make it any better? What if you fail a test and end up feeling horrible? Do you stay stuck in that horrible feeling, caught up in a part of you that is characterized by a sense of worthlessness, or are you able to engage in some activity that shifts your mood into another, more competent-feeling part of yourself? Or do you suddenly move out of a bad feeling into a space where there is no distress at all and you feel numb or calm? Do you ever find that you are suddenly immersed in an awful feeling and have no idea at all where it came from, or that your mood has shifted suddenly and you don't know why?

One of the reasons to do the work of healing is to make conscious what is held by the dissociated parts that encompass these responses. Then you have much more choice, much more volition as to how you experience the many parts of yourself. Your parts can work with you, and you can work with them, to create the quality of life you'd like to have.

Who's Responsible for My Actions, Anyway?

One of the important reasons for exploring issues of volition and dissociation is to answer the difficult questions about who is responsible for the actions of any given part of a person's entire psychological system. Multiples often have the experience of feeling that parts are taking control and doing things that get the everyday personality into trouble. This does happen. Yet, once you are in a therapy setting where expectations and boundaries are carefully set and explained, a lot of this kind of difficulty ceases.

Experience has shown that many multiples actually can control their behavior in surprisingly effective ways, once they learn that it is possible to do so.[20] So often, things *feel* out of control, and the behavior of dissociated parts seems to prove it. Think back for a moment to a time when you may have done something and then felt foolish or wished you hadn't done it, or a time when you got into trouble for something you didn't realize you had done. Once you understood what went wrong, you were in a better position to act differently the next time. It's the same with dissociated parts. Once you understand what happened, you can take steps to set up internal controls and strategies that help prevent parts from taking control in self-destructive ways.

A good example was presented at a recent conference on multiple personalities.[21] It involved a young woman who had been hospitalized after being arrested for shoplifting lipstick from a department store.

During therapy, the therapist explored which part of her had sho-plifted. The part responsible turned out to be a 14-year-old girl who wanted to wear makeup. The patient was a grown woman who didn't like to wear makeup of any kind, and the 14-year-old was furious. Through a process of communication and negotiation, arrangements were made for the 14-year-old to wear makeup at a certain time of the day, when it was all right with the everyday adult self. As is common in these cases, the woman hadn't realized that the 14-year-old part existed inside her and was baffled when she found herself with lipstick in her pocket. Once the teenage part was made conscious, a relation-ship was established and a more constructive day-to-day experience was arranged.

An important premise is that *the whole person is responsible for the actions of every part*. So, if one part begins to engage in some self-destructive behavior, it is up to the overall "system" to take action to stop what is happening. *This applies to non-multiples as well*. In fact, it applies to each and every one of us. Since everybody has parts, it is fair to say that we all have the fundamental responsibility—and capac-ity—to monitor ourselves in ways that allow us to live our present-day lives as constructively and effectively as we can.

Also, it's helpful to know that stress increases the probability that any dissociative strategies you may have developed as a child will be called into play in your adult life. As you move through the healing process, there may be times when you feel more stressed than others. If you notice that you are more dissociated than usual, you may suspect that there are internal or external stressors affecting you. As with any mechanism we use for psychological protection, an increase in dissociation is a signal that something is going on that needs your attention.

Healing and Dissociation

In healing, the purpose is not to stop dissociative processes altogether. Rather, it is to stop unconsciously drawing on nonvolitional forms of dissociation as a protection against knowing your feelings. Instead, you have an opportunity to learn to be present in your body and generally to have an integrated, ongoing awareness of yourself. To be truly safe in the world and to be able to function as the full adult you have the right to be means to be with yourself *consciously*. To have relationships that work means to be aware of what you are feeling, to have the freedom to act constructively on them, and to be able to communicate those feelings effectively to other people.

When you're dissociated as a result of trauma, it can be very difficult to do this, especially if you are a multiple. There may be just too many conflicting agendas, fears, and anger going on all at one time. For example, one child part may want to lash out at anyone who comes near, because to this part closeness means being abused. To another part, one that holds the hurt, for instance, it's unbearable to risk losing someone. This part may cling to people whenever they come close, and that may terrify another part for which the terror of having someone near is just too much to take. This part may feel an urgent need to run away when anyone approaches, emotionally or physically.

With all these mixed feelings going on at the same time, it can be exhausting just to get through the simple events of the day. You have a right to experience life more fully than that. But first you have to be in touch with yourself and how you came to be the person you are. You have to claim a more complete awareness so you can be a fully functioning human being.

It's important to remember that you don't have to have developed multiple personalities to have used dissociation to get through difficult childhood experiences. Keeping the dissociative continuum in mind can help explain why you act as you do at times and can remind you that you may have greater or lesser dissociative barriers at work in your unconscious. And, even if you didn't use dissociative strategies at all as a means of coping with a difficult childhood, you do have parts. Much of what has been described here is useful whenever the healing process demands a more conscious awareness of these aspects of your inner world.

We've been exploring how dissociation is called upon by a traumatized child, nonvolitionally and unconsciously, to get through overwhelming experiences. In the next chapter, we'll explore how the *therapeutic* use of dissociation, engaged consciously and deliberately, can lessen the power of dissociative barriers, help you soothe yourself, and give you tools to make getting through today, right now, easier.

3

Therapeutic Dissociation

A Better Way

In the previous chapter, we explored how nonvolitional, trauma-based dissociation helps some children cope with and survive an abusive childhood. Here, we will explore how the natural, *volitional* processes of dissociation, which occur in everyone, may be used to enhance healing and promote greater mastery in the present. I refer to this approach as *therapeutic dissociation*.

Therapeutic dissociation is but one application of the apparently normal and creative dissociative processes most of us have available.[1] Here, the concept of therapeutic dissociation applies to exercises and techniques that deal with healing childhood hurts and coping with the many ways those hurts may intrude upon and interfere with present-day life. It also encompasses the many ways that mastery may be enhanced in your current life by drawing on internal resources, "rehearsing" accomplishments and changes you wish to achieve, and accessing states of mind that provide new experiences and perspectives. It may involve reverie states, self-hypnosis, meditation, guided imagery, or any other approach that draws on natural dissociative capacities to shift attention from the outer world to an awareness of internal processes.

In the chapters that follow we'll look in more detail at ways you can develop your *adult observer*, an essential aspect of consciousness for being focused and capable in your day-to-day life.[2] It is the perspective of your adult observer that most directly allows you to deal effectively with life's daily challenges and opportunities. Using therapeutic dissociation, you can enhance this part of you by experiencing the difference between this competent, present-day aspect of consciousness and wounded child parts that are stuck in past hurts. In an exercise that follows, we'll touch on one way you can draw on your adult observer to recenter yourself when you unconsciously dissociate into a child state. In Chapter 8, we'll look more deeply at the potential for healing found in the use of therapeutic dissociation to explore the feelings, memories, and behaviors identified with particular inner child parts.

Using volitional, therapeutic dissociation has other benefits as well. For example, developing a stronger adult observer allows you to become more conscious of how your nonvolitional dissociative processes work. Becoming aware of how dissociation operates involuntarily within you can lead to greater mastery and an increased sense of control in the present.

Special Issues for Multiples

Before going further, I'd like to make some comments that apply to those of you who developed multiple personalities as a way of dealing with childhood trauma. First, while this chapter contains a number of techniques for using dissociative processes *volitionally* to support healing, it is important to distinguish these approaches from the ongoing process of therapy that is necessary for resolving traumatic dissociation. The following techniques, in and of themselves, are not sufficient to bring about healing. They will help, there is no doubt about that, but they are not the whole picture.

You may want to use the strategies offered in this book on a day-to-day basis to help you manage your dissociative process in new ways. But it's important to remember that, if you dissociated in child-hood as a result of trauma, involuntary dissociation has become a *habitual* response to stress. And so, at a fundamental level, when faced with distress or seemingly overwhelming challenges, you are likely to follow an internal rule that says something like, *when in doubt, dissoci-ate.*

The goal of this book is *not* to increase that automatic protective response. It *is* to allow you to become more aware of your dissociative process so that you can take some conscious, voluntary control over it and allow it to be useful to you in your healing. Your goal is to *increase* awareness rather than move away from it, and therapeutic dissociation can help you do that.

Some multiples, and their therapists, worry that engaging in exer-cises that involve volitional dissociation will create more parts. So far, inquiries into hypnosis and work with multiples have found no evi-dence that additional parts are created as a result of approaches that use therapeutic dissociative processes such as self-hypnosis, imagery or relaxation exercises.[3]

A MESSAGE FOR NON-MULTIPLES

If you are not a multiple, the exercises shared here will allow you to become aware of parts of yourself that are related to your past hurts. These naturally occurring subpersonalities and ego states may hold powerful, unresolved and unintegrated feelings, responses, and ways of thinking.[4]

As with all approaches having to do with psychological processes, you may find that certain exercises and ideas feel more useful to you than others. It's important to allow yourself to pick and choose what works for you. As you read through the material that follows, allow yourself to be curious about which aspects of therapeutic dissociation may to be particularly useful to you and which may not seem relevant to your needs at this time.

Also, please keep in mind that your ability to use dissociation voluntarily, as a resource, improves as you practice. Of course, getting results that make today easier to manage is a great way to motivate yourself to keep going.

Whereas trauma-based dissociation creates an unconscious, nonvolitional separation from a continuous sense of self, therapeutic dissociation allows you to be aware of yourself in two places at once. When you use techniques of therapeutic dissociation, it's easier to remember who you really are—*a present-day adult*—even as you observe and share the experience of parts of you that are locked in past hurts.[5]

Recentering into Your Present-Day Adult Self

Think of a time when you may have been involved with something at work or out with friends, and everything was going along just fine. Then, all of a sudden, someone said or did something that caused you to feel out of sorts. You may have become afraid, angry, worried about being competent, or catapulted into some other mood state that left you feeling more like a child than an adult. You may recall how much you wanted to reestablish your adult footing again, but you couldn't seem to shift gears back to where you were a few moments ago.

In this exercise, you allow yourself just enough breathing space to enhance the possibility of recentering into your adult state of mind. The key is to allow yourself to shift the vulnerable feelings back to where they really belong—in an inner child part of you—so your adult self can continue to deal with the present-day situation. Once you've succeeded in returning to your adult perspective, *then* you can offer needed support to the child part. Until then, you and your inner child will be drowning together, in feelings, sensations, and compulsions to act that relate to the past rather than today.

And so, focus on a recent time when you may have felt this kind of shift from your adult state of mind into feeling like a child. Allow yourself to imagine, for a moment, that you are experiencing those same feelings right now. Then, ask yourself, "What would it have been like if I had been able to imagine a child part of me that was the source of the feeling?" Pause here for a moment and let an image or "sense" of a child part come to mind. Accept whatever emerges this time. If nothing comes into your awareness, ask yourself, "If a child part *could* come to mind, what would it be like? What would my awareness be right now?"

Then, allow yourself to wonder what it would be like if you could allow the vulnerable or uncomfortable feelings to flow out of you and into that inner child part. This idea is hard for some people, because they don't want to hurt the child by giving it difficult or painful feelings. For now, let yourself experiment with the process, even if you feel guilty about giving the child feelings that are upsetting or painful. Just imagine that the feelings *are* moving from your present-day self and into that child.

The key to the exercise is that, once the feeling is "out there," in the child, you—the present-day adult—can do something to help. What if you could respond to and comfort that child in a soothing and reassuring way? What would help most in calming this part of you right now, or next time this shift occurs? Pause for a moment and explore whatever comes to mind.

Sometimes, what is most helpful is the very fact that you and the inner child part are *sharing the experience.* So often when we are hurt as children there are no witnesses, no one to acknowledge what happened to us. *One of the gifts you can offer to yourself is to become your own witness:* the adult part of you, once you are no longer engulfed in overwhelming childhood feelings, can be there with the child as a kind of supportive presence you may never have had before.

Now, as the next step in the exercise, ask yourself, "How might the experience I recalled earlier have been different if I been able to get back to my adult state of mind in this way?" What circumstances are you aware of that almost always throw you into these childhood feelings? Could you take a moment, now, to have a "mental rehearsal" of the next time you are in that situation? Observe how you will use your increased knowledge of this child part to help you stay centered as your adult self.

Each time you do this exercise it gets easier to identify the feelings, to allow the feelings to flow out to the child part, and to recenter yourself as the present-day adult right then and there, on the spot. At first, though, you may find that it is helpful to have practice time at home, using your imagination to replay events, as you did in this exercise.

For Alexis, an abuse survivor who had been tormented by an older brother throughout her childhood—and never protected by the adults in her family—this use of therapeutic dissociation proved an important element in dealing with a destructive work situation. From almost the first day on the job, Alexis felt insecure and on guard around a particular co-worker, a man who had a job equivalent to hers. Alexis felt her co-worker was trying to undermine her with their boss, which left her feeling vulnerable, angry, and frightened. At first she tried to ignore her feelings, to tell herself that she was overreacting. In spite of her efforts, though, a child part inside was terrified of being hurt, and the fear pervaded Alexis's experience on the job. There were days when she found it hard to focus, no matter how rational she tried to be.

As she learned to put her feelings of fear and frustration into a child part and view the situation from her adult perspective, Alexis discovered where the fear really belonged: in childhood experiences that had never been fully acknowledged or processed. She also realized that her boss played a central role in triggering the fear that she could be undermined or harmed by her co-worker. Tacitly, without ever saying anything, her boss set up competition among his subordinates, and the mood created simply terrified this child part of Alexis.

Over time, Alexis realized that the situation wasn't going to change and she moved on to a job in another firm. She also acknowledged that she had internal healing work to do. She realized that if she hadn't identified and listened to the frightened child part she might have stayed and participated in an unconscious recreation of a painful pattern from her childhood.

For Benjamin, it was different. When he started a new job in a busy clinic in his city, he found it hard to feel he fit in with his co-workers.

It seemed to him that they were unfriendly and didn't really want him to hang out with them. Because of the feelings that were triggered in him, some mornings it was hard for Benjanmin to get out of bed and go to work. He would begin the day filled with dread; it was a struggle just to make it through to the end of his shift.

As he allowed his feelings of rejection to flow into a child part, Benjamin discovered that his current situation tapped into powerful childhood fears of rejection. He was the only child of a relentlessly demanding and critical mother whom he could never seem to please. Because of the dynamics of that early relationship, as well as difficulties in school with other children, who often targeted him as a scapegoat, Benjamin had developed "super radar" for any sign of rejection from people in his present-day life.

Once he identified the child part involved with his fears of rejection and learned more consciously where the feelings came from, Benjamin also realized that sometimes he was seeing signs of rejection where there weren't any. For example, he and his co-workers were extremely busy on the job and didn't have a lot of time to hang around with each other and talk. At certain times during the day, Benjamin might notice one co-worker talking with another and immediately wonder why he hadn't been included. When this child part was activated, he didn't have his adult perspective available, a perspective that would have shown him that they were talking over a project they were both handling.

By regularly allowing his fears of rejection to flow into the inner child part, Benjamin began to feel more comfortable at work. While it didn't work every time, he did feel enough relief that he was able to recognize openings for him to interact with his co-workers. He also became increasingly aware of how painful it had been for him as a child to feel so criticized by his mother and left out by the other kids. This awareness helped him know the difference between his present situation and how it was for him in the past.

SPECIAL ISSUES FOR MULTIPLES

If you are a multiple, it may be difficult simply to "hand over" the feeling to another part that is outside you. The problem with switching into child states is that the child part literally "comes out" or "comes forward" in your consciousness and takes center stage. If the exercise for recentering yourself doesn't work at first, you might experiment with having a caretaker part come and "take the little one inside." Oftentimes, other parts can be conscripted as "helpers" who can bring about some improvements in a situation. It's not important to know how this works; simply ask and see what happens.

Also, once you have identified the child part that has been activated and have imagined that part as being in front of you rather than right there inside you, you might imagine that the child goes off to take a nap in a safe place inside. It's okay to call on a caretaker part for help at this point, too.

Teaching Your Hands to Talk

There are many ways to access inner awareness through the use of therapeutic dissociation, some of which focus on using the body to guide a developing conscious awareness of unresolved childhood hurts and to identify wounded inner child parts.[6] In this exercise, you can allow your hands to guide you to feelings, images, sensations, and memories you need to know that may, as yet, be unconscious. You do so by asking "yes/no" questions.

To begin, find a comfortable place to sit for a while, where you won't be disturbed. You may want to have paper and pen nearby, in case there is something you want to write down after you finish the exercise. Take a moment to focus your attention inside. See how it feels to close your eyes, take a few deep breaths, and just allow yourself to sense what it is like to settle into whatever is supporting your body.

Now, with your elbows bent, hold your hands in front of you so that they are facing each other. Discover what distance between your hands feels most relaxed and comfortable. Usually four to six inches will be about right, but there is no "correct" distance. Do what feels natural.

Next, notice that, in the space of those few inches, you may be able to sense a kind of energy—a push or pull—between your hands. If you don't feel the energy between your hands, that's fine, too. The important thing is that you allow yourself to be curious about what your hands will tell you.

Then, suggest to yourself that if your hands move together, even the slightest bit, or if you feel an urge to move your hands together, that constitutes a *yes* answer. If your hands move apart at all, or if you have an urge to move them apart, that constitutes a *no* answer. If they stay right where they are, you can assume that your unconscious is still processing the question and will give you an answer at another time, perhaps in a dream. When this happens, simply go on to your next question. There is no need to demand, no need to struggle. Just allow whatever emerges to be okay for this time.

The key to this exercise is to stick to the "yes/no" format. You can build on the answers with subsequent questions. For example, you might ask the following series of questions:

- Are the feelings I'm having related to something from my childhood?
- Would it be all right for me to become more aware of the origin of these feelings at this time?
- Am I alone when I'm feeling this way?
- Is there anybody else with me?
- Is it okay for me to see where I am when I'm feeling this way?

(When you ask this kind of question, wait a few moments for your hands to answer and then wait a few more to see if an image begins to form in your mind. If nothing comes, assume that a "yes" answer implies you *will* develop a more conscious awareness of what you seek to recall at a pace, and in a way, that is best suited to your current healing journey.)

As your hands answer the questions, you can focus your attention on any feelings, sensations, or images that come into your awareness.

Once you've gotten a handle on where the feelings really belong, you—the present-day adult—can take some time to soothe whatever distressed child part may be involved. You can also give yourself a few minutes to rethink the situation from your grownup perspective.

*   *   *

This exercise may be done anytime you have something stirring around inside and can't quite get a handle on what it is. For example, Naomi had a friend who had been her confidante for many years. Recently, this friend had met some new people and had begun to include them whenever she and Naomi got together. While Naomi wasn't sure what the problem was, she *was* aware that her stomach would twist up in knots every time she was around these people. It had gotten almost to the point of her not wanting to see her friend anymore, and yet she didn't know how to ask that they get together without the other people.

When Naomi sat down to talk to her hands, she wasn't sure anything at all would come to mind. She was desperate, though, to know why she was distressed and couldn't talk about it, so she went ahead anyway. What she discovered was that the new friends reminded her of three children who were neighbors when she was a child. She hadn't thought of them in many years, and had forgotten the cruel ways they had teased her. What was even more painful, though, was the fact that her parents never protected her from the taunts of these neighbors. Her father would tell her to "toughen up" and "learn to take it." It was hard for Naomi to admit to herself how much she wanted her parents to step in and help her.

By listening to her hands and becoming aware of childhood memories she hadn't processed fully, Naomi was able to deal more consciously with something she needed to resolve from the past. In the present, she recognized that she was waiting for her friend to sense her distress and protect her. Instead, she worked up her courage and told her friend she preferred to spend time with her alone. Naomi was surprised when her friend respected her request with no hard feelings.

SPECIAL ISSUES FOR MULTIPLES

Using your hands to talk to your unconscious can be very helpful in setting up more conscious communication with your internal system of parts. For example, if you are having a rough time at work or in a relationship, and you can't get a handle on which part of you is struggling so, using your hands to talk to parts of you can begin a process of settling down. By asking "yes/no" questions, you can allow parts of you a "voice" they may not otherwise have. Sometimes, when parts are engaged in a "yes/no" dialogue, images, memories, or other awarenesses come to mind that show you what has gotten triggered.

Then, once you have a better idea of what's going on inside, you may want to access a caretaker or helper part that can soothe the distressed part at deeply unconscious levels. Or you may want to dialogue with a part of you that may be interfering with your present-day functioning and work out some agreement that can meet both your needs. Talking with your hands won't solve the problem, but it will open channels of communication, giving you access to parts of you that may operate outside conscious awareness.

Your Inner Landscape:
On Becoming an Explorer

In Chapter 8, on dealing with inner child parts, we'll explore the concept of a *safe place*. It's an essential part of your inner world and something you have always deserved: a place to call your own, where no one may enter without your permission.

For example, take a moment to bring to mind what a truly safe place might look like. It may be indoors or outdoors, someplace you've been before—imaginary or real—or a new idea of safety that springs to mind now. What are the qualities that allow you to know you are *safe* there? Are there sounds, smells, or colors that convey a certain sense of comfort? How about the shapes and textures around you? Is there someplace you can settle in and just spend some time quietly resting?

The most important thing about your safe place is that it exists in *your* inner landscape and you have a right to experience a sense of security there.

At this point, it may be helpful to realize that, while your inner world may contain memories of frightening, hurtful, or severely traumatic moments, primarily it is a place of healing and empowerment. Most of all, there is a deep urge in the unconscious to move toward wholeness.[7]

For many of us who were hurt as children, journeys into fantasy, dreams, or nightmares may have left us frightened of our own imagination, of letting go and deliberately entering the realm of the unconscious. Or we may have used fantasy to get away from abuse, to create a sense of safety and mastery in the only way we knew how. This was mastery grounded in fundamental powerlessness to get away from what was hurting us. There is a price to pay for this kind of protective strategy, though. For some adults who were hurt as children, the world of the imagination is filled with frightening—as well as soothing—feelings and impressions. If you are one of those people, you may find it anxiety-producing when you first begin digging deeper into your imaginary inner world.

This is one of the many terrible effects of abuse. It robs us of a valuable and rich arena of consciousness: our spontaneous access to the healing symbols that are alive within us. Symbols are the language of the unconscious,[8] and when they involve scenes of abuse or images of terror, we may become cautious about entering this immensely important realm of consciousness.

In fact, if you were traumatized as a child, you may have felt, at times, as though you were an explorer in a dangerous land. You may reexperience this feeling—at first—when you close your eyes to take an imaginary journey. The landscape may seem uncharted and filled with creatures you can't see or hear but that you feel may harm you if given half a chance. When you've been hurt as a child, it's hard to convince yourself that the old dangers no longer exist.

Or you may be one of those people who had so little control over your childhood environment that, even when you *do* find a seemingly safe place inside, something comes along to intrude. For example, you may have discovered an inner landscape that you really enjoy only to find that, on a subsequent visit, the area has been damaged or destroyed. You may have no idea how this happened. All you know is that your images have turned from representing the hope of a new beginning to the familiar feeling of having no control in your world, as when you were young.

If something like this happens to you, allow yourself to be *curious* about it, rather than dismayed. Any evidence of destruction in your inner world arises as a result of childhood experience and learned expectations and contains something of the *quality* of what you learned to expect when you were a child. You need to know about these early learnings, because—with patience—they can be *unlearned*. Also, there may be parts inside that are afraid of hope or any kind of self-directed activity. If this is the case, it's helpful to acknowledge and communicate directly with these parts, which we will explore in greater detail in Chapter 9.

For now, keep in mind that you are, indeed, an explorer. The landscape of your unconscious is a wondrous place. What you may be surprised to discover is that you have in your consciousness, already, everything you will ever need to make this journey. Perhaps you can welcome any childhood fears that may accompany you. They, too, deserve to be healed.

SPECIAL ISSUES FOR MULTIPLES

Sometimes, it's a challenge for multiples to settle down and focus on internal imagery. If you experience this struggle, you may find that part of the problem is performance anxiety. There may be parts of you that are deeply concerned about "getting it right." Because you may not have had the opportunity to play safely and spontaneously as a child, it may feel unnatural and scary to let things just unfold without any demands about the outcome. It may feel too out of control to let yourself just be surprised by, and curious about, what comes to mind, without having an idea ahead of time of what to expect. Also, you may switch from one personality to another as images arise that have particular meaning to various parts of you.

If any of these experiences arise during your inner journeys, allow yourself to observe them, if you can, and then continue with what you are doing. There is no need to struggle. Sometimes, it's just too much work to focus on one thing. If it's one of those times, just let the exercise go and do something else, something that doesn't stress or upset you. There is no hurry. You'll get to your healing at the pace, and in the ways, that suit your needs right now. There is no right way to heal, no time in which you have to get there. Be gentle with yourself and allow your adult observer to note those times when inner journeys are easy and those times when they are impossible.

The same holds true for non-multiples. There need be no demands with this work. It is here as an *option*, an opportunity to explore your inner world. Whether you do so today, or tomorrow, or many tomorrows from now doesn't really matter. What counts is your willingness to learn about yourself in ways that are useful to you right now.

Discovering Your Inner Garden[9]

Within your inner world is a very special garden. It's special because, as is true of many places in the vast realm of the unconscious, the garden seems to have ever-expanding and unexpected sections in it. It's impossible to experience all of them at once, and you may find that different parts of the garden reveal themselves to you at different times. This can happen automatically as you go further into the healing journey that will take you deeper into your landscape of consciousness.

The symbolic language of the unconscious may be used to set up communication between your conscious, present-day awareness and the rich store of wisdom that is present within your unconscious.[10] For this reason, the symbolic process of working in the garden will translate into progress in your healing journey. Your symbolic activities may be translated, for example, into new awarenesses, such as forgotten memories that come to mind in dreams or at moments when your mind is drifting, new responses to situations that would have been difficult in the past, and perhaps, a new perspective on yourself and the world in which you live.

For this exercise, begin by sitting or lying down in a place where you won't be disturbed for a while. Through the use of your active imagination, you can draw on your natural ability to remove your attention from the outside world and focus it somewhere inside. Your eyes may be open or closed for the exercise, although it's easier to concentrate when you eliminate external, visual distractions.

Allow yourself to take a few moments, now, to imagine yourself entering a beautiful garden. It may be a vegetable garden, a flower garden, or any other kind of garden that comes into your awareness. It's helpful to hold an attitude of curiosity, discovery, and exploration, and to allow yourself to be intrigued and pleasantly surprised by what comes to mind.

Remember that the language of the unconscious is comprised of symbols. When you allow yourself to be open to images that support your healing, you never know, ahead of time, what may emerge. One of the delights of entering your internal landscape in this way is the potentially helpful and "just-right" symbols and images you may discover during the journey.

To help focus yourself on how it feels to be in the garden, become aware of the surface underfoot, the sounds, colors and smells around you, and the overall quality of the air itself. And remember, this is a *safe* place. It is a *healing* place. Give yourself permission to discover how your garden communicates these qualities to you.

Allow yourself, as well, to notice if you feel any sense of *not* being safe. It's worthwhile to be curious about these responses and to recall that they reflect early childhood learnings. If they do arise, simply notice them, if you can, and set them aside to explore later. If they persist, allow yourself to discover what inner child part may be feeling them and take a few moments to soothe this part of you.

Your purpose on this particular journey is to connect with a place where feels good to spend some time. It is a place to rest or to sit for a while and think over some issue about which you have questions. Most of all, it is a beginning place for extending your internal experience of safety and mastery.

For this particular exercise, simply spend some time, now, enjoying this part of your garden. You may want to explore more closely what's growing there, soak in the view, or just lie back, relax and breathe in the fresh air. Give yourself whatever gift of safety and ease you need at this time.

If you've had experience with imagery exercises, you may know already that finding a safe place in which to spend time can be useful in a couple of ways. First, you may want just to stay there for a while and allow yourself to soak in any good feelings you discover. Or you may want to find a place in the garden where you can sit down and settle in to go even deeper into the imagery and have a dialogue with an inner part, for example. It's entirely up to you. The garden is yours. The journey is yours.

*   *   *

Over time, you can extend your explorations into new areas of the garden. For example, you may want to find a sacred place, where you can focus more deeply on your spiritual process, perhaps to tap into a sense of connection or support that comes from a larger context that makes sense to you. Or you may want to find an especially private place in the garden where the silence can be a healing presence.

In the next exercise, a journey through the garden becomes a way to communicate actively with your unconscious about your active choice to engage your healing process. For example, as you take the following imaginary journey, consider what the different images can convey to your unconscious about your willingness to go more deeply into the process of healing from childhood hurts at this time.

Weeding the Garden

Imagine that you are strolling through your garden. On one side, you may see an area where things are growing perfectly, just the way you want them to be. It's obvious that you have been taking care of this part of the garden. There are no weeds. Everything is watered, fed and pruned appropriately. It feels good to be here, and you know that it represents the things that you are doing well in your present-day life. Give yourself a few minutes to soak in whatever good feelings you have about this part of the garden.

Then, notice that off to another side there may be a plot of ground that is filled with rich, brown, moist earth. You can tell that you have been digging here, unearthing things that you needed to remember. The ground is now ready, prepared for the seeds of new ideas; allow yourself to sense how good it feels to know that you have done the work necessary to be able to accept new ideas and try out new responses as they come your way.

Further back, in a part of the garden that may be much less accessible, notice that there is an area that is overgrown with weeds. The ground may be parched because of lack of water, or it may be swampy or flooded because needed drainage channels haven't been created. This is an area of the garden that needs your attention. How does it feel to think about digging in and clearing up what has been neglected for so long? What does it bring to mind to think of beginning to uncover what has been left outside your conscious awareness until now?

Notice, as well, that the neglected part of the garden may be surrounded by beautiful, healthy areas. You may find something reassuring in the discovery that what has been left over from the past doesn't have to dominate the entire landscape, and may coexist with surprisingly healthy and strong parts of you.

From time to time, you may want to spend some time working in the neglected area of the garden. When you do, your unconscious will understand—through the language of symbols—that you are willing to dig more deeply into unresolved areas of your past and clear them up. For now, all you need do is the symbolic work of weeding, hoeing, digging up what might be buried there, and generally clearing away what has outgrown its usefulness.

Also, it's helpful to know that you don't have to spend lots of time doing imagery work. Once you set something in motion by engaging the imaginary task, your unconscious understands and continues with the process.[11] This occurs even after you have reoriented your awareness to the outer world of daily activity. For example, it can be a real delight to check in and notice that sprouts have begun to show in the plot of land that was ready for the seeds of new ideas or to discover that you have cleared away more of the neglected part of the garden than you had realized consciously.

*   *   *

It's important to remember that there is no "right way" to do this exercise. The symbols and imagery in your unconscious will have personal meaning to you. If you don't understand them at first, that's fine. In time, it will all make sense. Sometimes hindsight is the only way to grasp what healing has occurred as you have worked with the images.

Howie comes to mind. At first he was frightened by the idea of weeding the garden. He had been hurt brutally as a boy, and he was not eager to unearth the feelings of those early years. What he discovered was that he could weed at his own pace. There was no need to rush, no need to push himself into digging any deeper into his early wounds than he was ready to handle. In fact, he discovered that the weeding process could keep pace with the internal strength he was building in therapy; he could take his time, discovering all the tools he needed to do the job well.

He weeded and cleared away one small section at a time, learning a great deal from the fact that he could stop and take a rest whenever he felt he had done enough. He also began to have dreams that helped him get in touch with feelings that were just too much for him to handle when he was a child. As a result of following his own pace, his unconscious was able to communicate important awarenesses without overwhelming him.

Rosie's garden was different. At the back of her garden was a section that had been neglected and allowed to become swampy. Water kept flowing into the garden, but it wasn't channeled appropriately and so it backed up in places. This created areas of stagnant water. Rosie had learned that water often symbolizes feelings, and she wasn't too surprised to find that her own inability to handle her feelings was reflected in the flooded areas of her garden.

With the help of her future self, a part of you we'll explore in Chapter 10, Rosie slowly began to create channels in which the water could flow. She allowed herself to dig into the stagnant areas and discovered what feelings were stuck there. As she worked with the garden imagery, in conjunction with her work in therapy, Rosie learned how it felt to channel her emotions constructively by soothing inner child parts rather than being flooded by feelings she didn't know how to handle.

Dialoguing with Parts

Just as you can access inner child parts and interact with them using therapeutic dissociation, you can also access other kinds of parts and interact with them. These are parts that contain deep wisdom, talents, capabilities and points of view that are different from the wounded parts of you.[12]

It's important, if it feels all right to you, to give yourself permission to access these wise parts, since they can be invaluable in helping you discover new ways to deal with present-day interactions. For example, the future self, discussed in Chapter 10, is a particularly powerful part that arises from a deep wisdom within your unconscious. In your relationship with the future self, you can discover how it feels to live in a body that experiences more confidence and security than you may experience at present or to explore new ways of responding to previously upsetting situations.

Choosing to dialogue with inner parts of yourself is time well spent. Each part of you has a story to tell: as when an inner child part reveals the source of vulnerable feelings, something to add to your awareness; or when your future self shares a new point of view on an old feeling or gives you "advice" that may help resolve a current difficulty; or when an inner guide shows you an image that represents a way out of a dilemma.[13]

SPECIAL ISSUES FOR MULTIPLES

As you develop your own ways of dialoguing with the various parts of yourself, you may find that you draw on a surprising array of vehicles to enhance a more conscious connection with your inner world. For example, some parts aren't allowed to talk, because to have talked as a child would have brought terrible punishment. With these parts, you may find that drawing or writing poetry creates an avenue for communication. For other parts, music, movement, or dreams will be the ways in which their stories are told. For still others, simply asking to know more and then realizing that something new has dropped into your mind may be the way communication unfolds. The means of communication isn't important, as long as it is not destructive to yourself or others. What does matter is that you allow yourself to be creative, to find your own ways of making contact with all the parts that comprise you.

Mini Stress Breaks

One skill that can help you enhance your day-to-day functioning is the ability to recognize when you are becoming stressed. For adults who were hurt as children and who used dissociation as a protection against abusive experiences, stress increases the probability that dissociative processes will become more pronounced. This means that it's more likely you'll fall into a child state when difficult things happen.

To help manage the demands of daily living, mini stress breaks are helpful. Following are a few exercises that can provide a way for you to reinforce your adult perspective when the going gets tough.

TWO-MINUTE TIME DISTORTION MINI STRESS BREAK

Using whatever self-hypnotic or relaxation technique you find works best for you, take yourself inside to your safe place.[14] Once you are settled there, let yourself see, in your mind's eyes, a clock that shows the current time. Then imagine how the clock will look two minutes from now. Ask your unconscious to bring you out of your mini break when two minutes of actual clock time have passed, and give yourself the suggestion that, at that moment, you will reorient to the external world refreshed and ready to begin again whatever tasks await you.[15]

During the two minutes, which you can stretch out to *feel* like two hours simply by giving yourself the suggestion that each second will be like a minute, you can rest deeply. You may want to imagine that you are swimming in a beautiful ocean. Perhaps you'd be most rested if you were drifting along in the middle of nowhere at all, with nothing in your awareness. It may be that what refreshes you most is to imagine that you are meditating during the passage of this inner time. Or, you may just want to spend the stretched-out two minutes engaged in imagined exercise.

The key is to allow yourself a *vivid inner experience* of whatever you have chosen to imagine during your two-minute break. Then, when your eyes open at the end of the two minutes, *you might suggest to yourself that you are getting better and better at recognizing the signals that tell you stress is mounting and you are in need of a mini break.*

GRAVITY-IS-YOUR-FRIEND MINI STRESS BREAK

In this mini stress break, all you have to do is take a deep breath and feel your body settle as you exhale. Once you become aware of how the support under you does all the work, take a moment to notice how the natural presence of gravity invites all of your muscles to become deliciously heavy and floppy. All you have to do is say "yes" to the invitation.

You can combine this mini break with a two-minute time distortion. Allow yourself to respond as deeply as you can, this time, to gravity's invitation really to let go and allow all the stresses to flow out of your body on the exhaled breath.

The important thing to know is that it doesn't matter how deeply relaxed you become. What's important is to interrupt the natural elevation in stress, which occurs when you go through the day unaware of how you may be responding negatively to events occurring around you.[16] As you experiment with this exercise, taking a deep breath and settling can become almost automatic as you unconsciously monitor your body's response to stressors and respond appropriately to bring your stress level down.

INVENT-YOUR-OWN MINI STRESS BREAK

For this exercise, ask yourself what you might do that would be particularly useful in bringing down your stress level. Some ideas may have come to mind as you have read this chapter. It's helpful to write down ideas as they come to you; you can go back later and develop them.

For example, think of things you really like to do that bring you deep pleasure. You may like to work with your hands in some way, perhaps through woodworking or needlework. You may love boating and would enjoy spending a few minutes working on a boat, or sailing it. Perhaps you enjoy looking at beautiful scenery and may find it relaxing to let your mind drift to lovely images you've seen. All of these activities may be experienced vividly in your imagination, giving you the sense of satisfaction that you experience when you do them literally and physically.

Give yourself an opportunity, now, to practice one of these mini stress breaks. Over time, you'll discover which ones work best for you and learn at what points in your daily life they are most useful in helping you regulate the amount of stress you experience. The key thing is to develop those mini stress breaks that allow you to tap into relaxation, to settle your body and mind. You have a right to regulate your relationship to stress and to take a break when things begin to build up.

SPECIAL ISSUES FOR MULTIPLES

It's essential for you, as a multiple, to discover ways to regulate your dissociative process. You have more potential to control the quality of your inner life, now that you are grown up, than you may have ever realized. As I mentioned earlier, stress increases dissociative processes and can cause you to switch from personality to personality in an exhausting and frightening way. Stress can leave you feeling fogged in and confused, as you dissociate actively, shifting from part to part. Dealing actively to reduce your level of stress offers one powerful way to tone down, or decrease, the amount of dissociation you experience on a day-to-day basis.

As with every aspect of your healing process, it is important to allow yourself to find what works for *you*. Each of us is unique, and no one technique fits everyone. You have a creative capacity that may be used to increase your mastery, to enhance your sense of well-being, and to provide effective means for you to deal—right now, today— with the results of having been hurt as a child. When you were a child, you may have dissociated unconsciously and involuntarily as a way to survive, to get through it all, and you *did* survive. Now you have a chance to shift away from dissociation as a protective response. Instead, you can draw, consciously, on dissociative processes that can enhance your capacity to be present with your feelings and to cope consciously and more effectively with life's challenges in the present moment.

In the chapters to come, we'll look at other ways in which volitional and therapeutic dissociative processes can be used to promote your healing journey. We begin, in the next chapter, with an exploration of what things may jump out at you in your daily life and send you back in time to childhood hurts. We'll look at some of the ways you can use these "triggers" to build bridges in consciousness between your present-day adult self and inner child parts that remain stuck in the past.

4

Identifying Triggers

WHY AM I SO SCARED?

As they face each day, survivors of childhood abuse meet the challenge of dealing with *triggers*. Those survivors who used dissociation as a way to cope with early trauma find that the effects of and difficulties caused by triggers are especially powerful.

Triggers are those cues, coming either from the external environment or from inside, that set in motion unconscious reactions and responses related to past trauma. They may seem to "come upon you" unexpectedly, out of the blue. For example, on a typical day, you might be working on a project, having a conversation with the boss, or going out shopping for groceries. As far as your adult mind is concerned, everything is going along fine. Then, suddenly, there you are, overcome by feelings of terror, panic, or shame. Something has come into your awareness from the outside, or into your mind from your own unconscious, that has tapped into feelings from childhood. When this happens, you may not know *what* has been triggered, but there is no question that things suddenly feel out of place, and you feel off center. It's as though you have been transported someplace else, to

another time, another experience—and your present-day adult awareness doesn't have access to where you've gone or what is happening to
you. Instead, you have tapped into a child part that is stuck "back
there," in a place you may not have remembered yet.

The hardest thing about triggers, until you get to know how they
operate, is that you may not have the vaguest idea what has happened
to you. Such experiences may leave you feeling helpless and frustrated.
It's important to know that they are an inevitable outcome of having
been traumatized; they are a "normal" consequence of childhood
hurts.

If you are an abuse survivor, chances are that you have had this
kind of reaction. Take a moment, now, to think about a time when
you may have felt perfectly fine when, out of the blue, and for a reason
you've never been able to explain, things suddenly seemed to change.
Can you recall how it felt to shift from an adult state of mind, where
you became worried about making mistakes or fearful of being hurt?
How did you cope with this shift in your internal experience?

Identifying Triggers

In order to feel more competent and masterful in your day-to-day life,
it's helpful to get to know your triggers. The more you know about
how you get triggered and *what* triggers you, the more choice you
have in how to respond. As you identify your triggers and trace them
back to childhood experiences, it's easier to remind yourself: *That was
then; this is now.*

This is, of course, easier said than done. When old memories get
triggered, it's as though you really are back there, lost in a childhood
experience that hasn't yet been translated into your adult awareness.
Sometimes you're back there in your feelings. What was safe a moment ago becomes terrifying now. Or you may be back there in your
body, with a sensation of pain, shortness of breath, or nausea that fills
your entire awareness in the present moment. When this happens,
your body may be caught in remembering some event from child-

hood, even though your conscious mind may not have a clue as to the content of the memory.

If you're a multiple, there may be times when you suddenly hear a voice in your head saying things like, "I hate you. You're stupid!" You may believe what the voice is saying and respond as a child would when verbally abused in this way. For example, you might try to appease the voice by stopping any activity and sitting very still, attempting to be as invisible as possible.

The first step in identifying triggers is to become aware of your feelings, of when your mood shifts from a sense of well-being to an overwhelming feeling of discomfort or vulnerability. Once you notice that your mood has shifted, you can then begin to explore what may have been going on that triggered you.

Jennie, an adult who was abused as a child, has lots of triggers related to her childhood experiences. Before she started exploring her triggers in therapy, a particularly troublesome one often caused her problems in her daily life. It had to do with the intense discomfort and sense of danger she felt whenever tall men wearing glasses came near her. Every time this happened, she would feel a compelling need to run away, even as she would tell herself she was being ridiculous. It didn't matter if she were on a bus, in a theater, at a lecture, or walking down the street. The fear and dread that came over her seemed irrational, but knowing this in her adult thoughts didn't make a dent. She was terrified. Most of the time she would leave or change her seat in order to feel safer.

Over time by paying attention to her feelings and getting to know important inner child parts that were related to her earlier abuse, Jennie has come to realize that this kind of man reminds her of a childhood abuser.[1] When she realized this, the trigger of tall men with glasses began to fade. Now when there's a tall man with glasses around, Jennie may feel momentarily startled, if she feels anything at all, but she no longer feels compelled to flee. If she does get triggered, she treats the response as she would any habit. She "talks herself down" by reminding herself that the man she used to fear doesn't exist in her adult life, that *there is a difference between then and now*.

Pockets of Time

How is it possible to be focused in the present one moment and then catapulted into a seemingly unrelated reaction the next? *This happens because of the timeless nature of the unconscious.*

Unprocessed, dissociated childhood experiences exist in an eternal now. They are like *pockets of time* in the unconscious that have no relationship to your present reality. Instead of being part of your ongoing adult awareness, they continue to be filled with all the feelings you had as a child.

To explore the concept of pockets of time, think, for a moment, of something you did last week, a year ago, or ten years ago, that you wish you hadn't done. Let it be something you recall readily. If you've thought about it many times and have talked it over with friends, chances are that it no longer has the same charge it did when you were younger. You may no longer get that terrible grabbing feeling in your belly when you remember what you did. It's just something that happened, and it's over now. The memory has been processed. You've made it part of your adult awareness and have come to terms with it; it no longer has the power to pull you into uncomfortable feelings.

If, on the other hand, you still feel a rush of intense shame and discomfort when you think of something you did that you wish you hadn't done, chances are that aspects of the memory continue to remain, unprocessed, in a pocket of time from childhood. When you get triggered, all the feelings and thoughts from that unprocessed pocket of time suddenly flood into your awareness, bringing with them the responses you had back then.

An important part of the healing process is gaining access to these pockets of time and bringing their contents into your adult awareness, where they can be processed in ways that were impossible when you were a child. Until this happens, these old experiences aren't really memories. They are more like flashbacks, more like actually *being* there. As long as they exist in this way, you remain vulnerable to shifting without notice from your everyday adult awareness into a frightened or enraged child part.

Your Cognitive Tree

As you increase your conscious awareness of the difference between now and then and consciously learn more of what you experienced, you add branches to your *cognitive tree*. The cognitive tree is a metaphor for increasing your adult understanding and awareness of your experience. It allows you to know where to "hang" feelings as they arise, and provides a context to explain what you are experiencing.

For example, the concept of pockets of time represents a branch on your cognitive tree. If you understand about pockets of time, you have a way to give meaning to your experience and to explain to yourself what is happening when you suddenly shift from a competent adult state into an irrational feeling of terror, for example. You have something to hold onto in the present, as you deal with the challenge of shifting out of the experience of a past trauma.

Actually, all of the material in this book can form branches on your cognitive tree. The more you know about what is happening to you, and the more options you have for dealing with it, the more you will be able to stay focused in the present.

An important distinction needs to be made between your cognitive tree and the psychological defense of "intellectualization." When people intellectualize, they actually seek to explain away their feelings in order to feel in control of what is happening to them. Instead of exploring their feelings, going into them, and working them through, they further bury awareness of unprocessed childhood hurts. Your cognitive tree, on the other hand, allows you to go more deeply into what is happening in order to move all the way through it to resolution and true mastery.

Be Gentle
with Yourself

Even as you develop your cognitive tree and come to understand why you respond as you do to triggers, there may be times when you feel foolish, or even angry with yourself, because you are triggered. As you struggle to keep yourself from acting on impulses that arise when you're triggered, you may berate or criticize yourself. You may yell at yourself for wanting to scream at the rude person on the street because the rage that comes up when you feel someone doesn't respect you is almost unbearable. At other times, you may feel humiliated or ashamed, just as you did when you were a child and couldn't seem to get it right when people demanded things of you.

It helps to remember that you aren't reacting on purpose. Instead, to some part of you—usually a child part—your adult life doesn't exist. The only timeframe in which this part lives is back then, when things were dangerous, when you were being hurt. Within the pocket of time, your adult self isn't real yet. The part of you that has been triggered doesn't know about adult options: that you can walk away, stand up for yourself without being hurt, or talk it through and work it out.

When you know this, it's easier to be gentle with yourself. Instead of giving yourself a hard time or looking around to be rescued by someone, you can observe your responses to different triggers. Also, you've added another branch to your cognitive tree when you realize that, until the memory is processed and the contents of the pocket of time have been brought into the present, you can't help but be triggered. The nice thing to know is that it *can* change. Your adult awareness can enter the pocket of time and make all the difference in the world.

Building Bridges

It's extremely helpful to develop a fundamental *curiosity* about your triggers. So often, we seek to avoid things that make us uncomfortable. Instead of being curious about triggers, you may feel that you want to get as far away as possible from *any* awareness of them. Once you understand the value of your triggers, though, their power to ruin your day lessens. Instead, you come to see that they are doorways into your history, *bridges to your past*.

As strange as it may seem, sometimes you may experience real gratitude when triggers are activated, because it means you have found yet another avenue into healing. As long as your past remains locked in pockets of time that are closed to your adult awareness, you are a prisoner to that past. You need all the bridges you can find to help you move from then to now, to allow you to be in the present moment without the fear of being pulled back to a terrifying moment from a time that you already survived.

There are lots of ways to build bridges in your consciousness. We'll look at some of them in Chapters 5 and 8. For now, it's helpful to keep in mind that every time you are triggered you have an opportunity to build a bridge from past to present. The more bridges you build, the more your day-to-day life will be free from the often puzzling and extreme shifts from adult to child states of awareness.

At times no amount of adult understanding can keep you from being triggered, because you haven't yet completed the healing process around a traumatic childhood experience. It's helpful to acknowledge that this is a normal part of moving through healing. It's not the end of the world. It doesn't mean you've failed. It just means that the feelings coming up are still held in a pocket of time that hasn't fully been brought into your current psychological timeframe. With practice, things *will* change and you will have a much greater ability to use these moments to increase your sense of competence, safety, and mastery in the present.

Alexandra comes to mind. When her children were growing up,

Alexandra liked to help her son work puzzles at a table in the corner of the playroom. Things would be different, though, when her daughter wanted her to sit down and have a tea party at the same table. Then Alexandra would feel a sense of dread come over her and she would feel an impulse to grab her daughter and run from the room.

Because she was in therapy, Alexandra had learned that she didn't have to act on her feelings, even when they were powerfully compelling. She knew there was some kind of memory, held in a pocket of time, involved in her response.

At first, before the bridges between past and present had been fully developed in her consciousness, Alexandra would excuse herself when she was triggered, taking a few moments to check in with the inner child part that had been activated by the tea party setting. Once she had settled down a bit and reminded herself of the difference between then and now, she could go back into the playroom and suggest another game to play with her daughter.

In time, Alexandra remembered that her father used to come to play "tea party" with her, before carrying her into his bedroom to "play a different game." As the memories became more conscious, Alexandra found herself less triggered by her daughter's playtime. Eventually she reported feeling relatively comfortable, although tea parties never became her favorite game.

Alexandra learned some important things in her struggle to become conscious of what was triggering her. First, she made a choice not to act on what she was feeling.[2] Her curiosity allowed her to draw on her adult state of mind, so she wasn't carried away by the impulse to flee. She developed one of the most important and challenging adult skills for healing: *the capacity to sit with your feelings without flying into action either to get away from them or to make them better*.[3]

When you sit with what emerges, you offer yourself an opportunity to process the feelings with your adult consciousness, to build a bridge between past and present. This is a theme I'll repeat many times, because it's so important. Sitting with your feelings allows your adult awareness to enter a pocket of time and become aware of something that has tied you to the past. It doesn't mean that it all gets better right away; with practice, though, the bridge gets stronger and the potential for getting triggered lessens unexpectedly.

Joseph found that he had to practice building bridges to one of his triggers many times. As an adult, he struggled a great deal with intimate relationships. He didn't know why, but whenever a woman looked at him in a certain sexual or seductive way, he shut down and withdrew. Sometimes he would leave, literally walk away, even though he couldn't really explain to himself why he felt such a compelling need to withdraw. To try to make sense of it and feel less out of control, he explained to himself that he just didn't know how to handle being committed to someone in an exclusive relationship.

What was most distressing for Joseph, though, and what he *couldn't* explain to himself no matter how he tried to frame it, were the powerful feelings that came over him when he was triggered. He felt then as though the woman he was with wanted to devour him and take away his freedom. He felt not only enraged but also desperate. In his adult mind, he knew he was overreacting, but he couldn't talk himself out of it.

As he explored the trigger of the look in a woman's eyes, Joseph became aware that his conscious memories of having to "cuddle" with his mother when he was young contained feelings that had never been processed in his adult awareness. He hadn't realized how angry and helpless he had felt when his mother involved him in sexual play with her. He discovered that the trigger was the look in his mother's eyes when she snuggled up to him in bed.

As he explored the contents of this pocket of time, Joseph realized that the "look" came up in current relationships whenever a woman began to feel desire for him. Inevitably, this would happen if he dated someone long enough, and then the struggle would begin. As he worked with the feelings about his mother, Joseph realized that walking away from relationships wasn't the answer. Each time he did, he only reinforced his conviction from childhood that the look *was* dangerous. Instead of building a bridge to the present, he relived feelings from the past. The choice Joseph made, over and over again, was to learn to interpret what he saw in a lover's eyes in a new, adult way, as he dealt with the effects of his childhood sexual abuse experiences.

Claudette struggled both at work and in her personal relationships. As is true with most survivors of childhood trauma, her life was filled with fear. Sometimes she could go along and forget the fear or become unaware of it for a while. Then, inevitably, something would happen that threw her back into undefined terror, seemingly for no reason at all.

It might be when she was walking along the street, thinking of nothing in particular, and someone walked up behind her. Or it might be when she was at work and her boss would leave a note on her desk, asking her to come in for a meeting. The things that triggered her were many and didn't seem to follow any pattern she could get hold of in her conscious mind. Sometimes her triggers produced such dramatic responses that she was thrown into a full-blown flashback.[4] These experiences frightened Claudette, because she felt so completely out of control.

By recognizing that the terror offered a bridge to pockets of time that contained childhood trauma, Claudette at least had a branch on which to hang her understanding. It helped to recognize that the terror was about *then*, rather than *now*. Instead of feeling swept away, as though a tidal wave had picked her up and would carry her to her destruction, she could hang onto her cognitive tree for support. It didn't mean that the terror went away completely, right away. But it did mean that a part of Claudette's adult awareness had something to hold onto that made sense of her experience. Also, by using the triggered terror as a bridge, Claudette began to put together the many pieces of memory that made up her traumatic past. Daily living became easier, less burdened by the ever-present fear from childhood.

If your responses to being triggered are as pervasive and powerful as Claudette's, it's helpful to remember that you can enter your memories a little bit at a time, like putting your toe into a cold swimming pool. As you get used to the temperature, you can go in a bit further. As you add branches to your cognitive tree and enhance conscious awareness of pockets of time from childhood, you can let in more of the memories that throw you into the past, often when you least expect it.

The Infinite Array
of Triggers

Triggers can come in any shape, form, style, or quality. For example, powerful triggers are associated with smells that remind us of childhood experiences, smells we may not have thought of consciously for years until they come into our present-day adult experience. Then, all of a sudden, we are transported to a pocket of time where the smell is one of the core pieces of a moment from childhood.

I recall a moment when I first started therapy. I was talking about my father. My therapist asked me to imagine him and suddenly my senses were filled with the fragrance of the soap and aftershave he used when I was young. I had no conscious awareness of these fragrances, but they transported me powerfully into the past, to a feeling of being held by him, with my face up against his.

Other triggers may come from sounds that are associated with childhood experiences. For example, there may have been a dripping faucet somewhere nearby when you were being hurt by someone. Or a past abuser might have whistled a particular tune that you came to associate with upcoming abuse. Hearing someone wheeze may trigger a child part of you that recalls, within a pocket of time, the sound a frightening adult made.

Triggers can also be activated if someone touches you in a certain way that activates unprocessed memories from a pocket of time. For example, Helga couldn't bear to be touched on her shoulder by anyone, at any time. Inevitably, she would jump with a powerful startle response if someone inadvertently put a hand on her shoulder. No matter how much, or how reasonably, she talked to herself about it, she couldn't stop the startle response from happening. It related to some childhood experience that she hadn't yet processed consciously and that retained the power to trigger her in the present.

Intrusive thoughts related to past hurtful experiences may also create triggers into unprocessed pockets of time. For example, you may find yourself with a thought that says, "I'm bad. Terrible things are going to happen to me," that seems to come from nowhere and won't go away. The thought itself triggers fear and may make you want to go to bed and hide. Also, unexplained panic attacks may indicate that memory material has been triggered or is emerging into your present-day awareness. If you know that panic and unprocessed memories are related, you can increase your curiosity instead of your fear when this kind of experience erupts.

Other triggers have to do with good feelings. For example, it may be that you have learned to associate excitement or pleasure with having been hurt as a child. If you have pockets of time that contain unremembered childhood experiences of being punished severely even as good things came your way, you may find yourself filled with dread, panic, or depression when you are recognized for some accomplishment, rather than the pleasure you might expect.

Triggers may also come from certain times of the year, a particular feel in the air, or a season in which bad things happened to you. For example, if you grew up in a chaotic home where you never knew what to expect, going off to school might have been your only respite from fear. As summer approaches, when school ends and children are home until school begins again in fall, you might notice that your mood also changes. Or you may have had a particularly hard time at school, so that the end of summer signals a deepening feeling of loss or dread, as part of you anticipates being hurt when you are again at the mercy of your schoolmates.

Because these parts exist within unprocessed pockets of time that are about *then*, rather than *now*, the feelings can seem very real, even if they are inexplicable and truly baffling. For example, you may not realize at all, consciously, that you are responding to unconscious fears of being home for the summer or of returning to school, because these activities no longer relate to your adult life. But in that pocket of time there is no present. There is only the unprocessed feeling of *then*.

For some people times of the week become triggers. For example, the approach of the weekend brings with it increasing anxiety or depression. If the people who hurt you were home with you on weekends, and the only time you had relative safety was during the week, Friday can become a day when the world seems less optimistic, less hopeful. For others, the actual weekend days may be filled with discomfort or a kind of free-floating anxiety, as pockets of time holding memories of unprocessed abuse are triggered.

Certain dates, including holidays, may activate pockets of time that relate to unremembered experiences that occurred on these days. For many adults who grew up in abusive families, holidays are particularly difficult. So often, what was supposed to be a fun day, a special day, turned into tragedy, violence or chaos, leading to fear, anger or perhaps profound disappointment.

Not all triggers are overwhelmingly powerful. Some are vague, creating a slight discomfort that you may barely notice. It's important to remember that pain is relative. *Any* triggers you experience are important bridges back to unremembered experiences, whether those experiences were traumatic moments in time or the result of chronically unloving, unsupportive responses from your childhood environment. And so, even if your history doesn't seem to be as dramatic, or traumatic, as some of the cases described here, your discomfort is likely to be as powerful to you as theirs is to them. What counts is that you take the steps you can to identify and resolve childhood hurts that continue to get in the way of your day-to-day living.

SPECIAL ISSUES FOR MULTIPLES

For people with multiple personalities, being triggered is a constant challenge, as different parts respond to varying kinds of triggers from moment to moment. When a multiple is under extreme stress and there is a lot of switching from one personality to another, triggers may be experienced in the smallest moments, in the minutest events. Triggers may even be internal in origin, as when one part threatens another, a child part becomes overwhelmingly frightened over a proposed trip, or an abuser is hallucinated as being right there in the room.[5] It can be wearying and harrowing to be a multiple who is being triggered.

If you have begun to develop your cognitive tree and to build bridges of awareness between your present-day adult consciousness and other parts of you, it will be easier to deal with being triggered. It *is* a struggle. There is no doubt about it. But be assured that what I've said about dealing with triggers for non-multiples applies to you as well. It just may take you a bit longer, and it may feel like a bigger mountain to climb.

For example, certain interpersonal interactions may trigger feelings of fear or rage that threaten to overwhelm you with their intensity. At first you may move fully into your usual coping strategy, which may include switching into a scared part, a competent part, or an enraged personality that makes you feel stronger. Perhaps the only new thing you can do is use hindsight to explore what triggered you and how you responded.

Later, as your observing adult awareness develops, something we'll explore further in the next chapter, you may find that you become more aware of yourself *during* your response to being triggered. As more bridges are built among various parts of your consciousness, you will bring more of your current awareness with you into the pocket of time that has been triggered.

Specific triggers tend to be associated with particular personalities. For example, it's not unusual for multiples to have parts that express rage triggered by feelings of fear or vulnerability. It's as though a raging personality were created to jump into conscious awareness whenever unmanageable terror was felt in childhood. This strategy allowed the child to move from overwhelming vulnerability toward a powerful feeling of rage.

The problem is that when, as an adult, something triggers fear, rage may emerge and create significant interpersonal difficulties. For example, imagine that, during a conversation, a friend suggests you did something to hurt her feelings. Instead of experiencing curiosity and concern, you might first feel fear of being punished, immediately coupled with rage. Then the response to your friend might be anger instead of interest, lashing out instead of inviting communication.

It helps to remember that to the personalities created by a child who has been terribly abused there is only *then*, a time when there is potential for danger in *every* interaction, in *any* moment. *Now* doesn't exist yet. By using what triggers you as a basis for building bridges between your adult consciousness and the pockets of time that are related to the parts you created in order to survive, you can begin to create a more alive and realistic sense of *today*.

This, Too, Shall Pass

It's important to know that what you are feeling right now *will* change. Eventually, you *will* come out of the pocket of time into which you may have fallen. Sometimes it doesn't feel that way, but with experience you will develop the capacity to remember that feelings don't last forever, even when you're in the middle of the worst of them.

As you track your triggers and respond to the ever-changing events that make up a day, you'll learn more about the nature of feelings. When they are allowed to keep moving naturally, feelings don't stay in the same place. It's when we grab them and hold onto them for dear life that they—and we—become stuck. Over time, as you learn more about your history and build more bridges to the past, you'll also develop greater confidence in knowing that what's been triggered doesn't last forever.

Next time you are triggered, perhaps you can allow yourself to be curious about what will happen if you remind yourself that these feelings are about another time and another place. They are to be taken seriously, but not literally. They have meaning for you, but it's probably about childhood. So, rather than deciding literally that your boss is about to fire you because you've been asked to come to a meeting, or that your co-worker is about to do you out of a promotion by gossiping about you, remember that triggers are about someone else, somewhere else, doing something else.

It's natural not to believe yourself completely when you deal with powerful triggers in this way, especially when you are tapping into a pocket of time that contains an unprocessed traumatic memory. Part of you may continue to feel that you have every reason to feel afraid of your boss or suspicious of your co-worker's motives. In fact, there will be times when it *is* important to listen to your feelings. Something really will be going on that has to do with your day-to-day life in the present, right now. There will be times when what triggers unprocessed pockets of time actually does coincide with something that really is dangerous or really isn't good for you. Over time, you will learn the difference between unresolved childhood memories that are being triggered and a well-developed radar that says there's a real problem in the present.

Taking a "Bathroom Break"

A strategy that is particularly helpful when you get triggered and you can't go home and hide, when you simply have to keep working on whatever the day has required of you, is to excuse yourself to go to the bathroom. Rarely will anyone give you a hard time for "taking a bathroom break." Getting away by yourself can be just the thing you need to pull yourself together.

Once you've managed to find some private space, take a few moments to reflect on what just happened. First, focus on your breathing and settle yourself. Ideally, your goal is to build a bridge from the pocket of time into which you've fallen to your present-day, adult awareness. This isn't the time to go deeper into the memory material that has gotten triggered. Instead, it's a time to note what happened, become curious about it, and promise yourself you'll go back to it later.

Focus as best you can in your adult awareness, while giving yourself the kinds of reassuring messages we all deserved when we were children. Imagine that the feelings that have been triggered are moving through you the way radio and television waves do, invisibly, all the time. There's no need to "tune in" to the feelings. Just let them pass. Let your body settle. Allow yourself to find some comfort in the fact that you can learn to be curious about what has triggered you, rather than automatically assuming that there really is danger in the present.

The bathroom break represents an opportunity to reinforce your adult self. You might want to look at your hands and realize how big they are compared to how little you may be feeling inside. It's also a time to remember your cognitive tree and draw on your understanding of how triggers work. Remind yourself that you have been triggered and that some memory from childhood must have been activated. Even if you have no idea at all what the memory is about, you can still reinforce your understanding that your reaction is about then, not now.

The bathroom break can allow the feelings to flow from inside you out to a child part, so you can recenter yourself. Or you might want to sit quietly and ask your hands some questions in order to discover what has been triggered from the past. You may want to call on helper parts to soothe and calm frightened child parts. If you have developed a support system of friends, perhaps this would be a good time to make a brief phone call to help you recenter yourself into your present-day adult self. If you can't find a friend to talk to, you might take a few moments to have a dialogue with yourself. You might say something like, "Wait a minute. It's_____*(fill in the current year)* and I'm in_____*(fill in where you are right now)*. I'm_____ years old *(fill in your age)*, and I'm going to be okay." Then, you might promise yourself that you'll take plenty of time later, when you're home and it's safe and appropriate, to go inside and find out what happened. Until then, it helps to remind yourself, over and over, what year it is and where you are right now.

"Buying Time"

One of the issues with which many abuse survivors struggle on a daily basis, in just about every relationship, is *compliance*. When you are abused as a child, you learn all too well that you have no choice in what happens to you. Like it or not, you must comply with the demands of another person. Your body is not your own; your wishes and needs don't count.

As an adult, you may find that it is difficult to say "no" to people who make requests, even when you know you don't want to do what is asked. Instead of saying "no" or negotiating mutually acceptable solutions, you may go ahead anyway and become resentful or angry with the other person or yourself. Because of this tendency, it is helpful to develop ways to "buy time" and give yourself a chance to think of what you want to do or say.

A good way to buy time for yourself is to respond to most requests with comments such as: "I need to think about it and get back to you," "I need to sleep on it," "I'll get back to you later." Without being rude, you have given yourself some space within which to bring your adult self to the fore, instead of responding automatically in ways you had to as a child. The sense of control that comes when you are able to buy time is very satisfying, even though it may be accompanied—at first—by guilt or fear.

What's important to tell yourself is that, even if the other person continues to push you, *you have a right to take some time to decide if you want to honor any request or offer that may come your way.* You may have had no choice as a child, but now, as a grownup, you can politely insist on some time to think things over. In time, and with practice, you can discover how good it feels to respond to the demands and needs of others in a way that feels good to you and that is free from the old feeling of "no escape."

Reviewing Your Day

All of the suggestions offered in this chapter are focused on one basic development: increasing your awareness of the fact that you have been triggered. Once you realize that you've been triggered, you can choose what you want to do about it. Immediately, the situation changes a bit. The mere presence of your adult awareness adds an element and begins to build a bridge, even if you continue to have no idea at all what memory relates to the trigger.

The next time you find yourself in a difficult interaction, take a few moments, as soon as you can, to go over what happened and see if you can identify the trigger that set you off. You might think of this as a review of the day that can strengthen the bridges you are building between the past and present. It's essential, though, that you be gentle with yourself and not use the review process to beat yourself up for not doing things "perfectly" or to prove how incompetent or wrong you are.

In your review, you might ask yourself about the key element in what you remember. What was the most charged moment? When did you first notice that you were feeling different? Did someone do or say something that sticks in your mind or that comes to mind as you think about it? Did someone move in a way that frightened you or looked scary to some part of you? Was there a noise or odor that set you off? Were you thinking about something just before you started to feel so awful? *Remember to be curious.* It helps to engage your adult awareness in the search for the trigger.

It doesn't matter whether or not you actually find the trigger or immediately shift out of the feelings it elicits. What counts is that you recognize where you are, what is happening, and that you have apparently accessed the past without intending to do so. The more you can think of it as an opportunity, instead of feeling victimized by it—or angry at yourself because of your inability to deal with it effectively every time—the more grounded in the present you are likely to feel.

It helps to remember that today, right now, an aspect of your healing process is to develop strategies for getting through the day that do not draw on the automatic, involuntary dissociation you may have used as a child. When you take the time to work with your triggers, rather than being thrown into old dissociative behaviors by them, you give yourself the gift of a greater sense of mastery and control. You give yourself something to hold onto in your adult mind when the past intrudes in your day-to-day life. There are other ways to hold onto the safety of the present moment, which we'll explore in the next chapter.

5

Healing with "Mindfulness"

SOMETHING TO HOLD ONTO

As we saw in the last chapter, a fundamental task in healing from childhood abuse is to learn to experience the difference between parts of yourself that are related to unresolved past trauma and your present-day adult awareness. We looked at how difficult it can be to attend to things you have to do today when you fall into unprocessed pockets of time that contain memories, feelings, thoughts, and behaviors related to hurtful childhood experiences. In this chapter we'll explore some of the many ways you can train yourself to return to your adult state of mind more readily.

When overwhelmed by the past, how can you reclaim your present-day awareness? This question comes up over and over again in the lives of abuse survivors. Being able to recenter yourself and handle life's challenges effectively is an important element in determining the *quality* of your day-to-day experience. It also allows you to pace your healing so that you have times when you are free from the intensity and immediacy of past abuse experiences.

Whenever we become immersed in an inner child state and lose our current, adult perspective, we temporarily lose touch with our present environment and with a range of options for dealing effectively with life's challenges. Take a moment to recall how, without your adult observer present, it's easy to forget yourself. It's no longer now, but then; it's no longer here, but there. When it is then rather than now, you are more likely to draw on *childhood* coping strategies than on the more appropriate and effective choices available to your adult self.

As we saw in the last chapter on triggers, it is extremely helpful to be able to return to your present-day awareness when a child state emerges spontaneously. The more you develop your adult observer, the more mastery you will experience as you deal with life in the present.

It is important to distinguish the observing part of your adult awareness from detached, cut-off parts that may arise from early experiences of abuse. For example, many adults who were hurt as children describe having an inner critic who constantly watches and comments on their every action. While this part may seem to be an observer, it is, in fact, usually a representation of some abuser from childhood. Another kind of seeming observer is described as a part that remains aloof from other people and finds fault with just about everyone. Again, this part represents wounds from childhood and actually operates to fend off closeness with other people. *Your healthy adult observer doesn't criticize you or cut you off from others.* Instead, it *recenters* you.

This part of you represents a valuable and *compassionate* resource. From it emerges a point of view that acts to reassure in ways you needed and deserved as a child—and would have internalized as you grew up if you had you been treated with respect and care. All of the strategies that follow are based on a commitment to *gentleness* and a request that you explore what it is like to return to your present-day awareness as best you can whenever you realize you've gotten triggered into the past.

SPECIAL ISSUES FOR MULTIPLES

Throughout this chapter I focus on the adult observer as an important part of developing mastery in the present. For some of you, this may be a difficult or frustrating concept to explore. For example, some multiples don't experience the presence of an adult part of themselves. If this is your experience, you may, instead, feel as though you were comprised of "a herd of children and teenagers," as one multiple put it. The concept of developing an *adult* observer may feel impossible. If this is the case, perhaps you can allow yourself to be curious about how and when you may begin to become aware of this part of you, perhaps—first—as a "present-day" observer. It's important to know that, even though it may not be part of your ongoing, conscious awareness right now, the potential for you to have this observer is in you. By learning to focus on your immediate experience, you can explore what it's like to be aware, rather than to react. It is through the process of coming back to *this* moment, of noticing what you are feeling and what is happening to you *right now*, that the observer part of you will develop naturally.

The Magic of the Breath

In recent years, many books have become available that deal with an approach called *mindfulness*.[1] Mindfulness is a form of meditation that invites you simply to notice what is passing through your awareness. This awareness begins with the breath—with simply noticing that, "Now, I am breathing in. Now, I am breathing out." This is a fundamental approach in certain forms of Buddhist practice. What follows is drawn from many of these approaches and is adapted to the needs of adults who were abused as children.[2]

　　Your breathing is something that is with you every moment. It never leaves you, although you may find that you learned how to *stop* breathing when you were a child. Often, when we are frightened or in pain, we don't breathe. Children who grew up in stressed-filled or abusive homes know a lot about holding their breath. It happens automatically, and it helps you to become invisible. It helps you to freeze and hold all the feelings in your body. It helps you not to feel. It is an automatic and necessary response to trauma.

　　Take a moment, now, to check in with yourself. Were you just holding your breath? Did you suddenly inhale when you read that sentence? As you pay attention, can you notice whether your breath is deep and slow, rapid and shallow, or someplace in between? Can you tell whether your breath is focused up in your chest or down in your belly? Commonly, people who were traumatized as children take what they think are deep breaths in the upper part of the chest. Do you feel as though you don't have access to your belly, the place where deep breathing occurs when you're safe? As you continue to read, see what happens if you let yourself check in once in a while and become aware of the quality of your breathing.

By learning to return to the breath, you reclaim your right to feel, to be in your body, to be in the present moment, a moment you had to escape by any means available back then. Whenever you simply notice your breathing, you bring yourself back to the here and now, automatically. Inevitably. It's impossible to be stuck in the past, or the future, when you focus on this breath, and then the next. It brings you back to your body and back to where you are, right here, right now.

Usually it's hard to calm your breathing right away when you find yourself engulfed in terror. At these times, it's enough to say, "Now I am breathing in and out rapidly, and I am afraid." When you do this, you bring the fear into your adult awareness. Your adult observer becomes more involved and you give yourself a moment of respite, some detachment from the childhood feeling. You strengthen your ability to be aware *of* it, instead of being lost *in* it.

Thich Nhat Hanh, a Vietnamese Buddhist monk, talks about holding intense feelings gently in your awareness, as if they were cradled in your hands, as you continue to breathe.[3] Instead of experiencing your feelings as an enemy with which to struggle, focusing on gentleness and the awareness of this breath, and then the next, can allow you to observe your feelings without being carried away by them.

Many adults who were abused as children find that, when they practice ways to return to the breath, the benefits of doing so become greater over time. Jayne comes to mind. She had been sexually abused from an early age by one of her caretakers. One of her ways of coping with the abuse was to become very still, to have a quiet voice—to do everything in her power to be invisible. For years Jayne had been burdened by a feeling of self-consciousness that left her feeling anxious and ashamed whenever she had to talk to people. This response was as powerful with friends as it was at work, and it left Jayne preferring to spend her time alone. Her constant worry was that she would say the wrong thing and upset someone or that she would have nothing worthwhile to say. As she practiced returning to the breath and becoming focused in the present moment, her automatic response of agonizing shame began to lessen.

Before learning to focus on her breathing, Jayne would become so caught up in her internal dialogue of self-blame and self-hate that she had no adult observer available to help her shift away from the child state that had been activated. At first, it was hard to remember to come back to her breath. When she *was* able to remind herself to notice her breathing, it allowed her to access just a little bit of her adult observer. Even a little bit was enough to shift her perspective slightly. Even a small amount of awareness that she was stuck in a child state helped her, eventually, to move out of it.

When you take time at home, in a place that is safe and quiet, to learn to focus on your breath, you develop an ability to do so more effectively when you're out in the world. Two things happen. First, your body learns how it feels to be settled and focused, instead of being caught in the throes of intense emotion. Second, learning to be present with the flow of your breath teaches you how to be present with the flow of your thoughts and feelings as well. You learn that you *can* tolerate the flow of awareness now that you are an adult and no longer in the powerless, vulnerable state in which you existed as a child. When you continue to breathe naturally and follow the rhythm of the inevitable in and out of your breath, you also learn that feelings *do* keep moving, that they eventually move through and then out of your immediate field of experience.

When we hold our breath, we also clamp down on our feelings. That makes it much harder to let them go. In fact, this is just like working with pain. The more you struggle against it, push at it, or hold onto it, the stronger it gets.[4] If you can let your feelings flow through your awareness, things change. You may notice that the feelings fluctuate from stronger to weaker and that they come and go.

When you observe rather than grab hold of them, they tend, eventually, to flow all the way through you until they are gone.

Many abuse survivors have found it helpful to spend a little time each day focusing on their breath. While you may not be interested in doing a formal meditative practice, adapting the meditative process to your own unique needs can be extremely beneficial.

SPECIAL ISSUES FOR MULTIPLES

If you are a multiple, you might find it especially challenging to be mindful of what is passing through your consciousness. Because you may have a number of personalities arguing, commenting, feeling, or responding to any given event or thought, it can be confusing, at best, to observe your inner process.

Even with all the confusion you have inside, it can still be helpful to return to your breath and strengthen your adult observer. That you currently function as an amalgam of parts is true. That you also have a present-day observer that can bridge among parts, no matter how undeveloped it may be as yet, is also true, even if it doesn't feel that way right now. A major accomplishment in your healing will be learning to recognize and return to a consistent adult observer when parts related to early childhood trauma become triggered. In addition, becoming centered and grounded in the moment can be soothing to many parts of you and can help you develop a greater sense of safety in the present.

For those of you who haven't as yet developed a reliable sense of an adult part of yourself, the breath can still become a place of focus, one where you can develop an adult observer over time. For example, each part of you has a relationship to the breath. Some may be frightened child parts that breathe rapidly. Some may be parts that forget to breathe altogether. Others may be parts that simply aren't aware of their breathing at all, as yet.

As you practice returning to the breath, you can ask "translator parts" to help you teach the other parts to calm down by paying attention to the breath. Translator parts are good to know about. They are parts of the self that operate to put words to feelings that child parts may be too young to know. They can help bring into conscious awareness feelings that may be too far inside to reach easily. In this exercise, they can help translate your learnings about focusing on the breath to other parts. As I have said before, there's no need to understand *how* helper parts operate. It's enough just to ask.

Meditations on the Breath

There are many beautiful meditations available that focus on the breath. Following are a couple of exercises that draw from various sources:[5]

First, settle yourself in a sitting position someplace where you can be comfortable and undisturbed for a little while. Then, simply begin to observe your breath. When you inhale, say to yourself, mentally, "breathing in." When you exhale, say, "breathing out." Whenever you find your mind wandering, simply invite it back to the breath. If you discover that you have a tendency to criticize yourself for getting off track, take just a moment to be curious about where you learned to be impatient with yourself. It's always helpful to have your curiosity handy. That way, you won't miss the little clues that often crop up and tell you more of your childhood story. Someone taught you to be unkind to yourself. You can wonder who that might have been.

In a traditional meditative practice, you wouldn't bother with your curiosity. You'd simply come back to the breath, always back to the breath. At this point, though, it's helpful to remind yourself that you are as you are for a reason. The ways you were treated as a child—in the family, in school, in church or synagogue, in your community—all taught you things that became part of the fabric of who you are as an adult. When these are things that keep you locked into a traumatic past, you have a right to identify them and let them go.

If you wanted to do a more traditional meditation, you would save the curiosity for another time. For example, you might decide that, after meditating, you could choose to acknowledge the many clues that come into your awareness throughout the rest of the day, as best you could. Then, during your meditation, you would be free to focus on constantly returning to the breath without deliberately giving your attention to anything else. If you are interested in a more standard meditative approach, there are many good books available on the subject.[6]

Throughout the process of focusing on your breathing, your mind *will* wander. Most of us are amazed to discover that we can successfully focus on the breath for no more than several seconds at first. It takes continuing patience simply to observe how often your mind goes off track and how good it can feel to come back to the reliable presence of your breath.

If you'd like to do something that may speak to you deeply, as well as providing practice in focusing on your breath, you might do the following exercise. It is adapted from one of Stephen Levine's meditations:[7]

> Breathing in, mentally say to yourself, "May I dwell in the heart of healing." Breathing out, say, "May I heal into my full self."

There's no need to do anything else. Simply breathe naturally and repeat these two statements mentally as you inhale and exhale. You may discover how quickly you settle into a quieter state of mind. Your body may also settle into a deeper level of comfort than is customary for you.

Focusing on your breathing won't take away all the feelings. It may not even change anything right away. In fact, for some people, focusing internally *at all* may cause anxiety at first. If this happens, simply notice your response, just as you would any other. What consistently coming back to your breath *can* do is allow you to remember who and where you are: the observer of your experience, here now, feeling these particular feelings. Whatever the source of your feelings, you have the right to breathe through them and then decide what you want to do.

The more you come back to your present-day, adult observer—or just to the breath itself, for those of you who don't as yet experience the presence of an adult part—the more you strengthen your ability to stay focused and centered in the event that unprocessed pockets of time get triggered in the course of day-to-day activities. It is within the perspective of your present-day observer that you have access to more constructive response options—such as reassuring yourself, opening lines of communication with a difficult person, or asserting your needs and wishes—that are so different from what was available to you in childhood. Your breath offers you a continuous way to reinforce your right to be free from childhood helplessness, to return to your adult state of mind, and to strengthen your sense of mastery in the present.

Leaves on a Stream

One of the popular metaphors to represent the stream of consciousness is a stream of water. With your mind's eye, take a moment, now, to imagine a stream. You might want to do this with your eyes closed, but that's not essential. The stream that comes to mind may be in a woods, running through a wide pasture, coming down a mountain, or somewhere else in nature. It may be one you've seen before in real life, or it may be a fantasy stream that comes as a creative image of your own. Either is fine.

Next, imagine that there are leaves floating on the stream. These leaves are like the contents of your consciousness—your feelings, thoughts, body sensations, pockets of time from childhood—and all of the *good* things available in your unconscious, as well—your dreams, wishes, talents, and other resources.

As you observe the leaves floating by, there are several different things you might choose to do with them. First, you can simply watch them go by, noting that they are there, perhaps noticing their shape and size. There's nothing else to do—just observe that they are present and that they are floating through your conscious awareness. You are noticing something that is passing through your experience and that's enough.

Staying focused in your present-day observer, simply note the leaves and then let them go. You might decide that you want to watch them float downstream and disappear around a bend. Or you might not want to watch them any farther than when they pass right in front of you. Notice how quickly they flow out of your awareness when you don't bother to follow their progress downstream.

Now, imagine that you are feeling anxious, scared, or angry. As with the leaves on the stream, you have a choice. You can simply observe the feeling as it flows through you. You can let yourself know that it's there. You acknowledge it. Sometimes, when a feeling is acknowledged consciously, that's enough. That's all it needed. It can then float on down the stream and out of your awareness.

Vera is an abused survivor who tried this as an antidote to her feeling of panic whenever she had to deal with authority figures. The thought of approaching her boss created a feeling akin to terror, accompanied by repetitive thoughts of being fired or making a fool of herself. Over time, as she practiced, Vera was able to take note of the panic she felt, acknowledge it, and let it go, just as if it were a leaf drifting by on her stream of consciousness. She realized that she didn't have to grab hold of it, or let it grab her, and that it was possible simply to observe it.

This strategy didn't work perfectly every time, but Vera did find that it became easier to express herself with her boss when she wasn't so totally caught up in her terror. And success breeds confidence. Each time she lessened the panic by letting the feelings float by, she learned that it was possible not to be at the mercy of her feelings. It didn't have to work every time. Knowing that it could work *at all* was an important discovery.

Another approach with the leaves on the stream is to reach out and take hold of one of the leaves and really examine it, *if you choose to do so*. The key here is that you have the right to choose how you want to deal with things. If, from the perspective of your present-day observer, you want to take some time to explore the leaf, you can. You may want to look at it from every angle. Or you may just want to stare at it for a while, to discover if you see anything you haven't noticed before.

In terms of getting to know your feelings, this approach would be like going inside to find the child part that is related to the feeling you are having. This is one of those times when you might choose to build a bridge of awareness between an inner child part and your adult observer by imagining a dialogue between these two parts of you. It would represent your choosing to take a few moments to explore the child's experience, to *share* the feelings.

For Tim, learning to identify his feelings, and then to take a few moments alone to deal with them, was an important revelation. Tim grew up in a chaotic, alcoholic family where there was a great deal of physical violence. He had shut out conscious awareness of his feelings, especially his anger. As a result, he had been at the mercy of a gnawing, but unacknowledged, irritation that constantly got him into unpleasant interactions with his friends and especially with his son. As he developed a capacity to observe his irritation with curiosity, as if it were a leaf on a stream, he discovered that at a deeper level he actually felt fear. When he took a little time to find the inner child part that was connected to the fear, he found that he was able to soothe himself to a point where his irritation level lessened.

Yet another approach is to reach out for one of the leaves and take just a moment or two to acknowledge it. Then, set it aside until later, with a promise that you will come back to it when you have time. This is like taking a moment to identify and briefly comfort an inner child part when you are triggered by something, then recentering yourself and promising to go back later, when you have time, to explore more deeply what the child was feeling.

If you choose to acknowledge a feeling and then put it aside until later, make sure that you do go back to it. Essentially, you are saying to your unconscious that you recognize something is going on, but you need some time and space to do other things first. You are agreeing to come back later, to look more deeply at this, if—for now—the feelings will subside. You are asking the unconscious to "put the leaf aside for a while," to free your adult observer to take care of some present-day matters, and you'll be back later to examine it.

Often, your unconscious will cooperate and respond by easing the feeling. The only requirement is that you keep your end of the bargain each time you ask for this kind of arrangement. If you tend to forget or choose not to take the time later to get in touch with what was going on with you, this particular strategy probably isn't the one to use.

Peggy discovered that identifying the feeling and coming back later to deal with it was a useful strategy during a busy school day. As a child, Peggy was given responsibility for her younger siblings and was punished severely if any problems arose. Later, during graduate school, she consistently had deadlines to meet and work to do. From time to time, she would experience a wave of anxiety and worry about failing her classes or not measuring up to a teacher's expectations. When this happened, it was hard for her to concentrate on the work that needed to be done.

She made an arrangement with her unconscious—or, more directly, with a helper part that soothed whatever child parts may have gotten triggered. Then, when she was through for the day, she spent some time drawing before she went to bed in the evening. Using crayons, she invited whatever child part may have been upset earlier in the day to draw a picture of what had caused the anxiety, from a child's perspective. Often, she drew a picture of some childhood event she hadn't thought about for a long time or hadn't brought into conscious awareness before. When this happened, her adult observer gathered important information about specific, unresolved childhood distress, information she could take into her therapy process. In the meantime, she did her best to soothe whatever child parts needed comfort.

The exercise of observing leaves on a stream can be relaxing and meditative in and of itself, and naturally strengthens your present-day observer. Sometimes it's nice just to sit for a while, knowing that leaves are floating by, that thoughts and feelings are present, and that you don't have to do anything about them. You can just look at the other side of the stream, watch a tree, a bird, or a butterfly, or just let your mind be deliciously blank, and allow the stream to keep on flowing.

Taking Some Time Off

Often, adults who were abused as children feel internal pressure to keep on with the healing, all the time, no matter what. And it *is* important, in the long run, to get through the pain, work through the memories, and heal the wounded places inside. It is equally important, though, to discover a balance that probably wasn't available to you as a child. There are times when it's all right to put the hard work aside for a while and just hang out. These are the times when you can let the leaves on the stream just float on by. They'll be there when you need them. *It's healthy and worthwhile to learn that you can have good things in your life, and fun activities, even as you deal with previously unprocessed childhood trauma.*

Too often, survivors of childhood abuse unconsciously overwhelm themselves just as they were overwhelmed as children. This happens when you ask yourself to dig more deeply than you're ready to dig. It happens when you insist on sticking with the pain even when friends have invited you out for some fun you secretly would like to have. Sometimes it's impossible to take time off from the healing. It's just too present and memories or feelings are emerging that you can't ignore. It's worthwhile, though, to be able to ask yourself what would happen if you did learn to take some inner, and outer, time just to be with yourself in a soothing way.

If you find that you cannot feel comfortable allowing yourself to have light moments along the way, ask yourself why. With your adult observer, become curious about what you fear might happen if you don't give it your all, every moment. You might discover something important about your childhood story, about how you coped in the face of experiences you were too young to handle adequately.

You have a right to choose. It's your stream of consciousness and it has many gifts to give you, gifts of awareness. When, how, and where you reach in and take hold of those gifts is up to you. The important thing to know is that you can choose to have both your everyday life of work and activities *and* your inner life of recovery and healing, at the same time.

"Big Surprise"

Another aspect of meditative practice that can be helpful has to do with *how you interpret feelings and events.* For some people, having any kind of feeling come into awareness becomes a cause for alarm or is interpreted as being out of control. Feelings are experienced as extreme—to have a negative feeling means something must be wrong and it has to be fixed *right now*. To have an angry response means things are terrible and shouldn't be that way. To have worked hard on an issue in therapy and have it crop up again means you are a failure. To have something unfortunate or painful happen to you is interpreted as awful, unfair, or evidence that your life isn't working well.

It helps to remind yourself that feelings are an important, and inevitable, part of being human, and that life inescapably contains a mixture of good and bad experiences. Life isn't always fair, and awful things do happen to good people. When we insist that unfortunate events never happen to us, and that it proves we are bad and deserve abuse when they do, we set ourselves up for constant distress in present-day living. It's not unusual for children who are being hurt to believe that if they were good, they wouldn't be abused. As adults, many of us continue to believe that if we are good people and do things by the rules, bad things will never happen to us. When things do go wrong, which they certainly will if we are at all involved in an active life, deep feelings of anger, fear, or sadness erupt in response to what was supposed to be a world free from any further hurts.

As your present-day observer develops and your cognitive tree adds more branches, your perspective on what certain feelings mean and how to deal with them can become more masterful. Basically, our feelings help us respond to the world and provide us with information about what is happening. They are an important source of information and mastery in the present, if we can learn to interpret them in ways that allow us to respond with our adult capacities and options.

With that in mind, take a moment to think about the feelings that most characterize your ongoing experience of the world. As a result of events in your childhood, you may find that certain uncomfortable or difficult feelings crop up over and over again in the present, depending on what happened to you. For example, if you lived in a home where you were chronically neglected or your feelings and needs were constantly overlooked, feelings of sadness, anger, and loneliness may be all too familiar. Fear of other people's displeasure might plague your adult relationships. If you were in a home where there was lots of physical violence, a hovering sense of panic or terror may be a constant companion.

One of the ways you can strengthen your ability to tolerate the feelings that come from childhood wounds is to develop an ironic attitude of "big surprise" when old, recurring feelings come up again and again, or when life presents a challenge you didn't expect. In some meditation approaches, "big surprise" is what the monks say when meditators find themselves plagued by repetitive and intrusive thoughts.[8] When you adopt this attitude toward your feelings, it's as though you're saying to yourself, "Oh yeah. I know you. Fancy meeting you here!"

You might even find that an attitude of "big surprise" towards feelings that consistently have brought you distress allows you to draw upon another helpful aspect of your adult observer: a sense of humor. If you can get a chuckle out of falling into the same old hole again, you may get just that little bit of distance that will allow you to go on with your day and get the things done that need your attention. Please be aware, though, that this is not at all like "humor" with which you may have been attacked as a child, under the name of teasing. Instead, "big surprise" is a gentle, soft humor, a kind of delight that you caught yourself at it again and became aware of yourself.

It also helps to remember that healing occurs in a spiral. We swing around again and again to the same old issues, but at different turns of the spiral. Each time we confront a similar feeling or reaction we have yet another opportunity to learn and to heal. Each time, we bring with us whatever new understanding we have gained since the last time we cycled through this particular difficulty.

As you get stronger, you'll be able to deal with your issues at ever deeper levels. Each time you resolve one level, you open to the next. It's important, though, to recall that, on the spiral, there are swings *away from* your pain, as well as back into it. Allowing yourself to say, "Ah, big surprise!" provides a light moment, a present-day perspective, that can ease the inevitable distress when you discover that the feelings are still there and you have to deal with them yet again.

Marla found the "big surprise" exercise particularly helpful. Because of her history of being psychologically abused—taunted and criticized at every turn by her older sister—she was highly vulnerable to any sense that she might displease others. Whenever she was with a friend, if she thought the friend didn't find her interesting or that she had said something the person might not like, she would fall into an old, familiar feeling of deep insecurity. She would go over in her mind how she could fix things with the other person, rehearsing again and again what she could say or do to make it better. She was lost in a worried child part, with no access to her adult observer. These thoughts would plague her, and she had difficulty getting away from them.

With this litany running around in her mind, Marla would begin to sink deeper into panic. All she wanted to do, finally, was make it all go away and pretend that nothing bad had happened. As she learned to access her adult observer by saying "big surprise" to her panic about upsetting people, she began to get some distance from the feelings. She found it easier to soothe herself with internal reassurance from this part of her, which brought some present-day reality to bear on her childhood feelings. Knowing that the feelings would come around again and that she could say "big surprise" many times also helped. No longer did the feelings signal a slide back into a place she couldn't manage. Instead, they became an opportunity to do some more healing of unresolved childhood hurts.

As you experiment with "big surprise," remember to be gentle with yourself. Avoid being critical or sarcastic. This exercise is intended to be a light reminder that, of course, the feelings are back again. Of course you're cycling around again to the wounded places inside. This doesn't signal something bad. It does allow you to recognize that the feelings are flowing through your awareness once more and you can choose simply to acknowledge that fact. There is nothing to do, nothing to change. You are allowing yourself to reconnect with your adult observer so that you can remember this is your area of vulnerability. It probably will be triggered often, but that doesn't mean you have to react to it. You have a right simply to observe and comment on it to yourself.

White Light Meditation

There are other ways, as well, to focus your attention in a quiet place inside, where you can take some time to feel centered and to strengthen your adult observer. Again, for those of you who may not experience an adult part as yet, you can allow this exercise to strengthen an internal experience of stability, perhaps unrelated to any specific part of you, that is becoming more available to you in your present-day life.

One way to increase your sense of centeredness is to meditate on a healing light. In many traditions, white light is considered to be a universal source of healing. If you are uncomfortable with white light for any reason, simply choose another color that connotes a positive, healing quality.

To begin, find a place where you can sit quietly for a little while without being disturbed. It may feel good to sit with your back erect, legs folded under you, or in a straight-backed chair with your feet on the ground. Experiment. There will be certain postures that feel more centering than others; find what works best for you.

Once you have settled, take a moment to focus on your breathing, simply becoming aware of when you inhale and when you exhale. There's nothing to *do* right now. Simply observe. Notice how your mind may want to wander, and then, how you can gently invite yourself back to the focus on your breathing. There's no need to criticize or force yourself. It's all right just to bring yourself back to the breath any time you find your mind has gone off to something else.

Then, imagine, if you will, a source of white light just above your head. The light may come from a sphere or some other origin that makes sense to you. The important thing to realize is that this is a *healing* light.

Now, without demanding or preconceiving what the light will do, allow it to flow down through the top of your head and fill your whole body. Notice that the flow can be gentle, yet powerful. It can fill all the *spaces* inside your body, even as you absorb it into your skin, muscles, and other tissues. It may even pervade your thoughts and feelings. If you are a multiple, assume that each part is experiencing the light in some way that is meaningful and healing.

As you continue to breathe comfortably and allow the light to flow all the way through you, notice that it moves out through the bottoms of your feet. You might imagine that this light not only nourishes you, but also cleanses you, carrying away any debris you don't need any-more—old thoughts, feelings, behaviors you have outgrown, present-day stresses and tension from your body.

Take a moment simply to experience the flow of the white light and the responses you feel inside. Allow yourself to soak in any pleasant sensations or good feelings that may arise. If you notice any areas of tension or anxiety, simply breathe and allow them to flow through your experience as the white light continues to fill you.

Then, notice that another light, which comes from the very center of the earth itself and conveys a deep sense of being grounded within your present-day self, begins to flow *up* through the bottoms of your feet. This light may be any color that comes to mind, as long as it represents something positive, rich, and deeply nourishing.

As with the white light, there is nothing to *do* but to allow this light to move up through your entire body and out through the top of your head. As it flows, your body can soak it in allowing the light to fill all the empty spaces inside. Your thoughts and feelings may also be pervaded by this light. As before, assume that all the parts of you receive a unique, healing experience as the light touches them.

Allow yourself to imagine that you possess a deep unconscious wisdom that knows how to utilize these two sources of light in support of your healing process. There is no need for you to be conscious of how this will happen. Focus on whatever sensations of being more centered and grounded in your present-day self may arise when you do this meditation, and leave the working of the light itself to your unconscious. If you have a specific request to make of your uncon-scious wisdom, allow yourself to dialogue with this part of you. You might think of it as your "center," your "higher self," or whatever metaphor makes sense to you. It's perfectly all right simply to ac-knowledge it as a wisdom deep inside that you don't know how to describe; you just know it's there when you experience its qualities.

Return, occasionally, to an awareness of your breath, simply noticing the natural "in" and "out" rhythm. Recall that your breathing
continues even when you aren't aware of it. It is something you can
count on. In the same way, the flow of the healing, centering light
from above your head and the grounding, nourishing light from the
earth itself continues even when you don't pay attention to it, consciously.

*   *   *

Use this kind of meditation to bring you back to yourself for some
quiet moments of just being. These moments are just for you, right
here, right now. They are gifts you can offer yourself that reinforce
your adult observer and enhance your ability to recenter yourself
when day-to-day living brings up unresolved feelings from childhood
or unexpected challenges that must be faced.

The approaches offered in this chapter just touch the surface of
what is available in self-help books and from therapists as ways you
can focus your attention to bring you back to the present moment and
to the awareness of your adult observer. Whether or not you are a
multiple, if you were hurt as a child, developing a present-day observer that is more present, more available to you is an essential part of
your healing process. This will increase your ability to function effectively and more comfortably in the present.

Another important aspect of healing from unresolved childhood
wounds, developing a strong and resilient adult observer, and living
your life with a greater sense of mastery involves increasing your
capacity to *contain*—rather than act on—your feelings. In the next
chapter, we'll explore how you can develop a capacity to sit with your
feelings and deal with what are often compulsive—and impulsive—
urges that take you away from what you need to know about yourself
and your inner life.

6

Containing and Sitting with Feelings

I FEEL LIKE I'M GOING TO . . .

If you are an abuse survivor, you know how difficult it can be to ignore what are sometimes powerful urges to act on your feelings, even if the consequences of acting may not be good for you. In this chapter, we look at a powerful way to make your life more manageable when these urges arise: containing feelings.

Containing your feelings involves allowing them into awareness without being compelled to seek immediate relief. Some people think that the concept of containing feelings is equivalent to "bottling up" what's going on inside. Instead, this kind of containing means *creating a safe space inside in which to explore and deal with your feelings.*

Often, therapy is described as becoming a container for the client's healing journey. It's a safe place to bring feelings and unresolved problems, a place where they can be held and respected as they are explored. When feelings are contained in this way, there is no need to *do* anything. Instead, you create safety and space for yourself, space in which you can learn things you need to know about your emotional life.

To contain feelings in a healing way, it's essential to acknowledge, first, that feelings are normal. Fully functioning human beings have both good *and* bad feelings, sometimes all at once, and certainly once in a while.

For so many adults who were abused as children, the world of feelings was intense and overwhelming. Often, we had no one to soothe our hurt, and we were too young to do it for ourselves. We couldn't learn how to contain our feelings because our world was out of control. In fact, for many abuse survivors, one of the most difficult effects of living in an early environment that was out of control emotionally is that they didn't learn to modulate feelings. It was all or nothing.

Growing up traumatized may have left you with a legacy of difficulty in expressing and managing feelings, especially if you used dissociation as a means of coping with childhood experiences. When you are dissociated, as well as immersed in a setting that is either stifled or out of control emotionally, getting in touch with feelings can feel dangerous or against every rule you learned about how to be safe in the world.

For example, you may have come from a family in which everyone shouted a lot and anger was acceptable, even when it hurt or frightened people. Or your family may have allowed only sadness and punished any evidence of anger, even if it were just "that look on your face." Your family may have been violent, expressing negative feelings physically. You may have grown up in a home where feelings weren't expressed at all, you never saw grownups fight, and you were never allowed to cry, stomp, or shout. Or you may have grown up in a family where someone was ill, and no one was allowed to show disappointment, jealousy, or neediness in response to the fact that other person got all the attention.

In *Recreating Your Self,* I described the early experience of infants and their caretakers.[1] When a caretaker is secure and knows what he or she is doing, the infant experiences safety at a basic level, without words. Upsets are calmed and eased. The infant is fed, changed, or rocked, and the world is made right again.

When a caretaker is anxious, everything changes. Instead of feeling better, the infant's distress escalates. Now the whole world is in chaos and there is nowhere to turn for comfort. The infant learns, instead, that distress leads to more distress; discomfort becomes acute and the little one goes on overload. As an adult, this person will have a decidedly different experience with feelings from the person who had a skilled and confident caretaker.

You have a right to live comfortably with your feelings. It is your birthright. It's awful when you have to go back as an adult and learn something that is natural and automatic for people who grow up in supportive and nurturing environments. But it is a journey well worth taking, because being at ease inside your own skin not only is a great way to feel but also allows you to live life with a sense of inner mastery and competence.

Your Emotional Style

So many people have shared their despair with me about ever being able to handle their feelings well. Some are people who always make promises, even when they know they won't keep them, because they can't bear the terror they feel when someone is upset with them. Their fear of another person's anger, of being hurt, becomes the motivating force in their choices. Others include those who can't seem to keep from overreacting and "coming off the walls" when they are upset. Often, they are unable to stop blaming everybody else or feeling victimized when things go wrong.

Think, for a moment, of the ways your family taught you to deal with your feelings—or *not* to deal with them. You may not be aware of all the patterns you brought with you from childhood, but others who interact with you will know them. Each of us has particular ways of dealing with our feelings. Some of them work, but many are relics of a childhood in which we often felt out of control.

The dilemma is fundamental. For example, if in your family loud anger was common but sadness was ridiculed, you had to find some way not to feel the sadness. If the sadness accidentally slipped into your awareness and you started to cry or had a sad face, you risked

disapproval or humiliation. If in your family *any* emotions were punished or considered inappropriate, you also had to learn not to experience your feelings consciously, so you could fit in. If you grew up in
an alcoholic or incestuous family, chances are you had to participate in
keeping a very big, and deeply upsetting, secret. In order to do this,
you couldn't let yourself know how bad it felt to live with someone
who was unpredictable, would hurt you, or broke promises all the
time. If you hadn't learned how to shut down your feelings, you might
have reacted to what was really going on and revealed the secret.

When you are taught not to feel certain things and not to express
others, or when you have to dissociate your feelings because they are
too intense to bear, you remove from conscious awareness some very
important ways of knowing yourself and your world. First, you must
learn not to notice or acknowledge the important place right in the
middle of your stomach—the place that flutters, grabs, or becomes
nauseated when something important is happening to, or around, you.
It's the place you may have had to learn to discount, even when the
sensations were—and still are—strong. Or it may be a place inside
that you don't even know exists, because you were so young when
you had to make it go away or go numb.

This leads, inevitably, to being out of touch with important information about your world. Later, in adulthood, being shut down emotionally may lead to becoming revictimized, as when you don't recognize danger signals in your body that tell you to get to safety. This is
one of the very real and immediate hazards of continuing to use dissociative strategies in adult life.

Being shut down emotionally may also create a sense of dissatisfac-
tion with others, as you struggle to get your needs met without really
feeling what they are. When you have to shut down your feelings, you
are robbed of a natural, developmental process of learning to experience and express your emotional reality effectively.

Discovering Your Feelings

When water is dammed up and not allowed to flow along its natural course, it will collect and eventually spill over. When it does, it may be impossible to predict where it will go or what may occur. There may be flooding. There may be damage to existing structures and carefully planned landscapes. Trees, objects, and even people may be swept away with the rising tide of water that has suddenly found a release.

When feelings are pushed away and not allowed to flow through your awareness, they also build up and spill over. Often, you can't predict where they will go. Sometimes unacknowledged feelings come out as physical illness or other physical distress. The body takes on what the emotions can't express. Think of yourself or other people you know who suffer from unexplained rashes or hives, headaches, stomach distress, allergies, and various aches and pains that seem to have no identifiable physical cause.[2]

Sometimes, if you allow yourself to listen to your body's distress, you can learn to translate it into feelings. For example, if you become nauseated and know that there is no physical cause, you might take a moment to close your eyes and focus your attention inside. In your imagination, you might have a conversation with your nausea, giving it a "voice." During your dialogue, you might ask it what it is trying to communicate to you and then pay attention to any images or impressions that drop into your mind.

For example, what if your nausea said, "I'm afraid." Then you could ask what it fears. As a response, you might get an image of a child experiencing something that is frightening. I remember one person who was afraid to go to a particular park in her city. When she asked her stomach what it was about the park that frightened her, she became aware of a large boulder near a carousel. As she explored what was scary about the boulder, she recalled that there was a rock near her childhood home that had always frightened her. As she worked with her fear and allowed herself to build bridges between the past and present, she got in touch with memories of being terrorized by an older cousin near the rock. The nausea eased as the source of her fear became more focused and she was able to soothe herself effectively.

At other times, disowned feelings spill over as sarcasm or destructive actions towards yourself or others. Because you may act from a basis of unprocessed, unacknowledged feelings, you may not realize the extent of the potential for damage until it's too late. Think of the times when you may have been hostile toward, or unaccountably enraged at, someone, only to realize later that actually you were frightened but unaware of your fear.

If you are a multiple, dialoguing with your feelings may entail asking one of the translators or other helpers to let you know what some part of you is feeling. There may not yet be bridges of awareness between you and the part that is having the nausea, for example, so you can't as easily just turn your awareness inside and ask your body what is going on. Over time, as you develop increasingly conscious relationships with the various parts of you, your dialogues may become more like those described above.

Of course, there may be times when you ask a question about what you are feeling and an answer will drop right into your head, just as it would with someone who didn't use as extreme a dissociative strategy as yours. It's helpful to remember that each person is unique; the means you develop for increasing your awareness of feelings will evolve in whatever ways are natural for you.

Translating Feelings into Action

One way many people deal with their inability to tolerate feelings is to engage in compulsive or addictive behaviors. These activities may feel as out of control as anything experienced in childhood, but often they seem to be the only way to deal with the buildup of unexpressed feelings. Usually, the compulsive behavior or addiction becomes the channel through which people divert the dammed-up feelings into activity without having to bring the actual feelings into conscious awareness.

Translating feelings into actions is something most of us do at least some of the time. Take a moment, now, to think about some of the ways you stay away from your feelings. Then, imagine how many times you may have "been around this same block." Have you noticed that, no matter how many times you may have repeated the same behaviors and seen that they don't really work well, things still don't change?

One of the problems with translating feelings into actions is that— each time you do so—instead of resolving anything, you actually lose an opportunity to heal. This is true for multiples and non-multiples alike. Rather than taking a moment to get in touch with what actually is going on, you divert your true feelings from conscious awareness by whatever actions you engage. Nothing is gained; in fact, chances are that you may end up feeling worse, not better. In psychology circles, moving away from feelings in this way is called *acting-out*.

Acting-Out

Once you've come to an understanding with yourself about acting-out, and learned just why it's such a problem, you have gained another valuable opportunity to further your healing from moment to moment in your daily life.[3] There's nothing inherently wrong with acting-out. It just wastes your time, because it diverts your feelings and robs you of a chance to come to terms with unprocessed childhood trauma.

Often it feels better, in the short term, to move into action and find relief, rather than to sit with what you feel and learn from it. For example, calling up your boss and making an excuse about why you can't make a presentation at a meeting might bring a momentary flood of relief and might even buy you some time. The problem is, what will you say next time you are asked to give a presentation? When will you deal with the fear of humiliation that overwhelms you when you think of speaking in front of a group of people? And what about the time you may have taken a tranquilizer instead of choosing to feel your anxiety and practice soothing yourself? What will happen if you feel a flood of anxiety and there are no pills available?

And what if some old, unresolved rage is coming up about someone who hurt you when you were young? Do you find you have a tendency to get into fights with people close to you, to get into blaming them for things, instead of dealing with the deeper, more difficult feelings from your past? Many of us fall into blaming and experiencing other people as the enemy when conflicted and painful feelings about important people from the past begin to surface. While it may be natural to feel this way, it's important to realize that blaming others just wastes another opportunity to heal yourself, to dig deeper and resolve the really hard stuff.

If you are a multiple, and your parts act out rather than deal with their feelings, you also lose an opportunity to heal. The problem is that you may be unaware of the actions other parts of you take until after the fact. You may ask, "How can I stop myself from acting out when I don't even realize I'm doing anything?" And you may feel angry and frustrated that you can't seem to stop these other parts.

At times like these, it's helpful to recall that in reality—even if you can't experience it at this point—you and your parts as a totality constitute *one* consciousness. Because of this, as your present-day observer develops, you may be able to cope with acting-out behaviors more effectively than you ever imagined possible.

Whether you are a multiple or not, as a good rule of thumb, it's more supportive of your healing process if you avoid acting-out. It helps to remember that, each time you act out, you put off the inevitable moment when you'll have to sit with those feelings and get to know them. Eventually, there is nowhere else to run.

To be sure, there are lots of ways we run away from our feelings. For Julie, who had been traumatically neglected as a child, a primary way of seeking relief from intolerable feelings of abandonment was to blame the people around her for her difficulties. Instead of allowing herself to acknowledge how frightening it was when people she cared about had other friends, Julie would yell at her friends when they made plans that didn't include her. Until she was able to admit that it was fear, not anger, that welled up inside her, Julie was stuck in the same old place, losing friends and not knowing how to change things. Until she could look inside and find the pain of having felt desperately alone and insignificant in her family, she continued to experience those same feelings in relationship after relationship.

Earl had a different way of getting away from his feelings. Instead of using anger, he used sex. From an early age, whenever he felt insecure, a feeling that would send him into a panic, he would masturbate or seek out a sexual encounter. It was hard for him to allow himself to sit through the urge to turn to sex because he had never learned that he could survive his feelings. He didn't know how to let them flow through him without being carried away by them. As an adult, if he couldn't find a sexual outlet for his internal terror, he would get high or smoke even more cigarettes than usual. For Earl, *any* means available to numb his feelings were a potential way for him to act out.

It was different for Alicia. As an abuse survivor, she couldn't bear the shame she felt when she disappointed someone or when someone was critical of her. The feeling was simply so overwhelming that she would fly into action and try to make things better. Phone calls, personal visits, gifts, and a constant internal dialogue about how she could make it better plagued her. It was only as she allowed herself to feel the shame fully, and trace it back to its origins in her childhood, that she could tolerate the displeasure of others.

Allen ran away from his feelings by drinking himself senseless. From the first time he had a drink, all he wanted to do was to be "completely unaware" of the feelings inside him. He had found a quick way to numb out, to get away from the realities he didn't know how to confront. For Allen to heal, he had to stop drinking and allow that important place in his stomach—the place where his feelings live—to awaken.

When he stopped drinking, Allen was surprised to discover that he had used extensive dissociation to survive an abusive childhood. While he was drinking, the blackouts, loss of time and other aspects of his behavior were all attributed to alcohol. Now, finally, he had a chance to focus on what really needed attention: his abuse history and how he coped with it as a child.

Sitting with Feelings

If you can relate to these experiences, there is a first step you can take, now, to learn what you need to know about allowing your feelings to come more consciously and fully into your awareness. To begin, it's essential to identify your basic acting-out behaviors. This requires being honest with yourself about how you run away from feelings. Initially, you may have no idea of how you divert yourself when feelings start to come up. Working with a therapist or support group will help you become more conscious of your feelings, your acting-out behaviors, and how you deal with them.

Once you've gotten a handle on what you do to seek relief, you are ready to learn some new strategies. When you become aware of a feeling and can sense that you have an urge to act out—to eat, drink, shop, fly into a rage, blame someone, get lost in a book or TV, or hurt yourself—*take just one minute and sit with the feelings before doing anything*. During this minute, ask yourself, "What does it feel like, right now, *not* to act out?" "How am I dealing with this feeling, *right now?*" Then, you might be curious about what you would feel or become aware of if you were to continue to choose not to act out. Notice what comes to mind. You may be surprised to discover what you are struggling not to feel or know.

This might be the longest minute of your life, but you give yourself a valuable opportunity when you ask yourself to stay put and feel whatever is going on inside. Then, if you have to go ahead and act out, at least you will have increased your awareness of what you are feeling. You will have given yourself an important moment of healing.

The next step is to sit for *two minutes* before acting. Again, the goal of sitting isn't just to count the seconds until the time is up. Instead, it's important to give yourself permission to become aware of what's going on inside. Above all else, be gentle with yourself. Acknowledge that feelings scare you, that you need to build up some tolerance for being with them.

Once you have developed the capacity to sit with your feelings for a few minutes instead of immediately acting out, you can extend the time. You will extend, as well, your conscious awareness of how you tend to respond to distress, whatever the source. Eventually, the urge to fly into action will diminish. As you reap the benefits of dealing with feelings instead of running away from them, you'll feel less inclined to act out. As you feel your internal strength and mastery develop, you'll look forward to increasing your capacity to sit with and manage your feelings.

The important thing to keep in mind is that each time you struggle to become more aware, rather than fly into action, your strength *does* increase. You may not even notice it at first; it just happens. On reflection, sometime in the future, it may even be hard to remember that you ever felt so vulnerable and out of control with your feelings.

It is also helpful, at those times when you act out and don't realize it until later, to sit down and review what happened, in detail. For example, allow yourself to think back to the moment when you felt the urge to act out. What was going on, or what may have gotten triggered earlier that you hadn't noticed, consciously? Then, review your choice to act out and the behaviors you engaged in as you did so.

The purpose of this exercise isn't to berate yourself or show yourself how bad you were. Instead, it is to raise your level of conscious awareness about how acting-out works to divert you from your feelings. It can be immensely valuable to allow yourself to become familiar with the kinds of situations that tend to elicit acting-out behaviors. With this information, you can develop a greater ability to choose to sit with your feelings as they arise.

Another unexpected discovery for many people is that—as they learn to tolerate painful or threatening feelings—good feelings also become more available. It's as though all the feelings live in the same place. If you avoid the bad ones, you lose out on the good ones, too.

For example, people who are healing from childhood abuse are often surprised when they have a lighthearted day. It may have been so long since they felt that certain kind of freedom or joy that they had forgotten such feelings were even possible. Sometimes it's devastating when you feel that precious lightness of being, only to lose it to a feeling of fear or anger. What's important to remember is that feelings keep moving. What you'll discover as you heal is that you'll move through more and more positive feelings and the bad ones won't last as long.

Learning to sit with your feelings and contain them safely, giving yourself space to deal with whatever you are experiencing, empowers you to be more fully yourself. As you increase your ability to tolerate your feelings, you'll discover that you carry inside you all you need to move through whatever may come your way.

For Brenda, sitting with her feelings was an alien concept. For as long as she could remember, she had been in constant motion, always involved with outside activities. As a child, she was a high achiever in school. Not only did she do well in her classes, but she also served on the student council and was involved in the school newspaper. Always caught up in a whirlwind of activity, Brenda was able to get through a very difficult childhood without fully realizing the injury she experienced at the hands of her abusive parents—or that her dissociated parts made it possible for her to do so.

When she first came into therapy, it was a constant struggle for Brenda to allow herself to feel. She had no experience with modulating her feelings, because her childhood pattern of never having time to be alone with herself had continued into adulthood. She didn't know that she had the capacity to *learn* how to allow her feelings into her conscious experience a little at a time. It seemed to her that her only choices were either to have no emotional awareness at all or to face a flood of pain and fear she felt she couldn't survive.

Over time, and with practice, Brenda learned to sit with her feelings, beginning with 10 seconds at a time. She wasn't able to do a full minute at first. It was just too long to tolerate the powerful, unprocessed feelings related to her childhood abuse. The dissociated parts of her that held the feelings were too terrified to allow them into consciousness. Beginning with 10 seconds allowed her, and the parts, to realize that she would survive. In her own time, she began to add seconds, until she did, eventually, learn to sit with her feelings for a minute. One minute led to two, with the most important insight being that, if she could handle one or two minutes of her true feelings, eventually she could handle experiencing her feelings for any amount of time.

For Milt, sitting with feelings was also a new idea. Historically, he became angry at others whenever he felt he was being controlled by someone else. At first it was a real struggle for him to stop from acting on his anger. He began by going off to the bathroom when he felt his anger rising. There, in privacy, he took a few minutes to check in with himself, to explore what might be going on that was making him feel afraid. Rather than raise his voice, and sometimes embarrass himself, Milt learned that his anger wasn't everybody else's fault. Instead, it was a signal for him to find someplace where he could be alone for a few minutes, identify what control issues had been triggered, sit with his feelings, and soothe himself. He found that the simple act of recognizing and sitting with his feelings eased them; once he had let them move through his conscious awareness, he could go on with his day.

Learning to sit with your feelings is a deeply personal process. It requires that you get to know yourself more fully and consciously than you ever have before. It also invites you to learn more about feelings in general, and to realize that in your emotional world complexity is the norm, that mixed feelings are more usual than one feeling alone. As you learn to sit with your feelings, you also learn an important capacity that you have as an adult: you can feel vulnerable *and* solid all at the same time.

The Middle Ground

And so, one thing to know about your emotional life is that it is normal—and inevitable—to have mixed feelings. If you were hurt as a child, it may be difficult for you to know what to do when you experience conflicting feelings. The reality is that most of us have mixed feelings most of the time. Daily living is filled with them. We love someone, and we can't stand certain things about them. We're happy about a trip that's coming up, but we're afraid of change or the unexpected. We want to go to a movie at the same time we'd love to be soaking in a hot bath. Part of us would be delighted to have an ice cream cone, while another part of us craves a bowl of chili. A new job brings the excitement of further professional development, even as it triggers deep feelings of insecurity or fears of incompetence.

Learning to tolerate mixed feelings is a powerful and comforting capacity to develop. If you had been fortunate enough to grow up in a family where emotions were handled in healthy ways, you would have been allowed to feel good and bad about the same thing at the same time. In healthy families people seem to know that feelings are just feelings. They aren't a call to action. They aren't an indictment or rejection of other people. They are just a way that we humans know about the world and our experience of it. It's the rare moment when something is completely one way or the other. To really *know* this makes functioning on a day-to-day basis much less stressful than it is when we believe we're supposed to be totally in favor of one thing or totally opposed to another.

Also, for many abuse survivors, there was a need to draw on the unconscious protective mechanism of *splitting*.[4] A child who draws on this particular way of coping with abusive caretakers creates a *good parent* and a *bad parent,* each completely separate in the child's experience. Because of this, the child is able to feel loved by the good parent during times when abuse is not occurring. Then, when the same parent becomes abusive, the child doesn't experience any loss of the good parent. This is an essential psychological protection, when you consider that it would be too overwhelming for a child to know that the parent who cuddles her and makes her feel good could turn into the one who hurts her so badly.

Justine's grandfather was her favorite person in the family. He would bring her ice cream and candy, and take her to the zoo. When she began her healing process, she recalled only the good things about him, the good and warm feelings she had whenever she thought about him. As she began to explore her true feelings, though, she discovered that her grandfather was also the person who sexually abused her, hurting her terribly. It was difficult for Justine to allow herself to know that this special man was the same person who had so affected her entire life as a result of the abuse he inflicted.

For some survivors, like Justine, allowing mixed feelings about people who are important to them is profoundly threatening at first. They don't realize that it is normal and healthy to feel both good and bad things about the same person, without that person becoming *all* bad. Often, they idealize people, finding no fault with them at all, until a point comes when something doesn't go well and the feelings shift to experiencing the person as totally disappointing. Early childhood splitting has taken away the middle ground.

If you are a multiple, finding the middle ground can be a real challenge, because different internal personalities often have decidedly different feelings about things. For you, it is essential to create an internal setting where you can come together with the other parts of you and communicate and collaborate about decisions.[5] In the long run, though, the comments and exercises offered here will apply to you as well. It's just that, in your inner world at present, mixed feelings are much more firmly defined than in non-multiples.

Take a moment, now, to get in touch with how you respond when you realize that you like somebody but you don't like something about them. Or that you are going to a party and feel excited but resent the intrusion of it on your time. Notice what you tell yourself. Do you believe that if you have mixed feelings then you can't *really* like the person or don't *really* want to go to the party? How does it feel to tell yourself that all it means is that you have mixed feelings?

When you are able to acknowledge that you have mixed feelings, without experiencing a need to act on them, you continue to develop an internal sense of strength. No longer is your world thrown this way and that just because feelings are present. Conflicting or intense feelings no longer mean chaos, or that things are spinning out of control. Deep inside, you stand on more solid ground. You have a better sense that the world really is made up of a vast middle ground. It's not all black or all white. The middle ground leaves lots of room to move between and among different feelings without having to take a stand at the extremes. And so, learning to stand in the middle ground is an important part of managing day-to-day living with a greater sense of mastery.

Most of us who were hurt as children have to learn about the middle ground as a new concept. Dyanne had this experience, as she struggled with mixed feelings about work. She wanted to enter a career that she loved, even as she did not want to challenge her mother's primary unspoken rule: Dyanne was not to have a more exciting, satisfying life than her mother had had. Having raised four children alone, Dyanne's mother resented the loss of her own career.

As Dyanne learned about the middle ground, she realized that it was possible to acknowledge a childhood fear that her mother would be angry with her while also being in touch with how much she wanted her own career. In time, she allowed the fear to coexist with her desires. The fear became a feeling, rather than something to act on, even as her wish to have a career became a motivating force behind going back to school.

Linda had a harder time finding the middle ground. As a child, she had been brutally abused, and all of her feelings were intense and threatened to overwhelm her. She had lived in a world of definite good and bad, and she had learned many strategies to do her best to be a "good girl." Because of this, any feelings of anger, disappointment, or irritation with others were pushed away whenever they came to the surface of her conscious awareness.

In her relationships with friends, Linda's feelings could be hurt easily. If someone said something that reminded her of her abuser, part of her wanted to run away from that person forever. The most powerful trigger occurred when Linda felt that someone didn't respect her or care about her opinion. When she experienced this with a friend, instead of feeling her anger or disappointment, she would shut the person out of her life. It took her a long time to realize that mixed feelings are normal, even in good relationships. Part of her was sad to lose friends and missed some of the people she had cut out of her life. She had never allowed herself to feel beyond what certain inner child parts felt. She hadn't even known that she had mixed feelings.

As she explored the middle ground, Linda learned that it was perfectly manageable for her, as an adult, to have vulnerable child feelings coexist with a different, more grownup understanding of her friends. When she would find herself wanting to push someone out of her life, she would go inside and explore the middle ground. Her first awareness would be that she was having mixed feelings, and this realization came as a great relief to her. It meant that she didn't have to act immediately. Instead, she could take some time to figure out what she felt and then decide what she wanted to do.

A first step in getting to know about the middle ground is to realize that it is the most powerful place to live on a day-to-day basis. Extremes come and go in the lives of everyone, but *to get through the day with a sense of mastery, the middle ground provides the best perspective.* It is the internal stance from which you can weigh the complexities of adult living with less urgency or impulsiveness than you may feel when you are experiencing the world as a black-or-white place to live.

Discovering the Middle Ground

One way to discover the middle ground is, first, to find an image to represent it. For some people, the middle ground may be imagined as a landscape that has lots of room in which to move around or that feels solid underfoot. For others, it is experienced, symbolically, as many shades of gray. If this isn't colorful enough for you, you might imagine that when the world is all black or white there is very little color, and so a middle-ground image might be a brilliant rainbow. How very different it is to live in a world of color, where there is a range of feeling and expressiveness, rather than in a world that is all black or white. Take a moment, now, to explore the difference between the colorful middle ground and a black-and-white world. What do you feel in each?

You may discover something surprising. There may be parts of you that are absolutely terrified of the middle ground. To these parts, a colorful, expanded world may be too spontaneous to be safe. There may be too much room to move around, too much potential for exposure and danger. If you feel this way, it will be helpful to develop your awareness of the middle ground slowly, as you also learn to soothe the frightened child parts inside.

Over time, you may well discover that the middle ground is a surprisingly comfortable place to live, because it more closely mirrors the ebb and flow of your true feelings. At first, it may feel a bit dull. Some of the intensity is gone. The adrenaline rush you've been accustomed to having in your life will diminish, and this may take some getting used to. What's nice to know is that, as you learn more about the middle ground, deeper levels of comfort and richness come into your experience. The highs may not be as high, but the lows definitely aren't as devastating. And, remember, a rainbow can have dazzling colors. Just because the highs aren't as high as they used to be, they still can be pretty wonderful.

Creating Symbolic Containers

Learning to sit with, and getting to know, your feelings is the most important way to contain them on a moment-to-moment basis. Developing this capacity gives you the ability to deal with whatever comes up, no matter where you may be. As part of the ongoing process of healing and the journey into unresolved and leftover childhood experiences, there are other ways to contain your feelings, too. These can make it easier for you to dip in and explore what would have been too overwhelming to deal with as a child.

One technique is to use imagery to create different kinds of containers in your inner world. It's helpful to begin with an image of a safe place. This can be a place indoors or outdoors. It can be a place you know already or one that comes into your imagination spontaneously. The important thing to know is that your safe place contains *everything* you need to help you on your healing journey.

"Scrapbooks"

For some people, an imaginary scrapbook becomes a helpful container. It's a place where you can put impressions of memories and childhood feelings as they become conscious. These impressions might take the form of pictures, colors, words, swirls, or just the sense that something is on the page that reflects your childhood experience, even if you don't actually "see" anything.

Once you have your scrapbook started, you can promise yourself that you will review these impressions from time to time. As you go over what you have discovered and become familiar with your memories and feelings, you will be less likely to feel flooded or overwhelmed. Instead, you will have a better chance of feeling comfortable as you allow yourself to be in touch with what is happening inside. You'll have an idea of what issues are surfacing and how you feel about them. This kind of awareness can help you stay in touch with yourself in the present day, rather than being swept away by unexpected feelings.

"BOWLS AND BOXES"

Sometimes a beautiful box or bowl with a lid becomes a useful container. This can be an actual object, out in the real world, where you symbolically place certain feelings you will come back to later. It can also be an imaginary container in your safe place. The nice thing about these containers is that you can dip in a little at a time, getting in touch with your feelings gradually, in doses you can manage. You can do this by imagining that you lift the lid just a bit, which allows some of the essence contained within to flow from the container into your awareness. You may become aware of a body sensation or a feeling, or a memory picture may flash into your mind. Whatever comes, working with the container will allow you to send the message to your unconscious that you want just a little this time. Little by little, the imaginary container becomes unnecessary, as *you* learn to contain the feelings within your conscious awareness.

"ANCHORS"

You can choose certain objects that you associate with pleasant or safe *present-day* experiences and allow them to become anchors for re-grounding you into your adult self.[6] For example, you may have a scarf, rock, piece of velvet, favorite sweater, or some other object that always gives you a good feeling when you touch it. You can even create special anchors as part of your healing process, by holding them when you are having a relaxed imaginary journey through your safe place or by meditating with them in your hand. The possibilities are endless; the fundamental goal is to give yourself something you can touch to bring yourself back into an adult state of mind when feelings need to be contained rather than acted out.

Another kind of anchor is a fragrance, something that reminds you of feeling safe or satisfied. Cinnamon is a good smell, although not if it reminds you of any abuse or holiday horrors. Certain soaps, incense, candies and sachets can be carried in your pocket as an anchor.

You can also create a physical anchor in your own body. One of the ways to do this is to put yourself into a relaxed state and access a feeling of comfort or safety. Then, use your index finger to touch your wrist, thigh, or somewhere else that feels okay to touch. When you do this, you create a place you can touch later, to reorient yourself to a feeling of comfort when you feel upset.

There can even be a special place in your home where you put your particularly vulnerable feelings when you have to go out. The message to your unconscious is that you have things to do in the adult world, and you'll come back later to deal with your childhood issues. Be sure to return to the issue you tucked away. When you do, the unconscious usually cooperates by reinforcing the effectiveness of the container when you're busy with something else. If you forget to come back and deal with what you promised you'd look at, you'll probably find that the feelings bubble up in ways that aren't as manageable as when you go in on purpose to deal with them.

SPECIAL ISSUES FOR MULTIPLES

There are several important considerations when multiples attempt to become more aware of, and contain, their feelings. First is the puzzlement many multiples feel when they first enter therapy. Often life has worked pretty well for them until now, even though they may have been depressed or had difficulties in personal relationships. All of a sudden, it seems as though coping strategies that have worked for all these years aren't available anymore. While no one can explain why, it's not unusual for dissociative processes to shift as we get older and to be less effective by our middle years. Finding new ways of containing feelings you never even knew you had can be a daunting challenge.

As I mentioned earlier, beginning the process may lead to more frequent switching from personality to personality or losing time. In other words, you may find that you dissociate more than you did before. *When this happens, it is a signal to slow down.* When all is going well and the internal system feels relatively safe, dissociative processes are lessened. Whenever you notice that you are having more pronounced dissociative symptoms, you will know that some part of you is feeling overwhelmed by some experience or internal event.

It's helpful to remember that the only way you had to contain your feelings as a child was to dissociate them. Now, as you learn new skills, taking it slowly will allow you to reestablish a sense of equilibrium and help you to function in your present-day world more effectively.

Sometimes there are personalities within a multiple's system that become mobilized to commit suicide or hurt the body when feelings begin to arise. if this has happened to you, you can again know that you need to slow down. You also need to be in a therapy process where you and your therapist can communicate with personalities that make it their business to stop pain at any price. With this contact, you can work with the feelings instead of acting them out.

For example, Fern began to tap into childhood feelings about emotional and physical abuse that she hadn't felt consciously before. Whenever any feelings began to surface, another personality, John, became agitated and threatened to kill Fern. His job was to make sure she felt no more pain, no matter what.

Over time, John was helped to realize that each time Fern was able to experience her feelings and process them, she actually became *stronger* rather than more vulnerable. I mentioned this dynamic earlier, and it is important to keep in mind. When John was asked to notice Fern's increasing strength, the threat of suicide was averted.

At other times, you may find that you want to hurt yourself—for example, cutting, burning, eating things that don't agree with you, smoking, drinking—when feelings begin to emerge.[7] If you notice that this kind of self-mutilation is increasing, it's another signal to slow down. There is nothing to gain by overwhelming yourself, and everything to gain by allowing feelings into conscious awareness one small bit at a time.

Also, it's helpful to know that most of us, whether multiples or not, inevitably return to old coping mechanisms once in a while. When you think that you've overcome a particular form of acting-out, only to surprise yourself by doing it again at some point, you might think of it as a signal that you are stretching in some way. Somehow, you are moving into the unfamiliar ground of change, and need something familiar to cling to for the moment. When this happens, you may notice that—even though it feels familiar—something has changed: your present-day observer may be more available and the behavior may not be as powerful. Awareness of the feelings associated with acting-out tends to make this less useful as a strategy. And so, when this happens to you, allow yourself to recognize that you are stretching and that you can let go of that old behavior as soon as you realize this.

There are many other ways to learn to contain your feelings— probably as many as there are survivors of childhood hurt. The most important thing to realize is that it is always up to you. Your own creativity and willingness to be aware of what is going on inside provide the best guidelines as to how you can contain your feelings and the impulses that arise with them. What matters most is to know that, as an adult, whether you are a multiple or not, you have capacities available that simply didn't exist when you were a child. When you were little, you didn't have much choice. You could either stuff your feelings down and put them out of awareness, or you could impulsively act on them, often to your detriment.

Now, everything is different. Each moment offers a choice you didn't have before. Each moment allows you to practice being with your feelings, exploring what they communicate to you, and discovering that you can experience the strength that comes with awareness. As you learn to contain and sit with your feelings, you can discover, as well, that this process applies to *every* possible feeling you might have, no matter how strong, how frightening, or how terrible they may seem. In the next chapter, we'll look at two particularly difficult feeling states—disappointment and despair—and explore how to contain and deal with them.

Disappointment and Despair

I JUST DON'T KNOW WHAT TO DO

Some feelings are easier to contain than others. In fact, some are so basic and so deep that it takes courage and practice to deal with them consciously. They are difficult even to acknowledge, much less to sit with and allow. Of these feelings, disappointment and despair are two of the toughest. I have talked with many survivors of childhood trauma who find that disappointment and despair present the greatest challenges to their daily functioning. Disappointment can wreak havoc in current relationships, while despair can elicit depression, frantic activity, or suicidal feelings.

This chapter is devoted to an exploration of these difficult feelings. As they are dealt with and resolved, greater mastery and strength in daily living become possible. Resolving the issues behind despair and learning to face and resolve disappointments lead to less overwhelming emotional ups and downs. Relationships with others improve. Both disappointment and despair arise within an interpersonal context, when as children we interact with the people we need for our survival. Learning more effective ways to handle how it felt to be so let down by these important people in our lives may ease old vulnerabilities and deep shame, as we come to terms with the depth of need we felt to be cared for adequately when we were children.

As with every other feeling that comes from a childhood of hurt, each time you feel let down by someone is another opportunity to explore how you learned to cope with disappointment. Do you fly into a rage? Do you withdraw emotionally but act friendly? Do you leave physically and write off the person? As with triggers, each time you find yourself struggling with feeling disappointed in someone who matters to you, it is another opportunity to learn more about what life was like for you as a child.

It's the same with despair. When you find yourself falling into the feeling that you are completely alone in the world, or if suicide seems the only answer to such profound pain, what do you do to manage the feelings? Do you withdraw from other people and isolate yourself? Do you actually toy with the idea of suicide? Each time you find yourself falling into that bottomless hole, where you feel completely alone and are convinced that there is no one in the world to help you, it's another opportunity to deepen your healing. Children who are traumatically hurt inevitably feel despair. When you were very young, there was no way to deal with these feelings, there was just no place to put them. Now that you have your adult state of mind available and can build your cognitive tree, you have a place to put these devastating feelings.

We mask the impact of disappointment and cover our despair in many different ways. How we deal with disappointment and despair is uniquely individual and yet embraces the universal urge to get away from the pain. Most of us play out the ways we created to deal with these feelings in our current interpersonal relationships. When we were hurt as children, so many needs remain unmet, so many wishes, hopes and expectations have been crushed. Usually, there is no real chance for these natural needs to be respected or honored. This sets many of us on a path, which we may follow throughout our lives, of searching for what we didn't get back then. This search, unfortunately, often recreates the very devastation we originally felt in childhood, bringing yet more disappointment and despair our way.

When this happens, we come to believe that there is no way out of these feelings. Even if we choose to avoid relationships, the unresolved feelings of disappointment and despair may color our inner life. What is important to realize is that as an adult, today, you can deal with these feelings and discover that not all human relationships need be the source of so much pain.

SPECIAL ISSUES FOR MULTIPLES

Multiples often feel overwhelmed just by the thought of dealing with disappointment and despair. Within a context of severe abuse, a child's neediness and vulnerability are so devastatingly assaulted that, as one person said, the feelings are "as big as the world."

If you are a multiple, take it slowly, one small bit at a time, as you move toward these feelings. There is no rush. In fact, the slower you go, the easier it is to absorb the true impact and effects of having been hurt as you were. If you feel an urge to hurt yourself, or if you become suicidal as you begin to deal with these feelings more directly, remember that these are signals to slow down. They let you know that you need to spend some time building your strength and developing your adult observer.

Also, remember that some multiples don't experience themselves as having a present-day adult self, which is an important element in sitting with and healing these difficult feelings. If this is true for you, remind yourself that your consciousness holds much more wisdom and mastery than you may realize. This is one of those times to ask for helper or caretaker parts to assist you in your healing process.

It's Not Fair!
I Deserve to Be Rescued!

Whenever I conduct workshops for adults who were abused as children, someone inevitably makes a comment that goes something like this: "It sounds as though you are telling us that we have to take care of ourselves. I've spent a lifetime doing that and now I want someone *else* to take over for a while. I don't want to do all the work. I want someone to take care of *me.*" Often, there is a good bit of anger and frustration behind these statements.

Usually these comments emerge as we explore the many ways in which the present-day adult can become an important source of soothing and comfort for inner child parts. For some people, the thought of becoming their own supportive presence creates a feeling of being cheated. It's as though, if they learn to take care of themselves, they will lose out on the possibility of getting what they always wanted—a good parent, a loving caretaker who can manage all the bad things and make all the good things possible.

If you've ever had feelings like these, take a moment to think about them. You might find that there is a part of you that believes that taking hold of getting your own needs met would mean giving up the battle for justice. It's as though there were a child part inside that demands fairness: what was wrong must be made right! It's intolerable to imagine that, eventually, no one will come along to rescue you. Becoming a competent, masterful adult who can resolve internal distress and deal with life's challenges doesn't feel like a positive development to this inner child part. Instead, it feels like an unbearable defeat.[1]

As you allow yourself to explore what comes into your awareness now, are you able to sense the disappointment that may lie just under the surface of your wish for fairness? Is it possible to sense the child's despair at never having been given what was needed? As you continue to read along, see what happens if you invite part of your awareness to wonder about how you deal with disappointment and despair and how you may have protected yourself from their full impact.

For children who were traumatized, there *was* an undeniable need to be rescued. Sometimes it's hard to let go of an experience that feels so real, so immediate. To imagine that you can take care of yourself might feel as overwhelming as it was then—and as unachievable. For these inner child parts, there is a desperate need to hold onto the wish to be rescued, because it is inconceivable to them that they can have any mastery of their own.

It's helpful to remember that as children we must keep ourselves from knowing consciously our true helplessness. Whenever I talk with people who recognized that their situation was hopeless, they also experienced an overwhelming and intolerable sense of danger. It's at this point, often, that survivors report a part of the self shutting down or splitting off, and taking with it any conscious awareness of the true nature of the child's situation.

Continuing to seek rescue helps a child pretend that it might be okay. If she can be good enough, then Daddy will stop hurting her. She can maintain the fantasy that she has control over her world and can fend off the despair that would result if she knew she were really powerless to make any difference at all in what happens to her. As long as we keep striving, we don't have to see that there is nowhere to go.

These inner child parts have another way to avoid the realization that things won't change, that they won't get better. Under the experience of hurt and helplessness, when people we depend on let us down, may be another feeling—a certain kind of anger or stubborn determination not to give in or give up. Have you ever heard a child say, "I don't want it! It's not the same thing!" when offered a substitute for something he really wanted? How many of us have felt this way at some time or another, even if we couldn't openly admit it, maybe even to ourselves?

Most of us have a secret place inside, where we wait—patient and determined—for someone to come along and rescue us. It may be, for you, a place where you find pain, loneliness, and discouragement. If you dig deeper, it may also be a place where you feel a strong, if unconscious, resolution to wait until that "just right someone" comes along to make up for all the good things you didn't get as a child. It may be a place where you dig in your heels and avoid taking steps that would lead you through, and then beyond, the need itself.

And so, your secret place may hold hidden anger and perhaps stubbornness. It may be a place that says "I *won't!*"—a place that protects you from having to face and deal with the inevitable fact that the time for childhood is over and the needs of childhood can no longer be met by others in your adult life.

It's as though part of us can't bear to experience what it was like to be let down so horribly when we couldn't do things for ourselves, when we had to depend on others. To have needs that *must* be filled by others, and to have those needs ignored, humiliated, or abused, brings about almost intolerable feelings of vulnerability. It's even worse because, as children, we can't *not* have needs. We can't turn them off completely. We are built to seek out cuddling, soothing, positive regard, not to mention food, shelter and comfort.

No child should have to live in a hurtful environment. No child should have to experience neglect, beatings, humiliation, or any of the myriad ways we may be hurt in an uncaring situation. The best many of us could do was stuff down the feelings and make a secret promise that someday we would get what we wanted.

While it is natural to want what you didn't get as a child, the demand that others must make it better for you causes all kinds of problems in adulthood. Mostly, it leads to inevitable disappointments with people who can't possibly measure up to the expectations and secret wishes that reside in this child part.

A Brief Story about Being Rescued

A client recently told me a story she had heard that relates to the wish to be rescued. The story goes like this: A man came home one day and discovered a moth cocoon near his door. He became curious and wanted to watch the moth emerge, so he took it inside and put it in a warm place. Soon the moth began to break through the top of the cocoon. It made a small hole in the top of the cocoon and then seemed to be unable to free itself further. As the man watched, he became impatient and worried because the moth seemed to be making no progress in breaking free. In an effort to be helpful, the man cut a larger hole in the top of the cocoon.

To the man's dismay, the moth emerged with a large, bloated body and small, withered wings. It couldn't fly and had great difficulty managing its unwieldy body. In his efforts to make it easier for the moth, the man hadn't realized the central role that a seemingly insurmountable effort played in the emergence of a healthy, viable adult moth. He didn't know that it was essential for the moth to struggle through the small hole at the top of the cocoon: it was the process of squeezing through the hole that forced the liquid in the moth's body out into its wings. Under normal circumstances, by the time an adult moth has struggled through the small hole in the top of the cocoon, its body is smaller and its wings are large enough to support it. Effort and struggle comprise the key to healthy development for the adult moth.

Coming to Terms with Disappointment

Perhaps one of the most difficult dynamics in adult relationships is what to do with the inevitable shortcomings of other people. It's as though we weren't allowed to learn that disappointment is a natural part of interpersonal relationships. It's as though we continue to view the world through a child's eyes, always looking for the good parent, the perfect partner, the person who will reflect back to us all the love and affirmation we missed when we were growing up.

When we enter current, adult relationships with a child's expectations, we forget that other people have their own agendas, their own wishes and hopes, which have nothing to do with us. To realize this would mean, to a desperate child part, a constant, intolerable threat of abandonment, a threat that what is needed will never be given. Needy child parts never learned about give and take. They are starving and want what they want *now*.

As you begin the process of healing the urgent neediness you may discover inside, it's important to be gentle with yourself and with the child parts that hold these feelings. The hurt and anger associated with profound disappointment can leave you feeling pretty raw. A soft touch goes a long way.

What Do I Really Want from This Person?

When you find yourself disappointed with someone who is close to you, explore what happens if you ask yourself, "What is it I *really* want from this person?" Allow yourself to listen deeply to the child parts of you. You may want to write down what comes to mind. Then, even after something comes to mind, ask yourself what need or want may have been under the reasonable one you just wrote down.

For example, you may say to yourself, "Well, I just wanted her to listen to this experience I had today. She acts as though it isn't interesting." If you listen more deeply, you may find a child part saying, "Don't you love me? If you cared, you'd be as fascinated with this as I am." You may be surprised by, or uncomfortable with, what comes into your awareness, but once you've identified the deeper need you can take steps to soothe yourself or to get the need met in ways that are appropriate in healthy adult relationships.

It's important to realize that the other person can't fix this for you, even if he or she were to try. What you are experiencing has to do with unresolved childhood hurts. This is a time when it's helpful to share your feelings with a friend, take them to your therapist, or do some inner work on your own. In whatever ways you choose to handle the disappointment, once you acknowledge the feelings coming from the child part, you have added to your healing.

If you find that all your relationships end the same way or that just about everyone you've ever trusted has betrayed you in some way, you might ask yourself, "How is this pattern similar to something I knew in childhood?" "How might this pattern express feelings of disappointment, now, that I couldn't let myself have as a child?" You can explore this last question more deeply by asking yourself where the person let you down, what your expectations were, and where your expectations and the other person's behavior collided. Sometimes, what feels like a betrayal is actually a situation where another person has taken care of his own needs instead of attending to yours.

The more deeply you allow yourself to delve into what you really wanted from this person, the more likely you are to find a child's need at the heart of your disappointment. Chances are you'll discover that the present-day person is standing in for someone else. You may find that you have been trying to get something from this person that you didn't get when you were young.

It may be as simple as wanting validation and affirmation at a time when the other person is too distracted or caught up in his own issues to be able to hear you adequately. To the adult part of you, it's usually no problem. If you stopped to think about it, you would have no difficulty understanding that there is nothing personal intended. To a needy inner child, though, this may replay old memories characterized by painful and humiliating rejections.

At other times, you may feel vulnerable and need someone to comfort you. If you call a friend or relative who isn't available, your adult self might wish it could be different but know it is okay. For a child part, though, it might feel devastating to be left alone when you are in need. It's at these times that it is helpful to know how to comfort yourself. Then, instead of staying planted in a place that requires the other person to make it better, you can do something you never could as a child: you can take care of yourself well enough to ease the aching need.[2]

On the Mountaintop: Identifying Unresolved Childhood Disappointment[3]

Take a moment, now, to think of someone with whom you are disappointed in the present. Write down all the things this person has done wrong recently, all the things that have really bothered you or made you feel unloved.

Imagine that you are standing on a tall mountaintop, from which you can see almost forever. Notice the color of the sky, the feeling of a solid mountain under your feet. Allow yourself to experience this as a safe place, as a vantage point from which you can see many things clearly.

Now, take all the disappointing things you wrote down and imagine that they make a list that stretches out in front of you on one side. You may sense them as words floating in the air, as photographs capturing a particular moment in time, or some other way that makes sense to you.

In front of you, on the other side, allow images or impressions to come to mind of people and events from your childhood that relate to the disappointments you are currently experiencing. Let these drop into the front of your mind from the back of your mind, because you want them to come from your deep unconscious. Allow yourself to be surprised at the many connections you discover between unresolved childhood disappointments and your current relationship.

Perhaps one particular childhood memory will capture your attention. You might want to take a few moments to review it, to discover what was disappointing and how you felt about it as a child. Then you might allow yourself to spend a few moments with the feelings, creating yet another bridge of awareness between your adult consciousness and an inner child part.

When you're finished, you might reflect on what you have been wanting from the person who has disappointed you. Take a moment to notice whether this is a need that really can be met by someone else, or if it is something you needed as a child that only *you* can give yourself now. Be sure to allow yourself mixed feelings. You may realize that there is no way anyone else can give you what an inner child demands from others, and yet it may feel unfair and awful that you have to give it to yourself. Over time, as you experience the benefits of meeting your own inner child needs, your increasing sense of strength when you do so may make it deeply rewarding to choose to take care of yourself.

Dealing with Despair

To begin the journey into a conscious awareness of despair takes courage, as well as some prior experience in dealing with feelings. Despair isn't something you can fix. Instead, it needs simply to be experienced, acknowledged, and validated. There is nothing to *do*, nothing to *change*. Healing comes through your ability just to *be* with the feelings and your willingness to allow them to flow through your adult consciousness to whatever degree you are able at any given moment.

Allowing the flow of intense feelings such as despair is like managing the flow of water backed up behind a dam. If the dam breaks and the water floods the land below, there usually is a great deal of destruction. When the flow is managed, by allowing just enough to emerge at a time, the land is nourished. Land absorbs water more efficiently when it is damp, when moisture has been allowed to flow in on a regular basis. When there has been a long dry spell, the water floods along the surface. It doesn't sink in; instead, it sweeps by, creating chaos as it goes.

In the same way, over time feelings lose their frightening intensity, even when they remain powerful reminders of past wounds. Healing occurs as feelings are allowed to move through your experience and become absorbed into your adult awareness on a regular basis. The hardest part is at the beginning, when, after years of having been shut away from your conscious awareness, the feelings may seem too big to manage.

When I think of processing despair, my mind fills with the many images people have described of their journey into this devastating feeling. Often they experience a dark void where a child drifts alone, unconnected to anything or anyone. It is a lost child, without hope, without comfort.

Many times, the child part that drifts alone in the void is unavailable to the adult self. There seems to be no way to reach in and touch this part quickly or directly, and there may be no response even if contact is made. It's helpful to remember that a child in despair has tried every possible way to make things better. Finally, she has given up and withdrawn into this dark, lonely place. It's just too painful to make contact with others. In this child's experience, any contact simply means a renewal of the pain of abandonment, the expectation that what is offered will be taken away.

Whatever image or metaphor you use to describe the experience of a child lost in despair, allow your imagination to make it real in a way that is meaningful to you. For example, you may discover a child curled up in a ball in the corner of a room or a child hidden deep in a cave. Wherever this child appears, allow the image (or sense of things, if you aren't visual) to guide you. Also, remember that—regardless of the intensity you experience—these are just feelings. They tell you a story and they cannot hurt you.

Lifeline: Opening Your Heart to Despair

One of the most powerful ways to tap into your despair is by creating a lifeline between your adult self and the child who is lost in that lonely place. This exercise involves a nonverbal communication from your heart to the heart of that child. Whenever you open your heart to yourself, something wonderful happens. Somehow, it seems, a deep part of your unconscious recognizes the willingness that is inherent in an open heart. It's as though you are saying, "Yes, I want to know. I want to connect with my feelings and my truth."

Now, imagine a beautiful colored light that fills your whole chest, especially around the area of your heart. There is no color better or more healing than any other. Allow yourself to connect with whatever nurturing and loving color comes into your awareness. Then, visualize a line of that light as it moves from your heart to the heart of the lost child. Be sure you send the line of light *gently*, so that it doesn't intrude on, or jab at, the child. You are simply *offering a connection* that needs no words and requires no response from the child. It is fine for the child to take it in at his or her own pace. There is no demand, no right response. Just observe whatever comes into your awareness as you continue to open your heart to this child.

Over time, you may notice that you become more aware of feelings of hopelessness, despair, and disappointment. *The lifeline that you have offered the child is also a line of communication from the very deepest place inside you.* There is no need for words, no need for thought. It's just an opening, an invitation to share the despair with your adult part.

* * *

When you invite your childhood despair into your adult consciousness, you foster an important healing relationship. You, the present-day adult, become a witness to the child's anguish. As you allow yourself to observe *and* experience the child's feelings, you become a bridge from past to present. Across the bridge travel unresolved and previously overwhelming feelings from a long time ago.

Witnessing the lost child's feelings may also mean learning to wail, cry, or feel rage on behalf of the child. By creating the safety of your adult awareness as a container for the feelings, it becomes possible to express them in a constructive way. In Chapter 8, we'll look in more detail at some of the ways you can do this.

For Jonathan, tapping into his despair was almost more painful than he could tolerate. He had been neglected as a child. His parents and older brother acted as though he didn't exist. He felt like an afterthought and was treated as a burden.

When Jonathan began to work with his despair, at first all he could do was imagine the void in which a child part of him was lost. He couldn't even bring himself to send in a line of light. It hurt too much to do anything but be aware of the darkness. Because he had learned to respect his own pace of healing, Jonathan didn't push himself. His adult consciousness slowly became a safe container for beginning to explore what were previously forbidden feelings.

Eventually, simply by sitting with his discomfort, fear, and awareness of the darkness, Jonathan discovered that he really could treat the journey into the void as if he were entering a pool of cold water. He really could go in "one toe at a time." The first thing he noticed was that after a while he really *wanted* to send in a line of light. There was fear, of course, but he could sense that he was ready. As he began, he further realized that he was *only* ready to send in the light. He was too frightened to allow an image of the lost child to come into his conscious awareness. Again, because he had learned not to push himself, Jonathan simply allowed the light to find its way in the darkness. Then, he trusted that whatever connection needed to be made had been accomplished.

It's important to allow yourself this kind of gentle acceptance. Jonathan knew himself well enough to realize that, if he pushed and went further than he was ready to go, he would just shut down and go numb. He'd lose any sense of the despair or of the darkness. He had learned to tap into his feelings just far enough to allow him to stay connected with himself. He knew that if he pushed ahead until he was numb, he would be recreating the overwhelmed feelings and dissociative response from his childhood. He realized that this would waste his time.

Eventually, Jonathan became aware of the lost child in the darkness. As he opened his heart to this part of himself, he also began to touch a depth of feeling he had never allowed before. Deep sobs expressed the child's anguish. An almost intolerable need welled up in him, and Jonathan had to remember to breathe through the devastating feelings that accompanied the memories he had about having to depend on people who humiliated and rejected him. The worst part was that as a child he couldn't get rid of his needs. He had no choice, and yet merely feeling needy was a powerful source of pain.

Each time Jonathan touched the depth of his childhood need for love and connection, he wanted to push it away. It took all of his adult courage to choose, again and again, to acknowledge these feelings and sit with them. He had learned to allow mixed feelings: just because he didn't *want* to connect with his despair didn't mean that he *shouldn't* go ahead and dip in a toe anyway.

As an adult witness, willing to observe *and* feel, Jonathan brought the despair into his present-day awareness. Over time, it eased. No longer was part of him lost in the endless darkness into which he used to fall, emotionally, whenever anyone rejected him. Instead, he had a conscious awareness of having felt despair as a child. Yes, it left some scars. Rejection will probably always be a sensitive issue for Jonathan. What has changed, though, is that the despair associated with being abandoned as a child is no longer as acutely alive for him in his current relationships.

And so, problems in his interpersonal relationships eased. No longer would he fly into a panic when someone rejected him. Instead, he was able to become aware that he was *feeling* rejected and abandoned and then allow the feelings to move through him. He learned that feelings are to be taken seriously, but not literally. He knew that there was nothing he had to *do* except to acknowledge that an old scar had been touched. Because he no longer fell into the darkness, he recovered more quickly from the fleeting feelings that were moving through him, even when they felt powerful.

Maureen's despair was different. It lived beneath a deep rage. As a child, she had been actively abused by various members of her family. As is true for most children who are traumatically hurt, the natural need for love and comfort from others had been driven underground. To keep it outside conscious awareness, rage became a protector, an emotionally safe place.

With her rage, Maureen could feel powerful. It gave her a voice in the world and allowed her to feel strong enough to interact with other people. Instead of feeling sad or panicked when people rejected her, she would become overwhelmingly angry and want to strike out at them. It took every ounce of self-control to restrain herself. Sometimes, she couldn't contain the rage and found herself calling people on the phone and hanging up, just to get back at them. As with all acting-out behaviors, the phone calls were a way Maureen diverted her attention from intolerable feelings.

As she began her painful journey, Maureen felt a great deal of resistance to the process. Because she had learned to respect her resistance and to acknowledge it as a communication of real value, she began right there. She allowed herself to sit with the feeling that her rage really *was* justified, that people really *were* treating her terribly. She noticed the panic she felt when she allowed herself to wonder if the rage were a shield, one desperately needed as a child, that now prevented her from moving on with her healing. She began to understand that, by holding onto the rage and refusing to experience the vulnerability behind her anger at other people, she protected herself from the unbearable despair she had felt as a child.

This is an essential realization for anyone who chooses to heal despair. We need to know how we protect ourselves from our childhood feelings. Strategies for survival when we were children were absolutely essential then, but they get in our way as adults. As we are willing to experience the feelings that are behind, or under, these strategies, we reinforce the bridges we are building between past and present. This, in turn, makes life in the present more manageable.

Over time, Maureen became increasingly skilled at allowing the rage to become a signal that she was feeling needy or vulnerable in some way. She learned to move through the rage to the underlying feelings and built bridges to her adult awareness that brought deeper healing. Eventually, the rage itself lessened, because it was no longer needed as a protection against feelings Maureen was now allowing into consciousness.

As you deal with your own despair, please remember that, no matter how huge or overwhelming it may seem at first, it is a *feeling*. Whatever brought you to the point of despair in childhood no longer exists. It happened a long time ago, and you have lived many moments since then. You have a right to move beyond your despair. You have a right to choose to feel it with your full adult awareness, so that your current relationships can be free from the pull of unresolved childhood wounds.

What may be most surprising about dealing with both disappointment and despair is how different it feels to interact with other people when these early responses are resolved. As you heal the deeper levels of your personal world of unresolved need and anguish, the world outside becomes a safer place to be. No longer do you have to depend on others to meet needs that weren't met in childhood. Instead, you have a better chance of being in relationships that are reciprocal, adult to adult. When you recognize that you want to be rescued, instead of acting it out with someone, you can take some time to go inside and sit with the feelings. You can create new and stronger bridges between your adult awareness and wounded inner child parts. In time, the demands you make on others to meet the needs that were so powerful in childhood will lessen. Then, if they come up at all, they are relatively easy to identify and resolve with your present-day strategies of internal soothing.

Some Comments about Anger

It may be evident from what I've said about disappointment and despair that intense anger or rage is often an integral part of these difficult feelings. In fact, anger, as one of our natural feelings, is almost inevitably turned into rage when we are hurt as children.

Few of us who were hurt as children grew up in homes where anger was expressed in constructive, healthy ways. For most of us, anger was either forbidden as an unacceptable emotion or expressed in violent ways, verbally or physically.

And so, when you get in touch with the deep, underlying anger or rage that may accompany your work with disappointment and despair, please remember that anger, when it is allowed to be a normal, healthy feeling, expresses the awareness that something is wrong, something hurts, or we need something to change. When we are allowed to express our anger naturally and spontaneously, we learn how to say no. We learn that it's okay to draw a boundary without having to overpower the other person. We learn to respect the boundaries of others as well, and to accept their right to be angry when we violate these boundaries.

As you work with the difficult feelings described in this chapter, it's helpful to keep in mind that your rage, no matter how powerful it may be in your experience, is still a *feeling*. As a feeling, it has a story to tell you. Your job is to listen to the rage, contain and sit with it, rather than acting it out, and explore what other feelings or needs it may conceal.

Remind yourself of the benefits of containing, rather than acting on, feelings. It's helpful to allow your anger to be a signal that alerts you to the fact that something is going on that needs your attention. Most of the time, if rage comes up, it will have to do with some childhood hurt. It is a bridge back to a past experience that has not yet been processed and resolved. On a day-to-day basis, using this strategy will save wear and tear on yourself and in your relationships.

In time, you will learn the difference between rage that is rooted in the past and anger that is telling you something important about today. It's an amazing feeling to discover healthy anger. It allows you to feel safer in the world. It doesn't feel scary, the way rage does. Instead, healthy anger is more a deep inner certainty that something doesn't feel right and needs to be changed. Also, it supports what is often a surprising new feeling: you have a *right* to say "no."

About Suicidal Thoughts
and Feelings

Perhaps some of the most frightening, and yet most common, thoughts and feelings that survivors of childhood trauma experience are those that involve suicide. If you've ever had these feelings—and you probably have, if you were abused as a child—you know how realistic they can seem: it's hard to imagine that there will ever be a time when you don't feel agonized and overwhelmed.

It's essential to remember that suicidal feelings are to be taken seriously, but not literally.[4] For children who are overwhelmed by trauma, it's almost inevitable to believe that to die would solve everything. It's as though thinking about suicide becomes a source of soothing, a safety valve or insurance policy that says that at least you have the power to stop it all if you choose.

The problem is that young children don't know the difference between a thought, a feeling, and an action. Wanting to die equals dying. The feeling that everything will be better if you are dead can seem so real, and yet, if you look deeply, most suicidal survivors of childhood trauma *actually have an underlying wish to be free from the pain, not to be finished with life.*

As part of both disappointment and despair, suicidal feelings can come up when there is a desperate desire to be rescued and then no one is there to make it better. When these feelings arise, it's often hard to reach out to friends or others who *are* available to support you. Because you were powerless to help yourself when you were young, nothing short of complete rescue feels adequate.

Suicidal feelings also can mask a deep rage at being hurt, a wish to get back at someone. Again, if you accept that this is a feeling like any other—and allow yourself to explore it without acting on it—it can become a bridge to the past and to deeper understanding, a bridge to further healing.

It may be surprising to realize, also, that touching on the experience of hope sometimes elicits suicidal thoughts or feelings. This may happen because any suggestion of hope brings with it the potential for disappointment. With disappointment comes the childhood pain of having been so alone and so much in need. If you find this is true for you, it's helpful to remind yourself that hope is sometimes related to disappointment. Then you can remind yourself of the possibility that, when you feel you are moving forward, you may also fall into the pit of despair or become suicidal. Once you know this, it adds branches to your cognitive tree and helps you tolerate and deal with these difficult feelings.[5]

SPECIAL ISSUES FOR MULTIPLES

If you are a multiple, suicidal feelings may come from yet another source. For some multiples, there are parts inside that feel compelled to kill weaker parts. If this is true for you, it is essential to work in therapy to develop communication with all your parts, to discover why one part may want to kill another, and to develop strategies for staying safe when a part that wants to kill becomes activated. Sometimes there are helper parts that can intervene and stop any acting-out that may be planned. To say the least, it can be terrifying to know that there is a part inside that wants you dead. The tragedy is that you weren't abused because of anything you did, not even because you were "weak." You were abused because someone in a position of power decided to hurt you, and you don't deserve to die because of that.

Sometimes, for multiples, there are parts inside that feel they must die because they are "bad" and feel responsible for the abuse. Killing themselves seems the only way to atone. If you keep in mind that these feelings arose in the mind of a child and that they need to be taken seriously, not literally, you can deal with them in the same ways you would any other powerful feeling.

Another source of suicidal feelings may occur when you realize, one day, that you are approaching middle age and nothing seems to have changed in your life. In fact, it may appear that things have gotten worse because your dissociative strategies have stopped working as effectively as they did in childhood. Also, you may have realized that you will never be rescued. Again, it is essential to remember that these are *feelings* about your life. They have something to tell you, but it probably isn't that you really want to be dead. Instead, they may address a deep—and understandable—wish to feel better, to have a life that works. If you have had these kinds of feelings, you might consider using them as a catalyst for going into therapy, if you haven't already. If you are in treatment now, suicidal feelings of this kind can be an impetus to explore even more deeply your wishes to be rescued. It may also help to keep in mind that the effects of trauma-based dissociation *can* be addressed in therapy with some success.

And so, one of the key strategies for dealing with suicidality is to make a basic choice not to act on these feelings when they arise. Instead, you can choose to sit with them and allow them to become a bridge to further healing. They reflect a childhood dominated by overwhelming experiences you weren't equipped to handle then. When you choose to use the feelings as a bridge to healing the past and increasing mastery in the present, you can then allow yourself to move through suicidal thoughts and urges just as you would any other feeling: you can be curious about what triggered them and use the trigger as a bridge to memories you haven't yet processed.

If you are ever afraid that you might act on these impulses, it's important to know that you can go to the emergency room of your local hospital and tell them what you are feeling. They will know what to do to keep you safe. In this way, you buy yourself some time to see how you feel once you have shifted back into your present-day state of mind.

There is much more that can be said about suicidal thoughts and feelings. For now, suffice it to say that to act on them would be to believe that you are still stuck back there in a childhood that hurt you and that made you feel overwhelmed. Now, as an adult, you have many more options. You deserve better.

Developing your skill to work with your feelings and access wounded inner child states increases your capacity to feel safe and competent in the world today. In the next chapter, we'll explore some additional strategies for dealing with these child parts from the past.

8

Dealing with
Inner Child Parts

WHAT DO I DO WITH THEM NOW?

Now that we've spent some time focusing on distressed inner child parts, you may be wondering how to deal with them on a day-to-day basis in a way that will help you feel more competent. The more familiar you are with your inner child parts, and the more practice you have in contacting and soothing them, the easier it is to deal with being triggered—with falling into one of those pockets of time that represents unresolved experiences from the past.

Over time, by working with your inner child parts, you can develop the capacity to bounce back into your adult state of mind more quickly. When you are able to identify which inner part of you has been triggered—and know what works best with that particular part—you can restore a sense of mastery with greater ease. In this chapter, we'll explore a number of strategies for soothing and healing these important parts of you.

Another aspect of working with inner child parts that we'll explore concerns the stories they each have to tell about what you experienced in childhood. To be free to live in the present, you need to know the childhood origins of unresolved and unprocessed experiences that interfere with your current life. It's not always easy to listen to the stories told by your inner child parts. Often, these stories contradict what you were told when you were young or how you were taught to see your family and your role within it.

Even though memory seems to be a process that is more fluid than fixed, [1,2] when you are working with the stories inner child parts bring into your conscious awareness, it is important to remember that memories are the way we represent childhood hurts. These stories address experiences you had that were hurtful or harmful in ways that continue to have an effect in your present-day life. As such, memories—whether interpreted as metaphor or actual fact—present you with an opportunity to access thoughts, feelings, body states, and interpersonal experiences that need to be resolved.

Fundamentally, when all is said and done, the greatest value of the stories inner child parts have to tell is to process and resolve *feelings, beliefs,* and *decisions* from childhood that continue to create problems for you in the present. Even if you can't prove that your memories are reflections of what actually happened, what matters most is that you gain freedom from the past. [3]

It takes patience to unravel the deeper levels of childhood learnings, experiences, and feelings. The process is like putting together a puzzle with many pieces. What makes it so challenging, at times, is that the puzzle is missing the lid to its box, so you can't see the whole picture ahead of time. Each child part is like a piece of the puzzle and each offers its own perspective and unique contribution to creating a full understanding of how you came to be as you are in the present. Some inner child parts hold feelings that have never been explored or remain unresolved; some represent thoughts and ways of thinking about how you came to understand your world; some encompass pictures and scenes, the content of metaphors, or actual events, representing memories that may previously have been outside conscious awareness.

There are times when inner child parts tell the same story from different points of view. At other times, they add their own, unique story to a developing sense of your history. Because they bring bits and pieces that, eventually, will add up to a whole picture, each time you go inside to listen to a child part, it's important to give yourself permission to be curious and open. Often you'll be on new, perhaps scary, ground, and it helps to remind yourself that, whatever these child parts have to communicate to you, you have already survived, you are here in the present, and you are safe.

You may find that there are other parts of you that have stories to tell, as well. It is not unusual for many of us who were wounded as children to have had equally difficult times during adolescence and throughout adulthood. These teenage and young adult parts of us have stories to tell, too, and it's important to remain open to them as you move forward on your healing journey. For example, take a moment to recall something from your teenage years that has never felt completely resolved. Many adults who were hurt as children had times when they felt ugly, isolated, or unable to figure out how to fit in with the other kids. Or you may have done things that still make you feel ashamed or guilty when you think back on them. How about your young adult years? Are there times you wish you could go back and live over again, so you could do things differently?

These parts of you can also become bridges back to previously unknown inner child parts. By allowing yourself to become aware of events that caused you difficulty or distress during periods of your life in which these experiences occurred, you create bridges back in time. Connecting with an adolescent who feels ugly, for instance, might take you back to even earlier, unresolved memories that left you feeling fundamentally ugly as a person.

And so, when you think of working with inner child parts, it's helpful to allow yourself to include any part of you that is from a time when you were younger than you are at present. You never know where healing information will arise, and if you allow for all the younger parts of you to communicate, you can enhance your mastery in the present.

More about Volitional
Dissociation: Self-Hypnosis

One of the most powerful ways to get to know your inner child parts is through the use of self-hypnosis. In *Recreating Your Self,* I described in some detail the process of self-hypnosis and how it can be used to develop conscious relationships with parts of yourself. If you haven't learned how to go inside and work with these parts, you might find it helpful to learn some self-hypnosis and imagery techniques.[4]

For many abuse survivors who used dissociation to cope with childhood trauma, going in and out of self-hypnotic trance is something that happens all the time.[5] Learning to utilize this process more consciously can give you a greater sense of control over your inner life.[6]

For now, I'd like to review some principles of self-hypnosis that can apply whether you go into an "official trance" or not. The most important thing to do when you connect with inner child parts is to shift gears from a focus on what's *outside* to a focus on what's *inside.* Usually, it's easier to do this if you close your eyes and if your body is comfortably seated and well supported. If you feel safer with your eyes open, that's fine, too. It's important to do whatever creates the greatest sense of present-day mastery.

I usually recommend that you do your inner journeys while sitting up, simply because it's easier to stay conscious of what you are doing. If you lie down, you may drift off, or fall asleep, and then you may not recall what you learned during your inner work. For some kinds of relaxation and self-hypnosis, drifting off is exactly what you want. But when you're developing relationships with inner child parts, you need to have your adult observer available on the journey so you can hold onto a conscious recollection of what you discover.

Once you've developed your own way to focus your attention on your inner world, you're ready to seek out inner child parts and develop relationships with them. You are also ready to discover what it is that distresses them, what they remember that you don't, and how to make it easier to cope with day-to-day living.

SPECIAL ISSUES FOR MULTIPLES

If you are person with multiple personalities, doing inner child work may be a bit more challenging than for less dissociated people. Because of the powerful intensity and focus of your inner parts, and because you may be in and out of spontaneous self-hypnotic states all the time, I recommend that you do this work only in conjunction with a trained psychotherapist.

There is no denying that it is important for you to get to know your various inner parts, and to promote communication and collaboration among them. It is also helpful to find out why you are triggered in the present, and how to deal with the triggered parts. It is equally useful for you to become more aware of how and when you switch from one part of yourself to another, and to develop ways to switch back into a more present-focused and competent part when you need to do so.

As a multiple, you may find that your inner parts, or personalities, are so well-defined and set in their ways that setting up more conscious relationships with them seems a daunting challenge. The work for you is likely to go more slowly than for non-multiples, and you will need to spend more time on relationship-building, getting to know and respect the feelings and perspective of each part and developing a collaborative approach that will decrease self-destructiveness and feelings of loss of control. One of your goals is to increase co-consciousness, to build the bridges of continuous awareness among parts of you, so that you have available all aspects of your consciousness as you need them.

Also, you may find that it is easier to identify child parts by how you feel in your body, your tone of voice, or what you are saying and thinking, than by working with an image of a child. As you come to recognize and identify those feelings, thoughts and behaviors that are related to various child parts inside, you increase your adult awareness of what is happening inside you. Then you might ask translator or other helper parts to become involved. For example, you might ask for help in soothing upset child parts, building bridges in consciousness among parts, and translating the story the parts have to tell you so you can work with and resolve the effects of early abuse.

Another of your healing goals is to learn to use less dissociative strategies for dealing with everyday life. It may seem puzzling, at first, to consider using a dissociative strategy to overcome your tendency to dissociate! It helps to recall that volitional dissociation allows you to increase your capacity to *observe* and *recenter* yourself into your present-day awareness. Over time, this capacity supports the use of coping strategies that keep you in touch with yourself, rather than splitting off awareness as happens in trauma-based dissociation.

For many people, a natural, automatic process of integration occurs as their present-day awareness encompasses more and more of their childhood story. This occurs as you get to know your parts and learn what they have to share with you. As a result, they tend to become less separately defined. While their talents, perspectives, and qualities of consciousness remain resources within your ongoing awareness, their characteristics as autonomous personalities may diminish. Then they can become more integrated aspects of your ongoing adult consciousness.

It's essential to reassure the various parts of you that becoming more integrated with your ongoing adult awareness does not mean that they will "die," which is something many personalities seem to fear. What you can convey to them, perhaps, is that they will be less lonely, less isolated, than they were before, and that their contribution to your total consciousness will never be lost. It's also helpful to allow yourself to grieve what may be a loss, for you, of "friends" you've had around for a long time. Moving from a dissociated state of functioning to that of an integrated individual is a big shift, in terms of how "populated" you feel in your mind. To be alone within your own consciousness can seem an alien and uninviting idea at first. What helps is to know that, once you are there, being nondissociated will feel more natural and powerful than you may be able to imagine right now.

For non-multiples, as well, inner child parts that represent unresolved wounds from childhood begin to fade as separate aspects of consciousness. This occurs naturally and automatically over time, as those wounds—and the feelings, behaviors and responses arising from them—become integrated into adult awareness.[7]

Discovering a Safe Place

Perhaps the most important starting point on your journey is to discover a safe place inside. This place may be indoors or outdoors. It may be a place you've seen before or one that lives entirely in your imagination. Within the safe place, there needs to be a gathering place, perhaps a room, where you can meet parts, and where they can come together and meet one another. It's also helpful for each part to have a room of its own that can be locked, if that feels safer. Also, your safe place may contain a special memory room, which we'll talk more about later, where you can go to preview stories that inner child parts may have to tell you. You might also want to include some quiet places of real beauty, where you can go and spend some time just being with yourself, encompassed in a sense of comfort and safety.

Over time, your safe place can become more extensive, as you explore your inner world more deeply. You can change things as you discover what works best for you. It's your inner world. It's your imagination. When you allow yourself to see what happens as you go along and to let go of those techniques that don't work as you develop the ones that do, you also give yourself permission to do this in your adult life. So often, when we are hurt as children, the world becomes an "either-or" place. We don't realize that, if things don't feel good, we have a right to change them. It's wonderful and liberating to discover that you no longer have to settle for something that's only half okay. You have a right to a safe place that meets your needs. You also have a right to an adult life that works for you.

Identifying Inner Child Parts

Once you have discovered, and gotten to know, your safe place, you can begin to meet your inner child parts. One of the ways to do this is to recall a situation in recent days that upset you or triggered you into one of those "pockets of time." Then, use the feelings that were present in the recent situation as a bridge and allow yourself to follow the bridge across time and space, back to a time and a place where you experienced something similar as a child.[8]

In order to use your feelings as a bridge, simply ask your unconscious to take you back. There is no need actually to see a bridge or even to feel as though you're going someplace. Because there is no time in the unconscious, you can be here, or there, or anywhere, with just a thought. Just keep in mind that you want to go back in time and become aware of a scene, or a brief impression, of a child who is experiencing the same feelings or thoughts you had when you were triggered.

One of the helpful things to remember, whenever you go inside to explore the story a child part has to tell, is to allow whatever comes to mind simply to be there. Later, when you've come out of your internal focus, you can analyze what you experienced and decide what felt real and what didn't. For now, remember that the stories child parts show you may be thought of as metaphors that convey the "felt-sense" of the experience. Just be open to whatever impressions arise. Sometimes it's hard for an inner child to tell his or her story, so you may need to let it come a little bit at a time.

After watching, or sensing, what went on, you might allow yourself to enter the scene and bring the child back to your safe place. Then you and the child can spend some time getting to know one another. As you do this, remember that developing a relationship takes time. Allow whatever the *child part* needs right now to be the focus of your attention. For example, the child may just need to be held and soothed, may need to go to sleep, or may want to sit nearby without touching you. That's fine. Just let it be, and stay open to whatever impressions come to you spontaneously from your unconscious. You are here to learn about what triggers you and how best to soothe yourself when this happens.

If, by any chance, you noticed more than one child in the scene, you may decide to bring all the child parts back this time or to return another time to tap into the other child parts' experiences of that same scene. For example, if you are aware of a child part that feels fear and also discover a child part floating on the ceiling or hiding in a corner, simply let this fact register in your conscious awareness. These inner children will have stories to tell, too, and they may add elements you hadn't known before.

Most often, only one inner child part will become obvious to an abuse survivor during any given journey back across a bridge. It's nice to know, though, that if more than one inner child shows up, the process is the same; there's no need to feel you have to push away any parts of you.

Learning to Soothe Inner Child Parts

As you get to know your inner child parts, allow yourself to discover what calms each one, what helps each to feel safe, and what creates the greatest soothing for each. You are likely to find that every child part has individual and unique needs.[9] Even if many of your inner child parts want to be held, each of these may want to be held differently.

For example, Erik discovered inside a four-year-old boy who represented his deep need to be acknowledged by his aloof and preoccupied father. When he reached out to this inner child part, he discovered that this boy felt most soothed and comforted when he was able to sit on Erik's lap with his legs and arms wrapped around Erik's body and his head on Erik's chest. Through trial and error, Erik discovered that this child part felt even more soothed when he heard Erik's voice speaking softly to him. Sometimes Erik talked out loud, and sometimes he spoke to the inner child mentally. What added to these healing moments together was that Erik had to think of things to say that would be soothing. That process alone helped him rehearse what he might say to himself during difficult moments in his present-day life.

A nine-year-old inner child part, on the other hand, preferred to feel Erik's arm around his shoulder as they sat side by side. Then, as they sat together, this inner boy would tell Erik about his day, about things that were important to him. He had never before had a grownup who would take the time to listen to him, and it was profoundly healing for this inner child, and thus for Erik as an adult, to feel valued and heard.

At other times, inner child parts might feel soothed most by having some time to play. Felice discovered this quite by accident one day when she was feeling particularly depressed. She went inside to discover which child part was feeling so unhappy and unloved, and discovered a seven-year-old who felt completely alone. Listening to a hunch, Felice invited this child part to accompany her on an imaginary trip to the carousel in the park. The child was delighted, and she and Felice spent some nourishing and fun imaginary time together.

For Eileen, as is true of many people, coloring soothes some of her inner child parts. When she's had a hard day or she's facing a difficult project, Eileen has learned to offer her inner children time for coloring or painting. She actually does this in her present world, rather than in her imagination. At times, she uses a coloring book and at other times large sheets of paper. She lets the child parts draw or paint whatever they like. Sometimes it takes only a few minutes of working with the colors and she begins to feel better. Recently, she has discovered that some of her inner children also like to work with play dough, and so she has added that to her repertoire of soothing activities.

You may find that some of your inner children like to hear stories. Ronnie found that she could gather together some of her inner child parts for storytime, and that they—and she—would feel immensely relaxed after she read everyone a fable or fairy tale. She discovered that actually reading out loud worked best, as it seemed more real to her when she could hear her own voice. As she did this, she would imagine that some of her inner children were cuddled in her lap and snuggled around her. As she read out loud, she experienced a satisfying feeling in her role as story teller. Not only was she soothing her inner child parts, but she was also affirming her own capacity to express herself in a loving, imaginative way.

Sometimes, when you are dealing with a very young child part, perhaps even an infant, the most soothing thing is just to hold the child. Often, it can feel tremendously comforting to wrap your arms completely around the child's body and really snuggle. At other times, as with one workshop participant, you may find that there are child parts inside that don't want to be touched at all. Janice's first contact with a five-year-old inner child surprised her. Her expectation was that this little girl would be glad to see her and would want to be held and comforted. Instead, this child part made it clear that she wanted nothing to do with Janice. All she wanted was for adults to leave her alone. She had learned to fear grownups and to expect to be hurt by them.

As she allowed herself to remain open and curious, Janice decided to do no more than sit down near this inner child and just be present. It was a relief to both of then not to make, or be subject to, any demands. It was enough simply to *be* there. The first thing Janice realized, as she sat quietly in her safe place with this inner child, was how much part of her childhood story had to do with having learned not to trust people. As she listened to the inner child's silent anger, she became aware of a great deal. She realized, more than she had before, just how much she had been hurt by the people who were supposed to have loved her. Through her willingness not to demand that this inner child part make contact in a preconceived way, Janice created an opportunity to experience some deep feelings she hadn't known existed.

With all your inner child parts, it's essential to be open to new and creative ways to make contact. The more you allow yourself to listen and respond to what the inner child parts seek to communicate to you, the more you will be able to tap into the story each part holds inside and gain greater mastery over what has previously triggered you.

The Power of the Mind-Body Connection

During those times when an inner child part needs to be held, deeply and completely, it's important to give your full attention to the way it feels to imagine having your arms wrapped around a child whose body is so much smaller than yours. If this kind of "holding" is to provide the most healing possible, it's helpful to draw on all your senses. For example, imagine how the child's body seems to relax and settle into your arms as you continue to hold him or her. Notice, perhaps to your surprise, that—as the child relaxes—your own, adult body seems to respond as well. The longer you spend time holding this inner part of you, the more your present-day body seems to feel comforted. The soothing you provide touches much more than just the past. It translates, instantaneously, into the present.

Such a translation is possible because of what underlies the healing that can occur when you do self-hypnotic work with inner parts of yourself: a powerful mind-body connection. What we experience and learn in our bodies, we carry also in our consciousness. We respond to what our body knows, and the body responds to what happens in consciousness. The more you can be aware of body sensations when you do your inner work, the more you engage the mind-body interaction and the more powerful the healing effects will be.

Examples of the mind-body connections abound. Imagine, for a moment, that you are peeling a juicy tangerine. Notice the orange skin. As you begin to peel, imagine the tangy smell that begins to fill the air. Let yourself recall the flavor of tangerines. Then, imagine that you take a bite. Has your mouth been watering as you've been reading? If so, this is an example of how powerful the mind-body connection is. All you've been doing is *imagining* a tangerine, and yet your body acts as if you actually were preparing to taste one.

Here's another example. When you do a deep relaxation exercise and imagine yourself walking along a beach or being in some other place you really love, bring into your experience all of the elements that make this a special place to be: the sights, the smells, the quality of the air. After some time of listening to the waves, or feeling the cool breeze blow across your skin, or watching butterflies flit around flowers, you may find that your body responds with a feeling of being soothed and refreshed. You may even come out of your relaxation feeling as though you actually have gone somewhere, with a clear memory of the sights and smells you experienced.

You may not be able to achieve realistic-seeming physical sensations every time you go inside to soothe a child part. But when you do you'll discover how good it feels when you are able to connect with what the child experiences as you offer comfort. The most delightful, and mysterious, part is that, as child parts learn to trust that you will be there to soothe them when they become distressed, something begins to change in your daily life, as well. Your own level of upset changes. When you do become upset, you settle more quickly. It's as though you are teaching yourself how to draw on the unconscious mechanism of self-soothing that children develop automatically when they are cared for in healthy, reliable, and respectful ways.

Living Heart-to-Heart with Inner Child Parts

It's important to know that there is more to coming to terms with what triggers you in the present than learning to soothe yourself, although learning to do this can improve the quality of your daily living to a significant degree. There is also the need to get to know, and resolve, those pockets of time that were created in childhood. As you get to know the child parts inside, you are, in a sense, saying, "Yes, I want to know how it was for me as a child. I want to know about the feelings and experiences I had then that have made me who I am today."

One of the most powerful ways to do this is to open your heart to your inner child parts. Just as you did with the child lost in the void of despair, you can allow your heart to speak for you and to become a pathway to awareness.

When you send a line of light from your heart to the heart of an inner child, something powerful happens. There is no need for words, no need to do anything at all. Your unconscious understands fully and uses the line of light as a line of communication from the inner child to your present-day awareness.

Gerry had this experience when she opened her heart to an inner child who appeared to her as she followed a feeling of fear from the present to its origins in the past. She was curious about the fear she had felt when her boss called her into his office to go over a project she had done for him. She felt her fear was unreasonable, but she was unable to soothe herself.

During her inner journey, Gerry discovered a 12-year-old girl in school, standing at the blackboard, totally humiliated because she didn't know the answer to a question. The teacher wasn't being understanding, either, and made Gerry stand there for what seemed like an interminable amount of time before letting her sit down, question unanswered. Apparently, Gerry had been humiliated a good bit during childhood and had a great deal of pain that needed to be felt and resolved. By opening her heart to the 12-year-old, Gerry brought into conscious awareness a depth of humiliation she hadn't realized she felt. By continuing to keep her heart open and letting the feelings flow into her adult consciousness over time, she was able to find relief in her present-day dealings with people.

As she opened her heart to the inner child, Gerry reached out to soothe that part of herself. She and the 12-year-old spent time talking together. They talked over the humiliating experiences, and Gerry offered her adult perspective, even as she gave this inner child plenty of room simply to say how she felt. Gerry's empathy for herself increased, and this translated into her adult life as a better sense of humor when she didn't do things exactly as she would have liked.

If you are someone who was hurt badly as a child, and it feels impossible to open your heart to all that trauma, please remember that you have the right to take it a little at a time. Getting in touch with the feelings and memories of inner child parts needs to have the quality of an archeological dig rather than an avalanche. Open your heart for only a second at a time, if that's all you can tolerate. Over time, you'll gain greater strength and you'll be able to take in more. It *never* serves your healing process to force yourself beyond your current capacity to process your childhood hurts. Listen to your heart. It will know how far it can open safely.

Are These Feelings and Memories True?

A question I hear constantly from people who are healing from child-hood trauma is, "Can I trust what I am experiencing? How can I know if these memories are real?" The honest answer to this question is that none of us can know for certain, without accompanying evidence that corroborates or supports any given memory, what constitutes accurate recall. This is because, beyond adding to and deleting from memories throughout development, we also seem, naturally, to emphasize cer-tain parts of a memory and leave out others.[10]

To realize how universal this last aspect of memory seems to be, think of a time you had a disagreement with someone and you tried to compare notes on exactly what happened that led up to it. Usually each person has a different version of what happened, with an emphasis on different aspects. Sometimes, you come away wondering if you both were in the same place, having the same experience!

If this thought upsets you, please keep in mind that, to heal from childhood trauma, it doesn't really matter whether you can *prove* what your memories convey, unless you are involved in litigation. For the purposes of healing, all that matters is that your memories become bridges or pathways to resolution of thoughts, feelings and experi-ences that have remained in your unconscious and have continued to affect your present-day life in difficult and painful ways.

The stories told by your inner child parts may be thought of as *metaphors for healing*. As with any metaphor, what matters is that your unconscious understands the *meaning* the story seeks to convey. When the mind-body link is activated during your work with inner child parts, healing can take place even if the metaphor is not a totally accurate representation of what happened to you. For example, many people have found relief experiencing past-life regression, and we generally can't prove whether these memories are actually true.[11]

Also, many of us who work with abuse survivors have come to trust in the body's ability to act as a bridge to memories of past trauma. What is accessed via body states may represent memories of actual physical trauma that occurred when you were young. Paying attention to body sensations, aches and pains, illnesses, and other forms of physical distress creates bridges back to childhood experiences that haven't been processed consciously. These physical states may also represent a child's attempt to cope with psychological trauma by translating it physically, as a way to avoid becoming overwhelmed. The problem is that it is impossible to resolve *emotional* distress when it constantly appears as *physical* symptoms, including stomachaches, respiratory difficulties, headaches, sore joints, menstrual cramps, or muscles that hurt.

Because of your body's reliability as a repository for unconscious material, you can learn to use its experience as the starting point for discovering inner child parts and unremembered childhood hurts. It's important to realize, though, that children sometimes translate nonphysical experiences into physical sensations. For example, a child who is being yelled at may experience the verbal assault as a physical beating, even when the child hasn't been touched by anyone. When you know this, it's not surprising to learn that there may be times when you discover a physical sensation and attempt to interpret it literally, but find that what you recall doesn't quite seem to fit or doesn't resolve comfortably. When this happens, you might wonder if you are translating a psychological experience into a physical sensation and see where that takes you.

Above all else, please allow yourself to go with whatever metaphors come to mind and see if you get some relief by dealing with them as they arise. Frequently, you will find that your unconscious uses memory metaphors to let you experience, release, and resolve unprocessed childhood hurts, whether or not you can prove that the memory material is factually true. At the very least, it is what you *experience* as being true, and that is the healing you seek.

Your Special Memory Room

An image that often can be helpful in delving more deeply into your memories is the "memory room." This room will look different to each individual, and what it contains will vary according to personal needs and preferences. In general, though, it is a room that contains everything you could possibly need to gather greater clarity about those physical ailments that represent unresolved pockets of time.

In a general way, the memory room is a private, especially safe and secure place. Often it is reached by going down some stairs, or down an elevator if that feels safe, or in some other way that suggests to you the quality of deepening. If it feels important to you, make sure that you are the only one with a key to this room and that you can lock the door after you when you have entered. Sometimes locking the door after you enter provides an extra sense of protection as you delve into your memories.

Your memory room may be more or less technologically advanced. It may contain files, a television monitor or movie screen, VCR equipment, audio- and videotapes, scrapbooks, a computer—whatever you might want it to contain. It's helpful if it has a comfortable chair where you can sit as you go deeply into your history. It can also have volume controls, a light dimmer, and any other kinds of mechanisms you need, to assure you that you can be more or less aware of any memory element that may come to mind.

Dreams and Other
Impressions

There are other ways to access memories, as well. Among the best are your dreams. When memories come in dreams, your unconscious creates a gentle—although sometimes frightening—way to introduce elements of unprocessed childhood trauma into your conscious awareness. You might experiment with asking your unconscious for dreams before you go to sleep and seeing what happens. When you decide to tap into your dreams as part of your healing process, it's helpful to have a notepad or tape recorder near your bed so you can record any dreams as soon as you awaken.

Memories may also come into your mind as unexpected flashes of scenes or feelings. As you recall that putting your history together is like putting together a complex puzzle, you might allow yourself to note impressions that fall into your mind from time to time. If you can keep from demanding that they all fit together right away or that they make sense as a whole picture would, you may find that—over time—your understanding of what happened to you as a child increases at a pace you can manage.

Another way to elicit or invite memories into conscious awareness is to write an autobiography, beginning with the very first thing you remember as a child. As you write, you may find that small bits of recall come into your awareness, and you can go back and fill in blank or sketchy spots in your autobiography.

Poetry, dance, art, and writing stories about other children are additional ways to tell your unconscious that you want to know more about what triggers you in the present. In addition, life transitions, having children, moving, changing jobs, loss, accomplishments, and other events in your current life may trigger memory material.

Regardless of what approach you use to connect with your memories, the most important thing is to give yourself permission to work with your memories a little bit at a time. There's nothing gained by overwhelming yourself. A piece here and a piece there will be of more benefit in the long run. Once you have enough pieces put together to sense what the whole picture might look like, then you can go inside and work with the total memory. By the time you do, it will no longer be as overwhelming. You'll know where you are headed, you'll have some sense of what feelings are involved, and you'll be better able to remind yourself that it all happened a long time ago.

Now That I've Got Them (Memories), I Don't Want Them!

It's not unusual for abuse survivors to feel a pressing eagerness to get into work with childhood memories. If you have felt this, you may also have been surprised to discover that as soon as memory material began to emerge you wanted it to go away! It's helpful to remember that memories are pushed outside conscious awareness for a good reason: because they were too much for you to handle when you were young. It stands to reason, then, that they will be unpleasant to experience when they begin to emerge.

A nice thing to do for yourself is to be gentle and accepting of your understandably mixed feelings. You have the right to slow down the process of working with your memories if it feels as though it is too much for you. As you gain more experience with dipping into and processing memories, you may want to push yourself a little. Only you will know how much is enough.

The goal in healing is not to overwhelm yourself with previously unremembered material. It *is* to take whatever time you need to *invite* unprocessed and unresolved issues into your present-day consciousness so that you can handle your current life more effectively. It *is* to allow yourself some rest and ease, emotionally, from the many triggers that elicit feelings and behaviors you no longer want to have in your life.

Mixed feelings are natural. You probably will have them. Remember, they are just *feelings*, and feelings are to be taken seriously, not *literally*.

Other Strategies for Helping Inner Child Parts

Working with memories is an ongoing process in healing, and so is dealing with your day-to-day life. Because of the effects of childhood injuries, it's helpful to have a whole range of strategies to use when inner parts get triggered. We've been exploring strategies that draw on volitional dissociation, as well as nondissociative approaches. In this way, you have alternatives to draw on that can apply more appropriately to a variety of present-day situations.

Over the years, I have talked with many adult survivors of childhood abuse who were desperate for some technique they could use to make it easier for them to get through upcoming experiences without falling into unresolved pockets of time. In this section, we'll review some of the many strategies available. Please remember that the only limitation in developing effective strategies is your own creativity. What is offered here are examples of general ideas. When you tune in to your unique needs, you may surprise yourself with the effective strategies you create on your own.

THE VISIT HOME

If you were abused as a child, or if you grew up in a family where dysfunctional patterns abounded, visits home can be difficult, especially when you are engaged actively in your healing process. During these visits, it's as though you have walked through the door and entered a "time warp," where you revert back to childhood roles and ways of coping.

One of the most helpful ways to deal with visits to family members is to arrange to have certain inner child parts *not* participate in these visits. You might find that it will be better for a child part to "take a nap" for the duration of your visit, so that it doesn't even realize you've gone home.

For Stephen, a young man who had multiple personalities, it was particularly important to find a strategy he could count on before he went home for his grandparents' anniversary celebration. He came from a family where physical and emotional abuse had been passed down through generations. Inevitably, whenever he spent time with members of his family, Stephen would "shrink." He would become one of his inner child parts, a boy of about five years old, who was very frightened. In fact, he was so frightened of being around these people that he would become disoriented at times and blank out.

Stephen's strategy was to have his inner children play in the basement of the house he had built in his safe place. He arranged for them to stay there for the duration of the trip, with the agreement that he would come and get them when he was on the plane coming home. Since there is no time in the unconscious, the inner children didn't know the difference between one hour and five days. All they knew was that they were free to play until Stephen came to get them.

After returning home, Stephen reported that the trip had been much easier than previous ones. He managed to keep his adult awareness more of the time, and he felt stronger. One of the additional strategies he had developed was to do a little reading each evening before going to bed. He found that, if he could read something that related to his present-day life, he could reinforce that he would be going home to his grownup world; that he was just visiting the family and wouldn't have to stay any longer than necessary.

If you are a multiple, there is something you need to know about visiting any family members who were involved in past abuse, either as active abusers or as people who stood by and allowed you to be hurt. For most multiples, going back into the family context is likely to create a need to dissociate actively. If you visit your family and find that you begin switching more, losing time, or feeling the urge to hurt yourself, it's important to recognize that you are drawing on the only strategy you had available when you were a child. Once you return to your present-day environment, and the context in which you function as the adult you are today, things should settle down. It's one of the prices you may have to pay for a visit home, unless you decide that, for the time being, until you are more solidly healed, these visits may not be a good idea.

Other people have come up with different strategies. Some of these include: imagining that inner child parts are going to the movies when a particular relative comes for a visit; imagining a child part going to the park to play while a relative is in your home; imagining that the child part is going somewhere, perhaps on a vacation with other parts inside, during a family visit. These are but a few of the infinite possibilities for keeping your inner child parts safe when you have to deal with your family of origin.

DOING SCARY THINGS

Among the many things we have to do as adults that may scare us are: making presentations, going on business trips, dealing with authority figures, taking tests, and for some, even going grocery shopping. Again, there are as many strategies for soothing frightened inner child parts as there are people who have these parts inside. Basically, they are variations on the techniques used when visiting the family. The fundamental premise is to take the inner children to safety or to arrange for the adult self to take center stage when inner child parts are present.

A particularly helpful strategy is to develop an ongoing, reassuring dialogue with inner child parts. What so many of us miss in homes where there is abuse or neglect is the natural reassurance that children need when things feel out of control or frightening in some way. With quiet reassurance, children often are calmed quite easily and our inner child parts are no different. Also, the more you, as the adult, practice reassuring your inner child parts, the more you may actually come to believe that everything really will be all right!

Bonnie faced a fear that is common to many of us. She had to make a presentation, and there was a child part in her that simply couldn't bear to stand up in front of all those people. After using her fear as a bridge to the inner child that was having such difficulty with the upcoming presentation, Bonnie became aware of feelings she had about not wanting to make mistakes. There had been lots of blaming and criticism in her family. To make a mistake was to become the target for vicious comments and attacks. Mistakes in Bonnie's family included not speaking up when spoken to, speaking without being invited to, accidentally dropping a glass of milk, leaving water on the bathroom floor, and any number of other infractions. Much of her childhood had been lived in fear of being blamed for something she hadn't realize she had done. To give a presentation in her adult life felt like a terrible risk, because she couldn't control the possible number of mistakes she might make inadvertently.

As she prepared for her presentation, Bonnie did two things. She listened to the pain and fear in the inner child part and also began to get in touch with her anger at having been treated this way in childhood. Then, in her imagination, she rehearsed being up at the podium with the child part hiding behind her legs. Each time a wave of fear washed over her, she would remind herself that the child could hide and that she, the adult, would handle the presentation. As she calmly reassured the inner child, she did so with an "as-if" attitude. Even though she wasn't one hundred percent convinced that it would be okay, she allowed herself to act as if she really were comfortable.[12]

Sometimes, when a child part is very, very frightened, you might arrange to have an older inner child or another inner part of yourself, hold hands with the little one. Setting up this kind of internal support can bring a greater sense of safety and soothing to a frightened inner child part—enough so, anyway, so that you can get done what needs to be accomplished in your present-day life.

HELPING YOURSELF SHINE

Many adults who were hurt as children weren't allowed to express themselves openly and spontaneously as children. To have done so would have been too dangerous or would have caused them to become a visible target for abuse or humiliation and teasing. Most of us have at least one inner child part that holds our talents, our urges to express ourselves creatively. Often these parts are buried so deeply in our unconscious that we don't even realize they exist. Sometimes, though, we are very much aware of them, and it is a constant source of grief that we could never express ourselves fully as children.

Imagine how different your current life might be if you had permission to shine. Imagine the positive things that might result if you were comfortable expressing yourself spontaneously and creatively. And now, imagine how you might feel if you were able to encourage the inner child part of yourself that has this capacity.

One of the strategies for helping yourself to shine more openly in your adult life is to create a safe, special room in your imagination where the inner child can dance, sing, and play without fear of criticism, humiliation, or punishment. An important element in this strategy is your willingness to become an admiring adult in this child's life. When you are present in the special room and watch the child's performance or participate in whatever play feels fun and healing to the child part, you become an important mirror. Your affirmation of the child's expression and energy becomes a reflection of self-esteem and safety. In time, what the child feels will translate into your adult life, and you may surprise yourself by becoming more open and expressive in situations where that is appropriate.

Of course, there are also fears that may be triggered as you encourage this child part to express itself. If you find that it's just too much to acknowledge and enjoy this spontaneous activity, allow yourself to back off and work with the inner children that carry your fear. This inner child isn't going anywhere and will be waiting for you when you're ready.

There is no right way to heal. You are the best source of wisdom about what is appropriate for you at any given time. Whenever anything feels wrong, or off-base, or potentially overwhelming, slow down and allow yourself all the time you need to get where you are going. This is especially true when dealing with issues around shame. In the next chapter, we'll explore this difficult subject and look at some ways to help resolve the effects of childhood humiliation and abuse.

9

Shame and the Disowned Self

I CAN'T BEAR TO LET YOU SEE . . .

Perhaps the most painful legacy of having been hurt as a child is the profound shame, buried deep within us, that we often carry into our adult lives. Even if we are not aware, consciously, of the breadth or depth of our shame, it can powerfully affect our current relationships. For example, it may create difficulties in entering into and maintaining intimate relationships. It may cause us to hold back and achieve less than we are actually able to accomplish as adults today, and prompt us to conceal who we "really are" in our interactions with others. It may also fuel the self-hate and self-disgust that so many adults abused as children secretly feel. When we experience ourselves as unworthy and undeserving, awakening to each new day can be pretty disheartening.

Shame arising from a childhood in which we were hurt may also rob us of the important experience of healthy guilt. Guilt and shame are fundamentally different in that shame is a comment about the whole self of a person, while guilt is a response to something we did that we want to do differently next time.[1] Guilt allows us to make changes in our behavior; shame takes us more deeply into feelings of worthlessness or despair about our self-perceived shortcomings.

Because of our shame, we are driven, unconsciously, to disown and disavow parts of ourselves that we feel were to blame for the hurts we suffered. Some of us think of ourselves as bad people who are too disgusting for anyone to see as we really are. Some of us think of ourselves as ugly, dirty, or tainted because of the things that happened to us when we were young. We tell ourselves, "If I didn't deserve it, it wouldn't have happened to me." We may secretly feel guilty because of the thoughts we have about the people who hurt us or the secret hate or contempt we feel towards people in our present-day life. Some of us even disavow the wonderful things in ourselves—such as our talents, love of beauty, and enthusiasm for life—because these were the things that brought disapproval, abandonment, or even abuse when we were children.

These aspects of ourselves—the good and the bad that have been shaped by experiences of hurt—create what can be called *the disowned self*.[2] You may already be painfully aware of your disowned self and the shame it conveys. For example, you may be quite conscious of your feelings of inferiority or discomfort when you have to deal with an authority figure or present a proposal at work or school. You may know, all too well, how it feels to be ashamed of yourself when you think you've said something ridiculous at a party. Or you may be most aware of your shame when you look in the mirror and see your face, or your body, and experience a feeling of revulsion or a need to look away.

Most of the disowned self, though, lives deep in the unconscious where you may experience it as waves of shame that seem incomprehensible but somehow deserved. When disowned parts of ourselves emerge into daily living or come into our ongoing stream of consciousness, most of us seek to push them away or hide from them. Our self-loathing, self-disgust, or fear of these parts can create an internal environment of acute discomfort. For many of us who were hurt as children, the biggest struggle of the day is to live with the internal voices, thoughts, and feelings about ourselves that carry on a ceaseless dialogue that points out every mistake, every flaw, every way in which people think badly of us.

The Shadow

There is a name for the disowned self that is drawn from the work of Carl Jung: *the shadow*.[3] Throughout this chapter, I'll use both terms— the disowned self and the shadow—to refer to the dynamic, unconscious aspect of the personality where we put parts of ourselves we cannot accept. It's important to keep in mind that the shadow also contains those elements that are beautiful in us. When we disavow our shadow side, we lose the energy and power of being a "full self."

A primary activity in the healing process that serves to empower our lives in the present is reclaiming the shadow, looking at and accepting those parts of ourselves that were pushed away when we were children—and that we may still continue to push away in adulthood.

A surprise awaits you when you embrace the shadow: as you accept and integrate into your adult awareness the disowned parts of yourself, a tremendous amount of energy and creativity are released into your daily life. This is a natural outcome of the work we explored in the previous chapter. As you allow your inner parts to tell their stories, to share their feelings and memories, you undertake a process of acceptance and integration of what have been previously disowned aspects of consciousness. No longer do you have to hide who you are. No longer do you have to fear that others will find out about the hidden self you keep tucked away inside. No longer will the voices that tell you how terrible, inadequate, or inept you are—or how awful it will be for you if you succeed—carry the power they may have at present.

We tend to believe these internal messages until we have allowed the hidden parts of ourselves into our ongoing, present-day awareness. Once we have come to terms with the parts of us we have disowned, there is no more power in the voices. They have no meaning. We know who we are, and it is okay to be fully human—good and bad.

Globalizing Versus Focusing on Specifics

One of the primary dynamics that fuels the experience of shame is our tendency to globalize the meaning of a humiliating experience.[4] For example, imagine that you were asked to do an important favor for a friend and somehow you forgot to do it. Imagine, also, that your friend was upset with you for forgetting. If you are someone who feels shame instead of guilt, your response to your friend's anger, and the shame of having let someone down, may reinforce feelings that you are a bad person, that there is something wrong with you. If you were able, instead, to look just at this one instance of forgetting and feel appropriately guilty that you disappointed someone, you could apologize and choose to do things differently next time. For example, you might decide that you want to get a daily calendar and write down chores you need to do. Or you might realize that you tend to forget things when you take on more than you can handle, so that perhaps you need to practice saying "no."

The key issue here is that a feeling of shame can distort your perception and lead you to feel that you are always going to forget or that you are a terrible friend. When you can think, instead, of the specifics of the situation as reflecting some changes you might want to make in your behavior, shame disappears and normal, healthy guilt can take its place.

Make a Mistake a Day

For many people who struggle with shame, making mistakes is almost intolerable.[5] Adults who were abused as children were blamed for just about everything. Think about how it was in your home. Were you one of those kids who happened to be in the wrong place at the wrong time when an angry parent came home from a hard day at work? Do you recall how you may have felt about having to walk on eggshells so you wouldn't accidentally do something wrong and get into trouble? Do you know now that what you actually did often had nothing at all to do with why you got into trouble? Are you able to feel, really *feel*, the truth that the problem had everything to do with your abuser and nothing to do with you, except that you were too small and too weak to protect yourself?

Were you one of those kids who was sound asleep and suddenly found yourself awakened by an outraged caretaker who demanded that you get out of bed and do some chore? Or were you shamed in more subtle ways, feeling the blame in the look on a parent's face or the tone of voice that conveyed the message that you somehow didn't measure up, that somehow you were a disappointment, a failure?

There are as many ways to blame a child—or anybody else—as there are people involved in interpersonal interactions. Take a moment to recall the ways you might have felt blamed as a child and the times when you have worried about making mistakes or have caused people to be upset or disappointed in you. Are these familiar feelings? Most abuse survivors know them all too well.

There is an exercise, a way of thinking about certain things, that you can do right now to learn how to make it easier, and more fun, to get through the day today. It is based on the premise that, *if you aren't making at least one mistake a day, you may not really be engaged in living, and you may not be learning anything new.*

Life is about being who we are and doing what is ours to do. When we are comfortable with ourselves, the "being" part of things feels pretty good much of the time. Then we are free to investigate new learnings that allow our "doing" to evolve and expand if we choose to explore our potential.

We human beings learn by doing. It's the natural way to get from here to there. We learn to walk by crawling, by struggling to stand up, fall down on our diapered bottoms, and then start all over again. If we are in a family that is loving and supportive, we might even get applause when we experiment with how to stand on our own two feet. If we are in a family that teases, shames, or expresses excessive concern for our safety, we might decide that falling down is a terrible thing and we had better not try anything until we know how to do it perfectly.

I remember a friend, from a long time ago, who couldn't wait to learn to water ski. We went to a lake together, along with some other friends, and she sat and watched everyone for a while. When it was her turn to try the skis for the first time, she was excited and animated. We all could tell that she was having fun. As is true with most beginners, she fell down almost as soon as she was up on the skis. What made me sad was that she just gave up after she fell. She insisted on coming back to the dock and she refused to try again, no matter how much encouragement we gave her. Instead of taking in the support offered by friends, she was held captive by the conviction that she should already know how to ski well enough to keep from falling down. Falling down felt like failure, and this was simply too humiliating to my friend. She didn't know that she *had* to fall down in order to learn how to stay up.

Much of what we learn is by trial-and-error. We have to make mistakes in order to grasp what we want to achieve. If you learned to ride a bike when you were young, chances are that you wobbled, or actually fell over, a few times, at least, before you developed the needed balance to ride well. If you ever learned to roller skate, you probably experienced something similar. Think of a time when you learned a skill that required you to wobble first. The basic fact is that, if you didn't falter, you couldn't develop the necessary equilibrium to accomplish what you set out to do.

It's the same with learning to do *anything*, even how to feel differently about something. Everything takes practice, whether you seek to acquire a new skill or learn a new way to handle your emotions. For example, take a moment to call to mind what it's like for you when you meet people for the first time. Are you comfortable? Do you have a good time and then go home and reflect on all the things you wish you had said differently? Or is it difficult for you the whole time because of your fear that you'll say the wrong thing, or have nothing to say, or somehow make a fool of yourself?

All of these responses can be thought of as driven by shame. They reflect feelings of not being good enough, of the inevitability that we will do something that will show people we really aren't worthwhile, that we aren't someone with whom they would want to spend time. And if they seem to like us, we tell ourselves it's because they were fooled and it will only be a matter of time before they discover the truth about us.

For some children, early learning experiences are made impossibly difficult because the child is not yet developmentally ready to accomplish them with ease. I have heard many stories of children who were toilet trained at very young ages. It's not surprising that when these children become adults they struggle with issues of control and often feel overwhelmed when new tasks need to be mastered. Other children were asked to do grownup chores before they had the coordination or skills necessary to do them well, leading to frustration, anxiety, and a basic sense of incompetence. For still others, being skipped a grade in school caused them to feel that they were never quite "enough," that they couldn't ever quite catch up with everybody else.

What is so tragic about shame-based experiences such as these is that they become a source of bad feelings about the self when, in fact, they actually represent stories about adults who misunderstood the natural developmental needs of children. Shame is counteracted when children's natural developmental capacities are understood and supported, and learning is acknowledged as a process that involves experimentation—which means learning from mistakes. Then children engage new experiences with their natural curiosity and enjoyment intact. When this happens, a feeling of competence and mastery can result from encountering and engaging the unknown. Can you recall a time when your curiosity was healthy and thriving? Even if you can't remember it, it's still likely to be there, deep in your unconscious, just waiting for you to rediscover it.

And so, back to our exercise. If some part of you can accept the premise that it's natural to make mistakes when you are involved actively in life, then ask yourself to do the following experiment. The next time you have to do something that makes you uncomfortable or something you haven't done before, allow yourself to be curious about how the process of learning will unfold. Instead of believing your feelings of shame—or whatever your thoughts or inner voices may tell you about how you will fail or appear foolish if you try something and do it incorrectly—see what happens if you remember that making mistakes is a natural part of learning.

It's helpful to keep in mind that the thoughts you have about how learning is supposed to work were created by a child's mind, a child who may have been confused, humiliated, or hurt in some way. If you can, allow yourself to feel compassion for the shame and childlike perceptions that are inherent in these thoughts and voices. Be curious about how the mistakes will help you do the task better. *Invite* mistakes. Their presence will assure you that you are learning something and that you are giving yourself an opportunity to discover what works best.

Of course, you may be like many adults who were abused as children. When you set out to revise your understanding of the voices that create shame, you may be unsuccessful at first, and then you may blame yourself even more! Please keep in mind that seeking to hear the shame-based thoughts and voices differently is, in itself, a new learning. Sometimes you'll be successful, and at other times you'll "fall down," as you learn to deal with those parts of your inner experience in a new way.

Elliot knew all too well what it meant to be filled with shame whenever he was among people. If he were home alone, he was able to carry on endless conversations with himself. He could be witty, intelligent, even eloquent. But when he was with other people, he became painfully tongue-tied and couldn't seem to put together a coherent sentence. His entire focus was on his need to say just the right thing. If he couldn't get it right in his head, he wouldn't say it. He couldn't bear the thought of being wrong or of saying something others might criticize. As a result, Elliot spent many evenings in quiet agony and many moments berating himself for being such an uninteresting companion.

In addition, the more self-conscious he became, the louder the voices in his mind became. It was as though he were turning in on himself and couldn't find a way out. As he was able to think of interactions with other people as new learning experiences—as experiments—it got to be easier. Instead of the grinding embarrassment of feeling like a fool or a dullard, he began to explore which kinds of interactions felt comfortable and which didn't. If he found himself floundering in a conversation, he thought of it as a "wobble," just like the wobbles he experienced when learning to ride his bike as a boy. He recognized that he needed the wobbles to let him know how it felt when he was becoming too self-conscious for comfort. Once he became aware of this, he could look inside to see if a child part were triggered, or if something else were going on, and take steps to care for himself.

After a time of learning to accept his mistakes and experience them as evidence of new learning taking place, Elliott reported something that a lot of people discover. His sense of humor about himself was improving. Instead of feeling dread in his stomach all the time, now he felt laughter, once in a while. It was quite different for him to be able to laugh *with* himself, to accept his human frailties as normal and natural. In childhood, he had been humiliated so often by his older brothers and cousins that laughter related to his behavior had always been a source of tremendous pain and shame.

For Josephine, shame about mistakes centered on her performance at work. Her fear of disapproval was massive and threatened to overwhelm her whenever she thought about making mistakes on the job. As a child, she had been repeatedly abandoned emotionally by her mother, who expressed almost constant disappointment and unhappiness at her lot in life.

On the job, Josephine tried hard never to make a mistake. What she didn't understand, though, was that her very best efforts would never be enough because it's impossible to do things perfectly. As she learned more about why she felt so fearful and ashamed, and as she practiced viewing mistakes as avenues to learning, life got easier. The most important change came in the way she talked to herself in her own mind. Instead of mercilessly blaming herself for being so stupid, Josephine began to tell herself more healing messages. For instance, she would say to herself, "Well, I wish I hadn't done it this way, but the world won't end. I'll straighten it out and know better the next time."

Learning to make at least one mistake a day isn't the whole answer to healing, but it helps. It's one more step in reclaiming your full self from a hurtful past. Instead of believing that making mistakes can cause the end of your world, the way they may have when you were young, you have the right to put them in perspective. You have the right to know that being human means having good and bad days, better and worse times. The goal in healing isn't to have things be perfect all the time; instead, it's to know that you'll be all right even when they aren't.

The Shamed Child

In *Recreating Your Self*, I talked about a very special inner child part, *the shamed child*.[6] This aspect of your disowned self can be envisioned as holding the essence of your shame, and much healing can be accomplished when you get to know this part. Imagine how it will feel when you are able to respond to feelings of shame, which may arise in the course of your present-day activities, with soothing rather than dread. What a difference it can make in daily living to be able to move through potentially humiliating experiences with a "lighter touch."

Take just a moment, now, to wonder what you might experience if you were to reach inside and put your arms around a child who may feel utterly unworthy and undeserving of love or nurturing. For some people, to connect with the shamed child is, at first, an extremely painful experience. Your immediate impression of the shamed child may be one of a distorted or ugly figure. The shamed child may have a face that is hidden or grotesque. It's important to allow your first impressions to tell you the story of the depth and breadth of your shame. You have a right to know how you really feel, because when you allow yourself to know, you open the door to healing.

Sometimes the shamed child wants nothing to do with you when you first make contact. There may be just too much hurt, too much shame, to allow any connection to occur. If this happens to you, just let it be. In time, the shamed child will respond if you will just be there, asking nothing in return. In time, you may be surprised to discover how willingly the shamed child turns to you for comfort. It's as though, at some deep unconscious level, the natural ability of children to respond to love awakens. Allow this to happen in its own time. All you need to do is be willing to open your heart to this disowned part of yourself. Your unconscious will know how to turn your open heart into healing.

Shadow-Boxing

One of the most profound, and important, dynamics of the shadow self has to do with how we experience disowned parts of ourselves in others. We all do this, automatically and inevitably. It occurs through a process called *projection*,[7] where we unconsciously attribute to others those qualities in ourselves that we cannot bear to accept as our own.

Along with projection comes the unconscious urge to control, eliminate, or overpower these disowned aspects of ourselves. On a social level, we do this when we project negative traits onto whole other groups of people. Racism, anti-Semitism, misogynism—all the "-isms" for that matter—represent a battle between us and disowned parts of ourselves.

As the first part of this exercise, think of a group of people you really don't like, or who frighten you, and make a list of the reasons why you feel this way. Notice that there will be certain things on your list that seem to prove to you that they actually are as inferior or evil as you had thought originally. As uncomfortable as it may feel, take a moment, now, to imagine that at least some of these traits apply to you, that they represent aspects of your disowned self that you haven't yet been able to embrace and integrate into your full self.

This isn't an easy exercise to do. Most of us want to wriggle away from any acknowledgment that the very things we despise in others are the things we refuse to see in ourselves. It's helpful to be understanding with yourself in this exercise and to realize that to be human means to be both good and bad. *That* is inevitable. What makes the difference between someone who is truly evil and someone who knows her *potential* for evil is *choice*.

Even as you come face to face with the less-than-lovely shadow parts of yourself, remember that at every moment you have the power and the right to choose how you want to behave. However, choice is only possible when you have become conscious of your true feelings and capacities to experience and express the negative side of yourself. As long as you remain unaware of your ability to think, act, and feel negatively, there is a risk that you will act out in unconscious ways.

On a personal level, we engage in shadow-boxing with loved ones, colleagues, bosses, and strangers on the street. When we shadow-box, we connect with the disowned parts of ourselves that we experience in the other person and then fight to destroy what we can't tolerate in ourselves.

For the next part of the exercise, think of someone who gets your goat every time. Choose someone who really rattles your cage, someone about whom you have strong negative feelings. It's probably best not to choose an abuser from childhood, because that will complicate this particular exercise. Choose someone from your present life or from the not-too-distant past. You may find that this particular someone represents a certain "type" of person who may appear in your life with some regularity.

Take a few moments to recall the behaviors or characteristics that really get to you and write them down. Once you have done this, sit for a moment and wonder what it would be like if you were to imagine these characteristics as your own.

In my own experience, I had a powerful realization with this exercise. Throughout my adult life, I've always had at least one friend who was difficult to get along with, whom other people really didn't like. What I didn't realize until recent years was that I *needed* to have at least one unpleasant person in my life so that I wouldn't have to acknowledge the unpleasant parts of my own personality. Instead, I could be the "good one" and feel secure and comfortable inside myself. Of course, I never *really* felt good about myself, but at least with a difficult friend around I could fool myself with feelings of superiority.

As I have worked with my own shadow-boxing issues, my life has become much richer inside. Now that I'm able to recognize, and own, the unpleasant parts of myself, I am a more complete person. I no longer need to have a difficult friend to protect me from that truth.

As you work with this exercise, be gentle with yourself. At first you may say, "No way. That person isn't anything like me. I absolutely won't accept that I'm shadow-boxing right now." That's fine. The reason we project our shadow selves in the first place is because we don't want to know about them. It takes time to open your heart to these parts of yourself, it's worth every moment of discomfort and gentleness, though. Remember, as long as these parts remain outside your conscious awareness, they tend to be expressed in unconscious—often destructive—ways, and may cause even more discomfort than is involved when you allow yourself to own them.

The Power of Choice

Earlier I mentioned that the most important element in working with your shadow self is the power you have to choose how you will act or *not* act. The disowned aspects of ourselves often include the following: racist feelings, sexism, "ageism," jealousy, hate, sadistic impulses, vulgarity, envy, vulnerability and feelings of helplessness, sexual impulses, power, bliss, hope, love.

You may be surprised to discover feelings such as power, bliss, hope, and love listed among your possible shadow aspects. For abused children, though, it is often important to disavow any experience of personal power, such as hope, excitement, self-respect, and other elements of self-esteem. To harbor or express positive or self-empowered feelings might lead to further abuse or to deep anguish when trauma reestablishes its terrible presence.

The reason we need to reclaim the positive, as well as the negative, parts of our disowned self is that if we don't we will project these qualities out onto others, just as we do the negative. Then it's the *other* person who is the source of our bliss. It's the *other* person who can convey love to us. It's the *other* person who deserves admiration and success.[8] And so, unless we embrace these positive qualities in our-selves, we assign them to others. We allow the good things to reside in "those special people out there" and rob ourselves of the experience and rewards of life-affirming qualities that are part of us.

We also reinforce our shame when we disown the good things about ourselves. We underscore feelings of not deserving to be treated well, or to be loved, or to achieve what we seek in our lives. On a day-to-day basis, if the good things belong to special people out there, then we're more likely to focus on input that underscores our sense of worthlessness. We're not as likely to "let in" affirming responses from our environment when we don't recognize positive qualities inside ourselves.

It's much easier to understand why we disown the negative aspects of ourselves. They seem to prove all the things our shame conveys about us. Once you are able to admit to yourself that you have feelings of which you disapprove or which frighten you, *then* you have availa-ble the true capacity to choose how you want to be in the world. People who abuse others make a choice, even if they don't realize it at the time. Instead of managing their own feelings, they choose to externalize those feelings and act out against others.

As you become increasingly familiar with previously disowned parts of yourself, it will also become easier to choose not to act on them. Once something that has been unconscious becomes conscious, it's much harder to pretend it belongs to someone else. For example, imagine that as a child you were constantly forced to do things you didn't want to do and you had no recourse. It wasn't possible to fight for what you wanted, so you had to swallow your rage and grudgingly do things you absolutely did not want to do. Now, as an adult, you may discover that you are constantly embroiled in fights. It may be that your doctor did something you didn't like, so you refused to pay the bill. Or you may have purchased something that didn't work correctly, and then you became involved in a long-running battle to have it replaced. By putting your time and energy into these external fights, you continue to disown your true feelings about the fights you never were able to have with your parents, for example. Once you reclaim these feelings, instead of projecting them out onto external sources, you also give yourself an opportunity to use your time and energy more constructively.

Or, imagine that you grew up in a home where promises were made and then broken. For example, someone may have been promised to take you on a special trip. Then, when the big day came, no one bothered to tell you that the plans had changed and you weren't going on the trip after all. Above and beyond the disappointment you may have felt in this situation, you were learning something important. You learned how people can be let down. If the capacity to break promises remains unconscious, you may discover that you automatically project it out onto others. For instance, you may find that you become outraged whenever you perceive that someone has been unreliable, even when the issue at hand is insignificant. You may feel an urge to strike out at them, verbally or physically. If you are able to recognize that your reaction seems overblown and can ask yourself what part of you the behavior might represent, you will have chosen a healing opportunity instead of another bout of shadow-boxing.

For Selma, the shadow issue that most dogged her heels was racism. As a child, Selma had been brutally abused and couldn't tolerate the feelings of being inferior and less than human that came as a result of the abuse. These feelings had been pushed deep into her unconscious and came to light only when she encountered someone she considered to be inferior to herself. This dynamic created some difficulties for Selma, because she worked in a job where she came in contact with a large cross-section of people. She felt under constant internal pressure and stress as she experienced aggravation, irritation, and disgust when dealing with people she felt were inferior to herself.

In essence, Selma had to see the powerlessness in others—had to get it out of herself—and then she could attack it the way her abuser had attacked her. In this way, she could feel strong and in control, and she didn't have to become conscious of the overwhelming feelings of powerlessness she had experienced as a child. At the same time, she was able to express, and justify, the abusive part of herself through her racist thoughts and feelings. She didn't have to wonder why she felt this way. She simply turned her venom on others without having to acknowledge that she was acting abusively. By clinging to her racist feelings, Selma continually missed opportunities for real healing. By projecting outside herself qualities that were painfully in need of attention within her, she prolonged her own discomfort.

The choice for William was different. His biggest trigger was elicited when someone else seemed to be distressed. He just couldn't tolerate it when he felt another person needed help. Even when people asked him not to interfere, William would jump in with both feet, getting involved where he didn't belong and making people angry because of his insistence on helping them. What he discovered, as he acknowledged that he was probably dealing with a disowned aspect of his own experience, was the desperation he had felt as a child. He *had* needed to be rescued when he was young, but no one had come to his rescue. He just couldn't bear any conscious awareness of his profound powerlessness. Unconsciously, he had dealt with these feelings by becoming conscious of the needs of others and then trying his very best to take care of them. He hadn't realized that he was really trying to take care of himself. As soon as William identified his own neediness, he was able to stop externalizing it onto others and to move inside his own process to do some healing work. William exercised his power to choose to deal with his own issues, and it made all the difference.

Balancing Hopeful Moments

One of the powerful things about dealing with your shame is discovering how deeply, and protectively, parts of you may respond to any hint of hope.[9] When we've been hurt as children, it's not unusual to have parts of us that guard against hope. Hope sometimes becomes a signal that bad things are about to happen, or it reminds us of times we were tricked or used because of our willingness, as children, to keep hoping it would get better. Disowned parts of us fight back with messages that say we don't deserve good things, that good only turns to bad in the end, and who do we think we are, anyway? The potential for even more disappointment is unbearable to some disowned parts of us, and so we may unconsciously fend off even the smallest signal that things are getting better.

Think back to a time recently when you felt that things seemed to be pretty much on track or you did something well and felt good about it. Did you notice that, soon after, you may have felt down rather than up, or had an urge to hurt yourself, or had some other experience that took away the hope? I can think of many people I've talked with who have so often felt depressed after something good has happened in their lives. I've also talked to people who get angry, frightened, or anxious when they have a good day.

Since one of the primary reasons for engaging a healing process is to allow you to feel better about yourself and your day-to-day life in the present, it matters how you respond to the many small achievements that create a more masterful and hopeful approach to living. If each step forward becomes the prelude to a potential step backward into an old feeling or an old behavior you thought you'd outgrown, it can be discouraging, to say the least.

When this happens, it's helpful to keep in mind that, when we "stretch" and reach into new responses or new achievements, sometimes it's necessary to return to old, familiar protective responses so we can reassure ourselves we aren't going too far. Over time, you may notice that your steps forward elicit less powerful steps backward, as parts of you begin to learn that expressing yourself doesn't automatically mean you will be hurt.

It's as though there were a part of the self, operating from the unconscious, that responds in ways that insure we don't get too carried away with hope. In my own life, and in working with clients and workshop participants, I have found that, if you balance moments of hope with moments that acknowledge and engage the shadow part, it becomes possible to take steps forward into a more positive feeling about yourself and your life without having to undo these steps by engaging in self-destructive responses.

One of the ways to do this is to take some time to sit quietly with yourself, after something good has happened, to have a reassuring dialogue with any parts of you that may be frightened by the step you have taken. When you take the time to acknowledge, consciously, that parts of you probably *will* be concerned when too much excitement or success comes all at once, you may discover that something inside eases. You may not even need to be aware, consciously, of the parts that are uncomfortable. Simply by assuming they are there and taking the time to reassure them, you may lessen the need to flee into old behaviors.

For example, you might talk to an inner part about giving you a signal, such as anxiety or a tingle in your hand, to let you know that some reassurance is necessary right now. Think of a time when you may have observed a young child playing and everything was going along fine. Then, all of a sudden, the child reached a point of over-stimulation and suddenly wasn't having fun anymore. If the person playing with that child were sensitive and stopped for a few minutes, the child may have settled down and been ready to play again in a little while. Had the caretaker kept going, chances are the child would have become increasingly distressed by the interaction.[10]

Then, bring to mind a time when you may have observed a young child who became frightened of something. If this child were fortunate, her caretaker may have taken the time to acknowledge the fear without humiliation or punishment. When this happens, a child can shift quickly from fear to curiosity. What is most important is to acknowledge and accept what *is* first, and then offer reassurance that you will pay attention to these feelings.

As you become aware of responses in you that signal a need to sit down for a few minutes and acknowledge your discomfort with the good things that are happening in your life, you give yourself a chance to be aware of, rather than act out, your vulnerable feelings. You have a right to know that it is safe to become your whole self and to learn that hope needn't be a prelude to despair. You also have a right to give yourself reassurance that you can take the process at a pace that allows all the parts of you to come along at their own speed. This doesn't mean that you must stop your forward momentum just because you are afraid. It does mean taking seriously the need to *acknowledge* your feelings and attend to whatever fears may have been triggered before pushing forward.

For Rhonda, the process of taking some time to go inside and acknowledge the feelings that were triggered whenever she felt hopeful proved to be a deeply meaningful practice. The trauma in Rhonda's childhood centered around severe abuse where there was no one to whom she could turn for any kind of comfort. Whenever any of her abusers seemed to offer kindness, the interaction turned out to be traumatic and painful. Because of this, almost any achievement could send Rhonda into a tailspin of despair, as a dissociated part would react to the tiniest hint of hope. For this part, good experiences were inevitably the harbinger of more abuse.

In her day-to-day life, Rhonda's biggest challenge seemed to come when she succeeded at making sales calls, which required her to be more assertive than was usual for her. When she had a good meeting with a client, part of her would feel a thrill of excitement in response to acting like a competent adult. Other parts, though, became frightened or angry at being too "out there." She would begin to feel hopeful that she was getting better, doing better, even as other parts of her would begin their descent into fear.

Because of this, a successful day had a good chance of turning into a depressed night. Rhonda would feel herself compelled to exercise until she was ready to drop, which she would bitterly regret afterward, or she would crawl into bed without giving herself the pleasure of a hot bath, which was a special treat after a hard day, or she would find herself compelled to go to a movie that she wasn't even interested in seeing.

At first, Rhonda didn't think it would do any good simply to sit down and acknowledge that she was afraid. As she practiced, she became more aware of the body sensations she had when she was beginning to get overloaded with feeling good about herself. Then she discovered that certain parts of her were soothed by the very fact that she recognized how she was feeling, rather than plowing ahead and being out of touch with the mixed feelings going on inside. She also found it helpful to say to herself something like, "All right. We've been doing a lot and now we're going to sit for a while and read a book. This can be a time in which we take a step away from the activity that is causing the fear." Instead of going to the movies, exercising, or spacing out in an unconscious attempt to deal with the feelings, Rhonda made a conscious decision to choose how she wanted to deal with her fears. Each time she made this choice, she also discovered an increasing sense of mastery: her life felt less out of control.

Davis had a different experience. His fears had to do with making friends and being around people. Davis also had been hurt badly as a child, both physically and psychologically, so interacting with people was fraught with expectations of being hurt, even when things seemed to be going well. Whenever he had a really good time with someone, instead of bathing himself in the afterglow of the pleasure of good company, he would begin to hear angry voices in his head. The voices would tell him he was bad, that he couldn't measure up, and that he shouldn't even think about having good times. These voices unnerved Davis, and sometimes frightened him. They never caused any physical harm, but their verbal abuse was deeply distressing.

Davis discovered that sometimes his discomfort lessened if, first, he acknowledged that parts of him must be afraid. Then, through trial and error, he found that if he spent some time walking in his neighborhood or puttering around his apartment, the voices in his head might calm down. The major work with these voices went on in therapy, but Davis was pleased to have developed some strategies he could draw on to use in his daily life.

SPECIAL ISSUES FOR MULTIPLES

If you are a multiple, feelings of shame may be so pervasive and overwhelmingly powerful that it is painful even to think of getting in touch with them. It is important for you to acknowledge that profound abuse creates profound shame. Go slowly into this area of your childhood hurts.

What may surprise you is how, within a context of safety and even to the smallest degree, healing becomes possible when you get in touch with parts of you that hold your shame. Each small revelation builds on the next, until you have developed a greater tolerance for what may have been agonizing feelings.

If you find that you feel more confused or split off from yourself when feelings of shame come to the surface, simply observe your response and slow down. Allow yourself to realize that for some parts inside it's still too painful to feel the shame. If you discover that feelings of shame make you want to act out or hide, observe that as well, keeping in mind that you can use each emergence of your shame to discover, bit by bit, how you cope and how different parts of you respond to these difficult feelings.

Over time, your willingness to feel, to observe, and to learn from your shame will create a strength in your adult observer and in your ability to soothe yourself that will make shameful feelings more bearable. It's helpful to remember that your shame arises not from who you are inherently but from what happened to you when you were too young to protect yourself.[11]

After Shame Passes

In the next chapter, we'll explore your future self, a profoundly important ally in your healing process. Getting to know the future self and allowing yourself to share the consciousness and physical sensations of this wiser, more evolved part of yourself can be deeply healing and have a positive effect on your day-to-day life.

For now, when you have been embroiled in feelings of shame and then they pass—as all feelings eventually do—take a few moments to write in your journal or sit quietly with yourself. During this time, you might reflect on where the shame lives in your body, what it communicates to you, and how you respond when you fall into this painful experience.

You might ask yourself what could have helped to keep your shame from being triggered to such an intense degree or what could have helped you once you were embroiled in shame feelings. This is a time of reflection, not blame. It's an opportunity to muse about what you experienced and to do some quiet pondering about what might make it easier next time.

You may want to take a few breaths and notice that, while you are able to remember that you felt shame, the intensity of the feeling may have passed and isn't with you right now. Whatever you may be feeling, notice how the next few moments can become moments of healing, of renewal. You have moved through another round of shame, and you have a right to rest.

Then, you may want to take a few moments to imagine that there is a source of beautiful, healing light above your head, like the one you explored in Chapter 5 on mindfulness. It's a gentle light, and yet powerful, of whatever color comes to mind. If it feels okay to do so, you might allow yourself to imagine that the light comes in through the top of your head and begins to fill your whole body. Because it's a healing light, it can be warm, or soft, or deeply comforting. It can touch all the nerve endings in your body and soothe them in a way that makes sense to you. This beautiful light can even fill all the secret and frightened places inside, offering a blanket of peacefulness for a little while.

If you choose to fill yourself with this light, notice that you can become a sponge and soak it into every particle of you—your body, your mind, your feelings. You can even gather some of your inner children together to experience the presence of the healing light with you. Then, recognize that this healing light is available all the time. It is a universal light, a limitless source of healing whenever you want to take a few minutes to rediscover it. You might also consider how it would feel to carry this light with you, to experience its presence whenever you need to throughout the day.

The important thing is to realize that you have successfully moved through your shame once more, only this time you may have had more of your adult observer present during the process. That's plenty to achieve any time you deal with hurts from childhood. It's enough for right now just to sit quietly and rest.

Shame is like every other wound from childhood. It heals at its own pace, a little at a time. That's the way you need it to be. Slow, steady change is reliable. It's the kind of change you won't lose when the going gets tough. And that's how it is when you meet your future self and become that wiser, more empowered you, slowly and over time. In the next chapter, we'll explore how to develop this relationship in powerful and healing ways.

10

Your Future Self

COULD THAT POSSIBLY BE ME?

One of the most powerful ways to make getting through the day easier is to call upon parts of yourself that feel more centered and convey a greater sense of mastery than you may experience at this point in your life. Within the timelessness of the unconscious, you can as easily draw on *resource parts* of the future as on wounded parts from the past.[1] Resource parts represent states of mind and body that communicate to your present-day self important new learnings, including ways of comforting yourself more effectively. And they come in many forms.

This chapter focuses on the *future self* as a primary resource in your healing journey, but there are other helpful parts as well, which I'll touch on a little later. In *Recreating Your Self*, I had a lot to say about the future self.[2] For me, personally, this construct has been one of the greatest supports in my healing journey, and I find it continues to be an important resource. Because of this, I would like to share my deepened understanding of this resource part with you.

How you envision the idea of a future self doesn't really matter. One way to conceptualize it is as an aspect of consciousness that exists in the *timeless unconscious*—that place inside where there is only *now*. From within that place where there is no time, you can access parts of you that represent past experiences *and* future accomplishments. Or you may imagine that the future self represents a "blueprint" that is inherent in your deep unconscious, the reservoir of your potential. Or you may think of it as a positive self-fulfilling prophecy—a suggestion you give yourself that becomes a positive self-hypnotic suggestion your unconscious follows.

As I mentioned in *Recreating Your Self,* your future self is that part of you, present in your unconscious at all times, that has already achieved changes you seek to make. However you conceive of your future self, it's helpful to realize that it represents a wiser, more evolved part of you, the essence of all you have the capacity to become as you heal. Sometimes it can seem as though the future self is an abstract concept, something that's "way out there" and not too applicable to everyday life. Nothing could be further from the truth. What I have learned, as I have interacted with my own future selves,[3] is that having a conscious relationship with *the healed self you are becoming* can be tremendously practical, right here and right now.

Let me illustrate with a personal example. It happened after I had ordered a new hypnosis chair for my office. The chair was scheduled to be delivered on a Monday morning, so on Friday evening I gave away my old chair. When Monday morning arrived, it was snowing hard, and as I started my walk to work I began to obsess about what would happen if the new chair didn't arrive. At that time in my life, I was still able to escalate worrying to heights that surprised even me, and on this particular morning I was really getting into it. After half a block, the thought floated into my mind that it might be a good idea to make a conscious choice to stop worrying, since I couldn't do anything about the chair. At almost the same moment, I realized I could ask my future self how she would handle the situation.

Almost as soon as I turned my attention to my future self, it was as though something clicked. I felt that click in my body as well as my mind, and I suddenly realized that the chair just wasn't a problem. Everything would be fine even if it didn't arrive. The accepting attitude of my future self flowed into me and a calm spread all through me. This was a very different state of being; to be calm when I felt a loss of control wasn't my usual response. As it turned out, the chair was delivered after all, and I was pleased not to have spent the morning tense and out of focus, worrying about something that really didn't matter. The exciting thing to have discovered was that I could access a new response by tapping into the state of mind of my future self.

It doesn't really matter whether you believe the future self actually exists. What *is* important is that you allow yourself to draw on resources that exist in your creative unconscious, which are available when you need them. The future self offers one way to symbolize, or concretize, the process.

I have heard from clients and others how they have called on their future selves at a moment's notice to help them shift gears when the going got rough. Jim, a workshop participant who came to a follow-up seminar, reported that he found it especially helpful to imagine the hand of his future self resting on his shoulder when things at work got tense. He described how the sensation of a strong, firm hand guiding him helped him recenter himself. It also gave him a sense of confidence and a feeling that he was supported. These responses served to soothe frightened inner child parts and gave Jim the inner strength he needed to deal with the challenges of daily living.

Eleanor, a member of a self-hypnosis group, discovered that she could imagine what it felt like to be hugged and comforted by her future self when she awakened in the middle of the night filled with feelings of loneliness and fear. It seemed that her body relaxed in response to the imagined presence of a comforting person.[4] She didn't go right back to sleep every time, but once in a while she would surprise herself by awaking in the morning and not quite remembering when she fell back to sleep.

As Eleanor's experience suggests, sometimes all you need is the sense of a supportive presence that conveys, "I'm here. It's all right. You're not alone and you'll be okay." When the message from your future self moves from your mind to your body, the sensation of being "held" can bring you back to a sense of equilibrium when you're feeling shaky.

There are as many ways to experience and get in touch with the future self as there are people seeking contact with this resource part. Allow yourself to find your own way of tapping into the help that is available to you.

The only thing that *is* the same for everyone, and something you have a right to demand, is that your future self be a *supportive* presence in your life. If you find that your future self is in any way negative or abusive towards you, you have probably tapped into what is called a "negative possible self."[5] This aspect of the future often reflects hurts you experienced as a child, and you have a right to put this self aside and *ask your unconscious to help you discover the future self that represents your best potential.*

SPECIAL ISSUES FOR MULTIPLES

There are some special issues that arise when people with multiple personalities tap into their future selves. As you might imagine, the various parts that comprise the total consciousness of a multiple have different viewpoints, styles, and ways of thinking. Because of this, it is unlikely that a single future self will be acceptable to the whole system of parts as representing someone those parts may become.

While each person is different and will approach the concept of a future self uniquely, there are a few general guidelines I like to suggest to multiples. First, if you have a personality that is most often the one who is "out" in the world, doing life as it were, then the future self of this part can become a friend or helpful adult presence to the other parts inside. The other parts needn't accept the future self as what they will become, but they often can accept, and draw on, its supportive presence.

In fact, if you are a multiple who feels that there is never any adult part present, the future self can become that presence for you. In time, as you naturally and automatically integrate this part, you can discover that you *have* developed an adult aspect within your present-day awareness.

When there are different future selves for different parts, it's okay to suggest that your future selves show you how it feels and works when your parts are able to collaborate constructively. Remember that the future self, as you are exploring that concept here, is a *positive, healed part of your consciousness*. Because of this, the future selves of your alters will express what is most positive in them. You can learn a lot by observing and experiencing what it is like when these wiser parts of you work together to further your healing process and make living in the world *today* easier.

A question that may come up for you if you're a multiple is whether or not working with the future self is like creating a new alter. Is it a way of continuing to use dissociation as you did when you were a child, to split yourself off into separate parts? My experience has been that, because of the automatic co-consciousness that tends to exist between you and the future self, this becomes an exercise in therapeutic, rather than protective, dissociation. It's an example of how dissociation may be used *consciously*, to increase, rather than split off from, an ongoing awareness of thoughts and feelings.

For now, give yourself an opportunity to explore the following information and exercises in whatever ways will be most helpful to you. Some may be quite useful, while others may not be workable for you at this time. As you complete each exercise, you might hold the thought that your experience of the exercise, and the learnings you have discovered, can be shared with all the other parts of you or at least with those parts that will find the learnings useful. Allow yourself to assume that this *will* happen in whatever ways are most healing for you.

How Would My Future Self Handle This One?

Because the unconscious part of your mind holds a tremendous amount of wisdom that is available to you by means of imagery, visualization, and self-hypnosis, you always have the option to reach inside and tap into new awareness and information when you need it. For this exercise, think of a problem you're having that you just can't seem to solve, a reaction you can't seem to overcome, or a challenging situation that you want to handle in a constructive way.

Using whatever self-hypnotic, relaxation, or guided visualization approach works well for you, take a few moments to go inside and connect with your future self.[6] Once you have accessed this part of you, you can reconnect by "tuning in" on an image or "felt sense" of the *presence* of your future self. There's no real need to see this part of you visually. What is most important is to *sense* what it's like when your future self is nearby, and to access that certain state of mind, or feeling in your body, that conveys the experience that you aren't alone, that there is a supportive part of you present.

Once you have connected with your future self, take a moment to review your dilemma. Go over the elements of the biggest problems, the situations you feel you don't know how to handle. Once you've got them in mind, ask your future self to show you how he or she would handle the problem. Your future self may show you this in a number of ways. For example, you might imagine that you step inside your future self and, in a sense, merge your two minds. Then, thinking as one mind, you may discover that a new idea or new way of seeing things comes into your awareness.

At other times, you might have an image drop into your mind that shows you what the future self thinks. Or you might hear something that makes sense to you. You might even have the experience of simply knowing, all of a sudden, how to respond in a new way, without really knowing *how* you know. You could also have an experience similar to the one I had about the new chair, where your thoughts, feelings, and body all move into a new state that conveys something helpful.

You may find that your new awareness comes when you sit down to do this exercise or later when you are engaged in some activity. For now, just take a moment to open yourself to the influence and guidance of your future self. Whether or not you become aware of something definite, sit quietly with yourself for a while, imagining that your consciousness is like a sponge and that you are soaking in whatever your future self is giving you right now.

Even if nothing comes right now, allow yourself to *expect* the help you have requested. Expect that, when you need it, some new awareness, feeling, or idea will drop into your mind from the mind of the future self. The important part is to ask, and then to say, "Yes, I will accept this help. I will accept this healing."

Discovering the Past Through the Future

When getting in touch with your future self, you may unexpectedly become more aware of unresolved past issues that hold you back in the present. If you are an abuse survivor, you may know how the moment-to-moment, daily challenges of life sometimes tap into old pain, fears, or angers. Sometimes you cannot be as effective as you'd like to be, because you get caught up in what used to be and can't deal with what *is* today.

For example, being triggered by certain kinds of people may really get in the way of work relationships. You may have had a sister or brother with whom you were competitive, but in ways that left both of you vulnerable and at risk of disapproval. You can ask your future self to show you how it feels when you're not competitive in these old ways or when you're not afraid of losing out to someone else and being judged a failure.

When you do this, you not only give yourself an opportunity to experience the present situation in a new way, but *you also tell your unconscious that you are ready to resolve this old fear*. By translation, this means knowing more consciously how it felt as a child to be driven into a competitive situation that didn't feel good. As with all unresolved feelings from the past, once you have them in your conscious awareness you can choose to do something about them.

And so, it's impossible to move toward and become your next future self without resolving what has been holding you back. It's a *choice*, and one you can feel good about making. Your unconscious knows what you are ready to deal with and what needs to wait till later. Since your future self emerges from a place of wisdom deep inside, you can trust saying "yes." You can trust that you will take your "next steps" in healing as you are ready to do so. That doesn't mean it won't be pretty uncomfortable at times. It also doesn't mean you won't wish, at times, that you could go back into the old place of not being so aware of what hurts, what makes you angry, what makes you tick. It does mean, though, that you have the right to choose to move forward in your healing process deliberately and consciously. For this reason, it's important to know that, when you say "yes" to the future self, you are also saying "yes" to moving more deeply into those unresolved issues that may have kept you from being the most effective present-day adult you have the capacity to be.

Again, I'd like to share this aspect of working with the future self from my own process, in a very practical example. When I first began to tap into my future self, over a decade ago, I didn't realize that saying "yes" to this part of me would mean moving more deeply into unresolved issues from childhood. As I look back now, with the benefit of hindsight, I can say, "Of course I had to deal with this or that issue. How did I think I could go forward without doing so? Why couldn't I see that before?"

In one case, the issue was my truly profound speaking anxiety. As I kept saying, "Yes! I want to be you," to my future self, I didn't realize that would mean becoming more active in teaching, speaking, and other kinds of public appearances. Actually, it's a good thing I didn't know ahead of time how much speaking I would be doing, or I probably couldn't have said "yes" to healing with such enthusiasm. As the healing process has unfolded around this particular issue, I have found myself extremely grateful that I plunged ahead and allowed my future self to guide me. Overcoming this fear has happened one step at a time, in "portions" exactly the size I could handle each time a new step had to be taken.

Accessing New Body States

One of the most important things you can learn from your future self is *how it feels in your body* to be more centered, confident, and safe in the world. What your body knows, your consciousness often follows, and what a difference it can make when, deep inside, you experience a

sense of solidity and security instead of the fear that may have pervaded your experience until now.

Also, for many abuse survivors, the body becomes a respository for
otherwise unremembered moments from childhood. For example, you
may have pains in your body that can't be traced to physical causes in
the present. When this is the case, and you have had a doctor investigate your complaints, you might wonder whether your body is reexperiencing some trauma or difficult experience from childhood.

For Lynn, the physical sensation that had bothered her all her life
was a pain in her upper arm. She just couldn't figure out where it came
from, and the doctors were equally baffled. The pain wasn't there all
the time. At first Lynn had no idea what caused the arm to act up. She
wasn't aware of any particular events that would bring on the pain.

It was only after exploring the issue in therapy that she realized that
her arm hurt whenever she had an argument with someone who was
special to her. At these times she unconsciously accessed experiences
with her mother, during fights in the kitchen, experiences which she
had not fully resolved. As she became more aware of the memories,
Lynn recalled that when her mother got upset, she would grab Lynn
by the arm and drag her around the room. Sometimes, when she was
really out of control, Lynn's mother would lift her by her arm and
throw her down on the floor. There was a great deal of fear and anger
associated with these experiences, but the feelings—and the physical
pain—had been dissociated from Lynn's ongoing awareness. In the
present, any argument or disagreement with an important person in
her life activated the sensations of that early abuse, without bringing to
mind the content.

It was helpful to Lynn when her future self showed her how it could
feel when she had an argument with someone and the arm didn't hurt.
That's when Lynn began to translate the physical pain into a more
conscious awareness of the *feelings* she had during those awful arguments. Her future self also showed her how it could be to have a
disagreement with someone and not have it become abusive or toxic.
As she "practiced" her new awareness, Lynn's body, mind, and feelings were learning a new way of responding. At the same time, Lynn
gave herself permission to look at more fully, and resolve, the difficult

feelings she had about her mother and the abuse that characterized so much of her childhood.

Jeff discovered that an awareness of his future self would come and go, depending on how stressed he was by present-day events and by how triggered he might feel in work or home situations. The burden of being a husband and father weighed heavily on him. In his childhood home, his own father was unhappy, overworked and emotionally unavailable. As Jeff learned to turn to his future self for help when he was upset, he found he had a new role model, a man he could respect. Over time, as the relationship between Jeff and his future self evolved, Jeff discovered that his way of thinking about his life and daily challenges changed. Now he sometimes was more open to thoughts of how things *could* work out, instead of his old, familiar focus on how out of control things were.

Jeff's experience is important because he had to learn to be patient with himself. Allowing the *body state* of the future self to enter his awareness didn't work every time, which is true for most of us. When it did, though, it taught him something important. It showed him that his present-day reality wasn't as overwhelming as he previously had been convinced it was. It proved to him that the weight he felt because of his adult responsibilities was, in large part, a reflection of unresolved childhood learnings.

Each time you allow yourself to blend your awareness with the body state of your future self, you create an opportunity for new learnings at very deep levels. Even if you have the same experience as Jeff, and you don't experience a different body state during a given journey inside to your future self, you say "yes" to your unconscious just by going inside and making an attempt. It's another way to support your healing journey and open yourself to those surprising moments when your future self shares a new body state with you, as often happens when you least expect it.

Living in Your Body in New Ways

Take a moment to become aware of your body. There's nothing to do but notice where you carry tension, where you allow yourself to loosen up a bit. Also notice, are you breathing? As I mentioned earlier, when we've experienced trauma as children, often we forget to breathe and we learn to hold our feelings locked tightly in our muscles. Your future self can help you learn to live in your body in new ways.

Bring to mind, now, a situation in the present in which your body tends to react in a way that causes you discomfort or distress. It may be that your heart races at times, if you're anxious. Or you may become nauseated if you're afraid. You may have general tension that you want to ease. If you choose to lessen the general tension in your body, it's important to remember that tension often holds unresolved memories and feelings from childhood. Remember that, for some people, beginning to relax sometimes brings feelings of increased anxiety or discomfort. When this happens, it's helpful to know that it is normal and that you can choose to ease only a little of your muscle tension at a time. As with any interaction you have with the future self, tapping into new body states is another way to say "yes" to healing.

Once you have identified what you want to work on this time, allow yourself to go inside, perhaps to your safe place, and contact your future self. Ask your future self to give you an experience of what your body feels like when it is free of the discomfort you have chosen to address.

Your future self may convey the new body state to you in several ways. You may discover an image, first, that encompasses the *quality* of the new body state. If this happens, allow yourself to explore what the image communicates to you. Then, enter the image and become it, so that you take it into your body. This coming together of you and the image provides an opportunity for you to experience the new state from inside your own body.

As with all inner work, it's helpful to allow impressions to float into your awareness in whatever ways come automatically. You may feel a physical sensation first, or you may become aware, initially, of a new state of mind. Whichever way the experience progresses, simply let your conscious mind *receive* what your future self wants to give you.

Sometimes your future self will respond by stepping inside you or by inviting you to step inside his or her body. If this happens, just allow your body to experience the sensations that exist inside the body of your future self.

It can also be helpful *to allow a color to come to mind that represents the new body state.* Over time, as the color and the new body sensations become linked in your experience, all you have to do is think of the color inside your body to access the physical sensations your future self has shared with you.

Then, when your present-day life challenges you with a situation that in the past would have caused you physical discomfort, you can practice what it's like to go into the situation with the body of your future self. If you have prior warning, it helps to do some mental rehearsal beforehand. You can do this by imaginging that you are in the difficult situation and that the color, sensation, or image that represents the new body state is already inside you. Over time, you and your body learn to shift into this new state, rather than sliding back into the past, where you previously accessed unresolved childhood hurts.

Following in the Footsteps of Your Future Self

Another way you can access new awareness, as well as say "yes" to change, is to follow in the footsteps of your future self. For this exercise, begin by thinking of a problem you want to solve, something you want to develop, or a change you want to make, for example. Then, imagine that you are floating on a fluffy cloud, flying on a magic carpet, or in some other way drifting along above the ground. The most important thing is that you feel safe. (If it is too scary to think of yourself floating above the ground, then allow yourself to walk on a path in a healing landscape.)

Next, with your future self in mind, notice that, below you, there are footsteps in the dirt, sand, or whatever surface is under you. These are the footsteps of your future self, made when your future self was in the process of moving through and resolving the issue that faces you now.

Realizing that these footsteps can show you the way into a deeper awareness of the issue and how to resolve it, allow yourself to follow those footprints until you find yourself there, with your present-day feet in the footprints left by your future self. Take a moment, now, to notice how it feels to know that you are guided, that there is a wiser, more experienced part of you that has already made the journey you are taking at this point in your life. You might even sense, perhaps, that your future self awaits you up ahead somewhere.

An important aspect of this exercise is to allow yourself to sense how it feels to *choose* to take one step after the other and to recognize any sensations, thoughts, feelings, or other awareness that may come to you as you proceed. Nothing need come into your conscious mind at this point. The important thing is that you are, again, saying "yes" to change, healing, and development of yourself.

Notice, as well, that a line of light may come back along the way you are walking and touch your heart. This is a lifeline from the heart of your future self. Become aware of whatever sensations or feelings come to you along this line of light. You might notice a gentle tug that reminds you that your future self is encouraging you to take the steps necessary to achieve what you seek.

If, after taking some steps, you feel a need to sit and rest for a while, allow yourself to do so. If, on the other hand, you have a sense that you want to rush forward, go ahead. The important thing is that you take each step your future self has taken and that you allow yourself to respond to the sensations and feelings that come alive in you as you make the journey.

You may find that your future self awaits you at some point along the way. If this happens, allow yourself to become the future self, to see the world through his or her eyes and experience whatever new point of view, understanding, body state, or any other awareness this more-evolved part of you is willing to share. If your future self doesn't appear, that's fine too. Just allow yourself to continue to follow in his or her footsteps, and consciously *accept* that positive change will unfold in your life.

The Future Self and Shame

The future self can be helpful in dealing with the residue of difficult experiences from a hurt-filled childhood, in part because of the capacity to "share" consciousness with your present-day self. Because shame is such a difficult and painful issue to deal with, I'd like to introduce the idea of drawing on the future self as it applies to an exercise that specifically focuses on moving beyond shame.

As you may be all too well aware, your body probably feels a great deal of discomfort when shame is activated. You may feel a grinding dread in your stomach, or you may actually double over with the physical sensation of needing to hide. You may stop breathing, or feel your heart speed up in your chest. Take a moment to recall any physical sensations that seem most characteristic of your own personal experience of shame.

You may also be uncomfortably aware of the terrible emotional state that shame elicits. Some people have such an intense desire to hide when deep shame is triggered that they become immersed in suicidal feelings. For others, thoughts and feelings may flood into awareness that convey a sense that it will never be okay, that things will never get better. Whatever your particular emotional and cognitive response to shame, it probably is decidedly unpleasant. Take a moment, now, to recall what kinds of thoughts and feelings you have when you feel shame.

What would it be like to have an opportunity to experience your body, mind, and emotions free of shame-related responses? As the shame is resolved, your body learns new sensations and your mind interprets interpersonal interactions in new, nonshaming ways. For example, you may discover that, when you are in the future self, you feel more solid right in the middle of your stomach, right where there used to be that awful feeling of dread. Or you may sense that your chest and your heart are more open, that the tightness or constriction you used to feel all the time isn't there anymore.

Also, you may tap into how your future self *thinks about* and *interprets* shaming experiences. And you may be surprised to discover that there are significant differences between how you conceptualize what is shaming and how your future self perceives it. For instance, you might explore how it felt to be turned down for a job. To your present-day self, this experience might represent your fundamental unworthiness and create feelings of hopelessness or despair. To your future self, who may have learned not to "globalize" the shame response, not getting the job may represent something else instead. For example, your future self might review the interview and see what you could have done differently, using the interview as a rehearsal for next time. What the future self is likely *not* to feel is that failing to get the job means that you are somehow unworthy as a person.[7]

Moving Away from Shame

Using whatever relaxation, guided imagery or self-hypnotic technique you like, take a moment, now, to close your eyes and settle yourself. Imagine, without demanding that any specific awareness or sensation arise, that your future self has come back in time to give you a healing experience about shame, to show you how it can feel as you move away from those old, familiar shame responses of childhood. As you begin, recall a particular situation in which you felt a deep sense of shame. Notice how your body feels as you review the awful feelings, thoughts, and body sensations that accompany shame.

Next, imagine that your future self is approaching from across time and space, moving through your inner world to where you are now. You may or may not "see" your future self. That doesn't matter. What is important is to allow yourself to sense that your future self is coming near.

When you feel that this has happened, imagine that you can step inside your future self so that, as in other exercises, it's as though *your body were the body of your future self.* Allow yourself to suspend any disbelief for a few moments, and simply accept that you are sharing the sensations, thoughts, and feelings of your future self, whether or not you are conscious of them right now.

As you explore what you are experiencing as you blend your body with that of your future self, allow yourself to hold the expectation that the sensations related to shame that you experience in the body of your future self may be quite different from what you carry in your present-day body. It's helpful to call on your natural curiosity and let yourself be open to any subtle, new sensations that may come into your experience. Take a moment, now, just to be with whatever enters your awareness.

Next, allow yourself to become aware of the state of mind and emotions of your future self as they relate to your remembered shame. You might do this, at first, by imagining that you are seeing through the eyes of your future self, that you have access to the perspective of this part of you. Give yourself plenty of time to pay attention to your inner experience, and simply take in any impressions that may come to you.

You may discover that your future self experiences shame in a very different way from how you currently do in your day-to-day life. For example, notice your body. How does it feel as the body of the future self, in all those places where the shame is held in your present-day body? Do you still want to hide? Is there a sense of strength anywhere that you hadn't noticed before? What new feeling or sensation is particularly soothing or reassuring to you this time?

To help you know how it feels to move beyond your shame, take a moment to look at your present-day self through the eyes of your future self. It's important to remember that this wiser part of you no longer carries the conviction that you are basically flawed or that you have awful things about you that no one should ever discover. Can you sense the self-acceptance that your future self feels? Is there a sensation somewhere in your body that conveys the quality of feeling good about yourself? Just continue to be curious and to realize that it may take some time before you're able truly to accept a less shameful perspective of yourself.

Now, give yourself a few minutes just to be with whatever you are experiencing, if that's all right with you. When you take this time just to be with the experience, you allow your present-day body to learn from the body of your future self how it feels to be free from the burden of shame. You allow your present-day self to learn how it is to feel good about yourself and to think well of yourself.

You may discover that you are able to learn these new feelings and sensations only a little bit at a time. That's fine; it's normal. Trust the small, slow changes. Each time you open your awareness to your future self, you give yourself the gift of moving further away from shame and closer to a healed sense of body and mind.

Spiritual Issues and the Future Self

For many people, the future self becomes a guide. Sometimes it feels like a spiritual presence. Because this part of you is wiser and more evolved than your present-day self, it's not surprising that it can appear, at times, to be a source of inspiration and guidance. If you experience your future self in this way, fine. What's important is to remember that *you are becoming this self,* one step at a time, as you heal. Even though some of your future selves may, at times, feel very far off from where you are now, each day offers an opportunity to take another step closer to that more healed self.

An important thing to know about "becoming" your future self is that there may be future selves that you never actually become in any way you can measure it in real time and space. Often a future self represents the development of an internal attitude or change of mind—or heart—that you need to bring into your *psychological* world. For that reason, it's important to know that, even if you aren't aware of it consciously, as one future self becomes the next, internal change and healing are happening. The process continues, even when you don't *literally* become the future self you are calling into your life.

One of the important things you may discover as you develop a more conscious relationship with your future self, is that you feel less alone. It has always seemed to me that one of the valuable aspects of having a spiritual focus in life is the sense it brings that we are not alone, that we are part of something larger, that there is support available within the world of our own rich consciousness.

If you find that your future self often feels like a spiritual guide, accept it. In fact, you might invite guidance by asking your future self, at the beginning of each day, to be with you and to help you cope more effectively with whatever your day-to-day life brings your way.

As with the other exercises described in this chapter, you can ask your future self to blend his or her consciousness with yours and *to show you how it feels to have a deeper spiritual connection*. Your future self may know, much more vividly than you do in your present-day awareness, the sensations and state of mind that accompany the feeling that you are never alone. Imagine what it would be like for you to have, in your present-day body, the sense that someone is always there, listening, offering guidance, even if you weren't aware of it consciously. For many of us, this is a very different experience from what we had in childhood.

Also, if for you the spiritual dimension includes expanded consciousness, or a more open heart, you can ask your future self to show you how it feels to have achieved these "next steps." It's as though you get a glimpse of a blueprint you are following and a chance to look ahead and get a feel for where you are going. As with many kinds of learning, once you have an idea of what you want to achieve, it can be easier to get there.

Other Resource Parts

There are other kinds of resource parts inside that are different from the future self. An important one is called the "Center" or the "deep self." This aspect of your psychological life may not be experienced consciously at all. Instead, it may be thought of as an *organizing factor* in your consciousness.[8] You might think of it as that part of your consciousness that not only contains all the wisdom of your individual self, but also connects you to universal consciousness, in whatever ways you may conceive that to be.

Your relationship with the Center may be different from the one you have with your future self. When you want or need help from the Center, it's possible just to ask, without necessarily having any conscious awareness of a response.

For example, if you are struggling with a reaction you have to someone or with a situation that inevitably triggers you, you might call on the Center to help you resolve it. Even when you're in the middle of an upset, the Center may be able to help you shift gears. For example, if you can't recenter enough to focus on soothing an inner child part yourself, you might ask the Center to activate a caretaker part to come and take care of whatever part has been triggered. It might surprise you to experience a change in your internal state, without conscious awareness of how it happened. Also, at bedtime you can ask the Center to give you dreams or help you resolve things while you sleep.

The Center has the capacity to send certain thoughts and feelings from your deep unconscious into your conscious awareness. An example of this is when you may be dealing with difficult feelings and memories from childhood, and you feel raw inside. At these times, you can ask the Center to send waves of comfort to accompany the waves of feeling. The waves of comfort may feel like a soothing balm that eases the rawness and residue of dealing with intense feelings. You can also ask the Center to send you a wave of awareness that lets you know you're stuck in an old coping mechanism or are viewing things from an old perspective.[9]

You might also think of the Center as another way of symbolizing what some people call the "higher self." The higher self may be conceived of not only as the organizing aspect of your total consciousness, but also as a source of spiritual connectedness and expanded states of awareness.[10] For many people, having a more conscious relationship with their higher self is profoundly comforting.

People with multiple personalities have identified yet another resource, called the *internal self helper*. This is a part of the self that seems not to be burdened or limited by the protective dissociative barriers that exist for the other parts. During therapy, and on a daily basis, internal self helpers may be called upon to offer advice, soothe little ones, or intervene in a variety of ways that help the overall system to function effectively.[11]

For those of you who aren't multiples, there are also helpers inside. They come in all shapes and sizes, and are there for the asking. All you need to do is focus your attention inside and call on them. They may appear as people, animals, colors, sacred objects, beings, or other symbolic representation.[12]

As you move along in your process of healing, it may be reassuring to know that your unconscious is filled with a rich array of resources, only some of which have been described in this chapter. Of equal importance is the support you can find in the outer world, among other people. In the next chapter, we'll look at the special challenges and opportunities you may discover in the world of interpersonal relationships, including intimate partnerships, friendships, and the many acquaintance relationships that develop at work and in daily living.

What about the People in My Life?

When you've been abused as a child, managing current interpersonal relationships can be quite a challenge. So many things act as triggers, and sometimes, on a feeling level, it's hard to tell the difference between the people you know today and the people who may have abused you in the past.

Even if you aren't currently involved in an intimate relationship with someone, if you are at all in the world, you have to interact with other people at one time or another. In this chapter, we'll look at many kinds of relationships, including friendships, intimate partners, business colleagues, and acquaintances from all arenas of your life.

That Was Then, This Is Now

As we explore these relationships, it helps to keep in mind the following premise: maintaining an attitude of curiosity and being willing to learn from your experiences with other people can help you to understand the story of your childhood more fully and allow you to gain greater mastery over its effects in your daily life.

For many abuse survivors, even going to the grocery store may be fraught with feelings of terror or, at least, apprehension. For example, if you were verbally abused or viciously criticized as a child, asking a store clerk for help may feel as dangerous as walking in front of a runaway truck. If you can recall that the feelings of terror are about *then,* when you were little, it may allow you to be more comfortable talking with the clerk *now,* when you are grownup.

Or, if you live with someone and have a hard time getting along, it's important to be able to distinguish between triggers that relate to past abuse and what may be actual present-day mistreatment. Sometimes it's hard to tell the difference, but it gets easier as you are more familiar with what triggers you.[1] Also, as your healing process progresses, you will become more aware of how you really feel when you interact with someone else. This increased awareness can help you to draw appropriate boundaries and know when you want to say "no" and when you want to say "yes."

For example, it may be that your partner's tone of voice, body odor, movements, or other characteristics remind you of someone who hurt you when you were a child. These qualities alone may trigger you at times. When this happens, it is helpful to take a few moments to go inside and find out what some part of you is remembering or feeling. Then you can take whatever steps are appropriate and available to you to create increased safety. For example, you may ask the other person to use a different cologne or to avoid quick or sharp arm movements. When the other person can't change what triggers a child part of you, then it is up to you to work towards perceiving the trigger in a new, updated way.

On the other hand, it may be that your partner really does speak to you critically or treat you in abusive ways. When this happens, it is appropriate to deal with the issue on a here-and-now basis, rather than working with your unresolved childhood wounds. This is why it's helpful to work with a therapist: you can get to know your triggers; also, when present-day mistreatment occurs with someone important to you, you will have a place you can go to work out the most constructive response and strategy for resolving the problem. As you get to know your triggers and move through your healing process, you can more effectively explore the differences between old memory feelings and current problems. We'll look more at the benefits of therapy in the next chapter.

Interpersonal Bridges
to the Past

For now, take a moment to think about a recent interaction you may have had in which you felt triggered into childhood feelings or found yourself experiencing a strong, reactive emotion in response to some person. Go over it in your mind, paying particular attention to the ways the interaction may have reminded you of how you felt as a child. If you don't have any conscious memories of difficulties in childhood, then notice how certain strong emotional responses may elicit a quality of vulnerability and helplessness that you might associate with a child's feelings. It may be that the current situation is acting as a bridge to the past, revealing to you how you felt, at times, during your childhood.

After you have reviewed the recent situation in your mind, give yourself a few moments to allow the feelings you had in that situation to come back into your awareness. If you find that it's hard to imagine them, ask yourself what the feelings *would* be like if you *could* recall them now.

Then, using the feelings as a bridge, allow your mind to drift back across time and across space to a time and place in childhood where you may have been feeling the same way you were in the current situation. Allow yourself to view the past scene as if you were watching a movie. Simply become aware of what is happening to a child who is "over there" in that scene.

In this exercise, you allow the person in the present to become a bridge to someone in the past. Once you have identified who it is that the current person represents, you may want to do some inner child work with that past experience or use another soothing or healing exercise that may come to mind.

The benefit of using this kind of bridging exercise is that it allows current triggers to become the seeds of healing experiences. It allows you to make use of the rich supply of awareness that you carry with you from the past and provides a means to remind yourself, once again, that *that was then, this is now.*

Finding Friends and Falling in Love

When we've been traumatized in childhood, our unconscious often learns to associate love with pain, punishment, or neglect. For this reason, it is difficult, if not impossible, for most of us to choose friends or lovers who don't in some way replay our childhood relationships. Even when we manage to find a person who doesn't fit all the elements of what was hurtful to us when we were children, chances are good that we will connect with someone who has his or her own store of old wounds.

It is unusual for abuse survivors to develop partnerships or deep friendships with people whose patterns of intimacy from childhood are completely healthy.[2] The other person may *appear* to be more to-gether than we are. And, in fact, he or she may actually be less wounded than we are. But the bottom line is that the people to whom we feel most strongly attracted usually will be those who in some way meet our unconscious expectations of what it means to be connected to someone else.

The issue of how one person in a relationship may appear to be so much more together than the other is important in resolving the effects of childhood abuse. In work with couples, therapists have long known that the person who looks less functional actually may be performing a great service for the other member of the partnership: the person who appears more together can hide his or her own vulnerability or other unresolved feelings behind the more overt difficulties with the partner.[3]

In fact, one of the things to know about healing from a traumatic childhood is that it will challenge your friends and partners to become more consciously aware of their own unresolved issues. As you get stronger and know more about developing boundaries, stating your wants, and saying "no" to things that don't feel good, for example, people in your life will have to become more aware of their own past wounds and ways of dealing with them.

For example, if you live with someone who is always in control of his or her feelings, what may happen when you are no longer the household volcano? Your partner may begin to experience anger that was unconscious before or become irritated when in the past *you* were the one who had cornered the market on irritation.

The shifts that occur in relationships as one member heals represent a real gift to both people. As much as change may bring discomfort and require the people who know you to get more in touch with their own unresolved issues, your healing offers an opportunity for others to deepen their own development, if they choose to do so.

It's probably not surprising that some people in your life may resist your healing process. If your change means they may have to deal with their own old patterns, they may pick fights, use old strategies to trigger you, or seek in other, usually unconscious ways to bring the relationship back to where it used to be. The more you recognize your triggers, and the better you become at building bridges to your past, the more aware you will be of this kind of dynamic. Then you can choose to deal with it, or not, or perhaps ask yourself whether it is a healthy relationship for you.

One thing to watch out for—and this goes against all the ways in which we have been trained to think about intimacy—is the feeling of being swept away when you meet someone and fall head over heels "in love." Often, this kind of sudden and intense connection is the product of two unconscious patterns of intimacy finding each other, because there are underlying, *familiar* was of relating that are held within the unconscious process of each person. When these patterns arise because of early childhood abuse, there is likely to be a repetition of these hurts, in some way, at some time, in the current relationship.[4]

For example, have you ever met someone and thought, "Finally! I've found the perfect person who will take care of me, love me in all the ways I always wanted to be loved, and make everything wonderful for me!" Then, several weeks, months, or years later, did you discover that the dream turned into a nightmare that was like living your childhood all over again—that your partner turned out to be just like the hurtful person you thought you had left behind?

Or, have you ever made a new friend, someone you connected with and felt drawn to like a magnet, only to find later that she was as neglectful or demanding as your family always was? This doesn't mean that we don't sometimes have the good fortune to connect with someone who really does live up to our expectations, but this may well be the exception rather than the rule.

Our culture enshrines the concept of "romantic love" and provides little in the way of role models for deep, ongoing, committed love between two mature adults.[5] For this reason, it is hard for most of us to know how healthy relationships begin, develop, and mature, and sometimes it feels as though there's no "life" to a relationship if things aren't intensely emotional.

And so, as you heal from the deep personal effects of childhood hurts, it's important to learn how to have more affirming and healthy interpersonal relationships. There are many books available that provide information about how healthy relationships function, what to expect from a non-abusive friend or partner, and how to help when you discover that your relationship needs work.[6]

Also, if you are a parent, it's important to know that the more you learn about your current relationships with others and how they have been affected by childhood experiences, the more you will be able to treat your own children in non-abusive ways. The more you learn today, the more you will be able to insure that abusive or hurtful patterns won't be passed along to tomorrow's generation.

Sometimes I Just Want
to Be Alone

The fact is that for many abuse survivors relationships are difficult and create endless stress. If you are dissociated, stress can lead to increased dissociation, which can leave you feeling out of control. It can also create confusion for people who are close to you. On the other hand, being isolated and alone is a problem as well; it may even be worse than learning to deal with the challenges of interacting with someone else.

There's not much difference between friendships and intimate relationships except that, with your intimate partner, you are likely to be triggered into even deeper feelings than you may be with friends. The issues are the same, though: how to deal with disappointment; what to do when you feel misunderstood; how to understand whether or not you are being abused in the present or are simply reacting to heightened sensitivity from the past; how to know if *you* are being abusive; how to share ideas and activities with someone and feel comfortable and safe; how to talk about things that matter to you without being afraid of humiliation; how to know that you are important to the other person. This list could go on and on.

When you are traumatized by other people as a child, what you learn about interpersonal interactions is hurtful rather than healthy. That's why you need to find people who are trustworthy and open enough to allow you to learn how to be with them. If both of you can agree that you are on a journey together, a relationship journey, then there may be enough safety to take the risks that are so much a part of deepening intimacy with another person.

Sometimes it may feel safer and easier just to forget having relationships at all. The problem is that you have natural, inescapable needs for the company of other people, for people with whom to share your fears, the stresses of your day, the things that matter to you. If you have no one in your life—either as friends, lovers or life partners—it's hard to build those healing bridges between past and present. You don't get any practice at learning healthier ways of interacting, and you may recreate the deep isolation that abused children so often feel.

It *is* scary to allow people into your life. There's no question about it. And, there are times you may get close to someone who isn't good for you. Most of us have done this—probably more than once. If you are engaged in an active healing process, though, these experiences can become opportunities to learn more about how it was for you as a child and what you learned to expect from people who are important to you. The more you understand, the more you are able to make choices about what you want to have in your life now.

SPECIAL ISSUES FOR MULTIPLES

For those of you at the far end of the dissociation continuum, where you have parts that lose time or don't know each other and sometimes are confused when they suddenly find themselves in unexpected situations, the stresses and challenges of relating can create many complications.

Recently I heard an example of how frightening it can be to discover yourself in a place with no idea of how you got there. A multiple had taken a vacation with her lover and was excited about going for a ride in the country that would take them to a resort. At one point during the trip, though, the multiple went to the restroom in a gas station and switched into a part who had no idea where she was or how she got there. It took some coaxing to get her to come out. It was the presence of someone significant in her life, whom this other part knew, that helped calm things down.

As this example illustrates, it is helpful if the people who are close to you know the various parts, understand their individual idiosyncracies, and have an opportunity to develop a supportive relationship with them. For example, if you have a young child part who huddles in a corner and doesn't want to be touched when she gets frightened, it's important for anyone who lives with you to be aware of what has happened if they find you behaving in this way. Otherwise they may do things that upset you even more or feel helpless and frightened themselves because they don't know what to do to help.

Also, it is *essential* that multiples with children seek professional guidance from a therapist who understands multiplicity and family issues. The stresses of parenting may trigger parts of you that don't know about dealing with a child, or certain parts may treat your children in ways that are hurtful to them. While research indicates that many adults who were abused as children never go on to abuse others, there is always a chance that there is an abusive part inside that may become activated in your parenting role.[7] Your children are too precious to risk handing over to a part that may hurt them. Also, when your children are included in a therapy process, they can deal with the confusion that often arises as a result of having a multiple parent. They, too, need to have support and a way of understanding what's going on.

If you are still in contact with your family of origin and with your abuser(s), chances are good that you will continue to dissociate whenever you are around them. Many multiples find that they have to take a vacation from contact with abusers in order to heal. After you have gone through the largest part of your healing process, you are in a better position to assess what kind of contact you want to have with past abusers, if any. As long as you are dissociating, you're really in no position to decide.

In terms of contact with former abusers, partners of multiples must leave it up to the multiple to decide when and where the partner also has contact. If you are the partner of a multiple, imagine how it would feel to the person you love to know that you would contact a past abuser without permission, that you would have a relationship with someone who hurt your partner so terribly.

Also, sometimes it's difficult for partners to participate when a multiple wants to continue to relate to a past abuser. It may baffle and anger a partner to think that contact is still allowed. Again, this must be up to the multiple. It can be hard to give up family members. In time, the multiple will decide what course to take in having or not having contact with past abusers.

For multiples anywhere along the continuum, an intimate relationship will be a challenge. It is a worthwhile challenge, though, when you have chosen someone who respects you, is non-abusive, and is willing to work on his or her own issues as you work on yours. Your partner must also be willing to risk change because as you heal you *will* change. As a multiple, you have never had the experience of being your whole self, all at once. It takes courage for both of you to face the unknown together.

Getting Support

It is also important to know that you both will need outside support as you take your journey of healing. Whether you are a multiple or a less dissociated adult who was traumatized as a child, your partner cannot provide all the support you will need on your healing journey. Even though it may feel safest to be with your partner, you will need people in your life—friends, a support group, your therapist—with whom you can talk about problems you may be having at home or share difficult and traumatic memories. You also may benefit from being around other people who have had experiences similar to your own. It's reassuring to know that you aren't crazy, that you aren't doing things that are so very different from what other survivors have done to cope with their abuse histories.[8]

It's also important for partners to have outside support. There will be times when the partner is simply overwhelmed by the emotional task of coping with an abuse history. When this happens, the partner needs a safe place to vent feelings of frustration, anger, or hopelessness. In addition, it's helpful for partners to listen to the strategies that others have used to deal with some of the difficult relationship and life issues that come up with people who were traumatically hurt as children.[9]

And so, just the two of you won't be enough to provide the amount of input, reassurance, and venting room that is essential when dealing with material from a traumatic childhood. Support may come from self-help groups, friends, and professionals—anyone with whom you feel safe and who understands the kinds of issues with which you both are grappling.

Whom Do I Tell About
My Past?

As you get close to people, perhaps one of the most difficult questions that crops up is whom to tell that you were abused as a child. If you are dissociated, it is even harder to decide with whom to share this information because of the potential that you will be misunderstood or become an object of fear or disbelief.

As with all relationships, it is important to get to know someone before you jump into sharing intimate information about yourself. Immediate intimacy may feel good at the time, bringing as it does a sense of connection and warmth. The problem is that you may tell more than you really wanted to reveal at that point in time, and you may end up feeling exposed and uncertain about whether your story will be respected by the other person. It's different when you've gotten to know someone first. Even though you may still experience some self-consciousness, or maybe even shame, you'll know deep down inside that the person can be trusted to treat your story with the consideration it—and you—deserve.

If you are dissociated, it will be helpful for your close friends and partner to know about how dissociation works and, specifically, how it functions in you. There is a caution, though, if you are a person whose dissociation is so extensive that you have developed multiple personalities. Many people who have been diagnosed with MPD have found that it has been worse for them after telling people specifically that they are multiples.[10] For this reason, if you are a multiple, it may be best, at first, simply to say that you are dissociated as a result of childhood abuse and then slowly to educate the people who are close to you.

Also, as a multiple, your choice of friends must be made with care, in terms of deciding with whom you want to share your childhood history. You may find that some people you thought were friends just can't take knowing what happened to you, whatever their own reasons may be. These people can be friends, or acquaintances, at a certain level, but they probably can't be reliable confidants. Too often, when friends are threatened, disgusted, or put off by traumatic abuse histories, they respond with rejection, doubt, or other judgments that can cause distress in multiples. It's a terrible feeling to have shared your very deepest pain, only to have someone minimize it or turn away from you. You deserve better than that. All the more reason to go slowly and test the waters a little at a time.

As I mentioned earlier, whether you are a multiple or not, if you were abused badly as a child your close friends and intimates need to understand what is happening to you when you get triggered, shift moods, suddenly go into flashbacks, or engage in behaviors that appear strange or threatening. When they do understand, they can provide needed extra support, or leave you alone if you can't stand to be disturbed, or become a bridge back to the present when you are having difficulty doing that for yourself.

For example, Maude and George had been living together for several years when they came in to do some work on their relationship. As they talked about the difficulties they were having with each other, it became evident that Maude was dissociated. George described what he called her "fits," which actually were abrupt shifts into a frantic, panicked part that emerged whenever Maude felt criticized. At those times, she would start to talk to George in an ever-escalating, panicked, and angry way, all the while defending herself from what she felt were unfair accusations. She had a child part inside that couldn't tolerate the fear of potential punishment for being accused of doing something wrong.

From George's point of view, Maude was out of control and didn't understand him. He would try to calm her by explaining that he wasn't blaming her, he was just trying to clear up something that bothered him. The more he would try to explain, the more upset Maude would become because he wouldn't just drop it. Between them, the interaction kept escalating until Maude would run from the room and lock herself in the bathroom.

George found himself increasingly angry that Maude seemed unwilling to listen to what he wanted her to understand. He couldn't figure out what the big deal was all about, but he did know that these exchanges wore him down. He described feeling overwhelmed and hopeless that these kinds of interactions would ever be resolved.

It helped George to understand that Maude basically became a child at these moments—a frightened child at that. She was terrified of being blamed for things she hadn't done. In her childhood, she was punished brutally for the slightest infraction, often when she hadn't done anything at all. Her response of panic, upset, and defensiveness represented her only way to try to stop George from blaming her.

As George learned about how Maude's dissociative process worked, he was able to shift his own gears when Maude became upset. He learned to sit down and ask her to come and talk with him. He learned how to remind her that he was George, it was today, and they were at home in their own city. Also, by making eye contact, George was able to help Maude reconnect with him in the present.

What was helpful to Maude was realizing that her rages were upsetting to George. All she could think about when this kind of situation was triggered was that she had to show him he was wrong. By using the situation as a bridge to the past, she was able to realize that the intensity of her response was related to her father, not to George, and that she was frantic to stop him from blaming her. George's real responses, and the effects of these interactions on him, rarely entered her mind. The child part was fighting for her very survival.

Also, and this is always an underlying opportunity whenever you allow yourself to explore relationship patterns, George had a chance to look more deeply at his own irritation with Maude and with his unwillingness to back away from the interaction once it began. He was able to open up his own childhood issues about feeling frightened and angry when he wasn't understood, as well as his deep need for Maude to be okay so he could feel secure in the relationship.

It is essential for you to realize, whether you are dissociated or not, that your actions *do* have an effect on the people who care about you. As I mentioned before, children who are badly abused learn that what they want, how much they hurt, or what they say doesn't have any effect in their world. The fact that they want the abuse to stop, or the abuser to love them, doesn't have any impact on what happens to them. Their wishes just don't matter.

Because abusers tend not to respond to the wishes or input of their victims, often it is hard for abuse survivors to believe that they *do* influence and affect their world now, as grownups. For example, it matters if you disappear for several days without telling anyone where you are going. It frightens people who care about you if you hurt yourself. If your feelings are out of control and you become enraged all the time, it hurts the people at whom the rage is directed.

If you are a multiple, you may inadvertently give conflicting messages about what you need or want from another person. When the person doesn't know how to respond to your mixed messages, it can be confusing and frustrating for both of you. It is helpful to be able to know that two different parts of you are making separate demands at the same time, on the same person.

For example, if one part of you wants to go to a movie and another finds it too scary to go out in the world and would prefer to stay home and read, you may be unaware that, in making plans with your partner, you have made two very different requests at the same time. For someone on the receiving end of your communication, it may be difficult to know how to respond as your priorities change. Then you may become annoyed because your partner doesn't understand what it is you want. This kind of interaction may well lead to irritation for both of you.

What can be particularly helpful is for your partner to say something such as, "You've said you want to do two different things today, and I'm kind of confused about which one you'd like to do more." Then you have an opportunity to become aware of your communication and you can go inside to figure out your real priority. When your partner knows it's okay to point out conflicting requests, he or she doesn't have to feel so helpless or take the interaction so personally. It gives both of you an opportunity to communicate with each other more openly and honestly and to discover that you *can* find solutions to what seem to be, at times, overwhelming difficulties.

Shadow-Boxing Revisited

In Chapter 9 we explored the area of the disowned self and the process of shadow-boxing that goes on within all of us. This is an especially powerful—and problematic—dynamic in close friendships and with intimate partners. In any relationship, there is a tendency to see in the other person parts of ourselves that we have difficulty accepting. When one or both people are adults who were abused as children, this tendency is even more pronounced. This is because of the powerful need to disconnect from those parts of the self that contain or represent unacceptable or dangerous feelings and impulses. If expressing these parts of the self can lead to further abuse, and possibly even greater danger, it is essential that they be disowned. Later, in adulthood, it can be a tremendous struggle to deal with these disowned parts as they show up reflected in people with whom we feel closely connected. Our response to important intimates who express qualities similar to these parts of us can be surprisingly strong. It's as though we've gotten a glimpse in a mirror and are horrified at what we see there. Our immediate response may be to get away or attempt to destroy what has been reflected back to us.

And so, even though we may feel attracted to someone whose early experience has created patterns similar to our own, that very attraction may also indicate that they have characteristics that mirror some of our disowned parts. In many relationships, the ongoing, never-ending cycle of arguments and hurts reflects the attempts of each partner to push away or destroy the disowned parts of the self revealed by the other person.

The problem is that these arguments erupt from a level of the unconscious that makes them unproductive and hurtful. They are not like the constructive conflict that couples can use to learn about each other, deepen their intimacy, and discover what works best for them.[11] Instead, they are efforts to continue disowning what is reflected by the other person and to get rid of it instead of exploring and integrating it into the self.

As I mentioned in Chapter 9, the key issue is what we decide to *do* about these aspects of our human nature. When we allow ourselves to become consciously aware of the parts of us that feel out of control or unacceptable, we build more bridges to the past and to wholeness within ourselves.

For Trinnie, the immediate problem was with her best friend, Greta. Trinnie and Greta spent a great deal of time together. They went to movies, out to dinner, took walks in the park, and generally were each other's most frequent companion. The problem was that Trinnie felt as though Greta needed her too much. In therapy, Trinnie constantly complained about feeling that she just couldn't say "no" to Greta, even though that's what she wanted more and more.

As we explored the problem, it became apparent that Greta's neediness mirrored an inner part that Trinnie couldn't bear to acknowledge. Using her response to Greta as a bridge to the past, Trinnie discovered a child part inside her who was desperately needy. This child part had been completely outside Trinnie's conscious awareness. As far as she had been concerned before this experience, she was independent, self-sufficient, and just fine on her own. She had never allowed herself to know about the deep vulnerability that was just under her experience of independence. Whenever Greta expressed her neediness, it just got too close to Trinnie's own unmet, childhood needs.

As she worked with this part of her, it became easier to be around Greta. It also became easier to say "no" because Trinnie no longer needed to feel burdened by Greta's need. She had faced her own.

Shadow-Boxing with Intimates

Take a moment, now, to think about someone you're close to, whether or not you spend a lot of time with them, who has some characteristic you really can't tolerate. The characteristic that comes to mind may be a feeling, a particular behavior or kind of appearance, or some other thing that just drives you up a wall.

Next, explore the quality or characteristic you have identified, and ask yourself what it is about it that is so distasteful or causes you such discomfort. You may come up with lots of reasons why you are justified in feeling as you do. And it's true that there may be good reasons why you don't like this quality or behavior. It may, in fact, be unacceptable or unpleasant. It may also be true that the quality this person expresses represents something in you that you have disowned, that you have refused to accept as your own.

Allow yourself to imagine what it would be like if you *did* have a part like this in you. What would you think of that part of you? What were you told as a child about behaving this way, looking this way, or feeling this way? Ask yourself, "If this really were a part of me, how would I feel about it? What would I want or need to do about it?"

To become further acquainted with what may be a very important part of you, you might draw a picture of it, write a dialogue between you and this part, or have an imaginary conversation with it in your head. It may have important things to tell you about your childhood, or perhaps about qualities in you of which you need to become conscious. It may, in fact, represent a valuable asset that is a problem only because it has never been accepted or allowed to find an appropriate expression in your overall way of being.

As you become more accepting of your disowned parts, you may discover that some of the repetitive arguments between you and this important person in your life begin to diminish in frequency and intensity; they may, in fact, disappear altogether. For example, you may find that what you thought were demands coming from this person actually reflect your own unmet needs, or that the person you thought needed rescuing actually is yourself. Or you may find that the one who tells all those apparently self-aggrandizing stories of success actually reflects a part of you that wants to be recognized or feels better than other people. On the other hand, you may find that what you don't like about this person really isn't about you and that you need to decide what to do about the relationship.

Remember that shadow-boxing can happen with positive qualities as well. You might do this exercise with someone you know and care about deeply, someone whose attributes seem far beyond your own present-day capabilities and yet feel so desirable. This person may be a friend, or a member of your family, who has always seemed somewhat intimidating or unapproachable to you because you experience her as so wonderful, so completely good. What you may discover is that you have these very qualities inside yourself, but you've never had permission to express them openly. In fact, sometimes when you allow qualities you have admired in someone else to blossom in yourself, you also begin to get a more realistic picture of that other person. No one is perfect. Everyone has flaws. Someone who is real is more approachable, more available to be a deeper friend or partner to you.

Just as you can stop shadow-boxing with the admirable qualities in those who are close to you and allow these qualities to develop in yourself, you don't have to continue carrying other people's disowned vulnerabilities. As you become stronger, perhaps they can reclaim some of their own helplessness, fear, or other unresolved childhood feelings. Take a moment to wonder, now, how would it be for you to know someone close to you as both strong *and* weak?

It is wonderful to watch couples, relatives, and friends deepen their constructive and healthy connections as *both* people in a given relationship become more aware of their unrealized and disowned parts. As each takes responsibility for his or her unresolved issues, a deeper, *safer* intimacy becomes possible.

What About Sex?

Sex for adults who were abused as children can be a conflicted and difficult subject. For sexual abuse survivors, especially, what is meant to be an expression of deep affection and a means of deepening intimacy can become a replay of the horrors of childhood.

Around issues of sexuality, the adult survivor of abuse must be in the driver's seat. This may be difficult for partners, as they find themselves suddenly in a relationship with someone who insists on being touched only in certain ways, at certain times. As difficult as this may be, many couples find it worth the effort. Otherwise they may discover that chaos can erupt as the survivor is thrown into a flashback, becomes triggered and freezes, or dissociates and becomes numb. For some adults who were sexually abused as children, a period of celibacy is essential for healing. Partners who face this crisis in their relationship may find this necessity difficult but worthwhile in the long run.[12]

For multiples, sex can create switches into parts that are specifically created to handle sexual activities. The problem is that, while the specific part may seem to be doing just fine, there may well be other parts inside that are feeling revictimized or enraged by the experience. Just because things look fine on the outside doesn't mean that there are no problems developing due to sexual activity with a partner.

Communication is essential, and it helps if the partner knows something about the multiple's inner system. With non-multiples, communication is equally important, and sexual healing needs to be handled just as carefully, because there may be parts of the person that, while not as fully dissociated, respond to sexual activity as if it were abuse.

Sometimes during sex adult survivors of childhood sexual abuse confuse their partners with the original abusers. For partners, these can be terrible moments, when their loved ones respond to them with terror or rage. At times like these, it is helpful for partners to seek eye contact, speak soothingly, and talk about who they are, where they are, and when it is. As with other kinds of flashbacks, it helps to have abuse survivors look around the room as partners point out familiar objects and decorations, things that can help reorient survivors to the present moment.

Books are now available to help individuals and couples find their way through the often painful process of dealing with sex as it relates to survivors of childhood abuse, especially sexual abuse.[13]

What about People at Work?

We've explored some of the issues that can come up with important people in your life who are friends or intimates. Problems can also be

encountered with work associates, bosses, and with people you don't
even know.

All that has been said in this chapter about dealing with other
people applies to those you interact with at work or in the course of
your daily activities. It's not unusual for adults who were abused as
children to have difficulties or conflicts with authority figures. For
some, bosses, supervisors, and other authority figures are frightening
people and relating to them may bring feelings of fear, panic, or even
terror. If you've ever had feelings like these, you can be pretty sure
that you have some child parts that can't distinguish between your
current boss and a past abuser. It's as though then were now and the
dangers of childhood are present on the job.

For others, interacting with authority figures may be characterized
by conflict, anger, or irritation, as bosses stand in for earlier authority
figures with whom the abuse survivor felt humiliated, helpless, or
enraged. If you've ever been in this kind of relationship, you may
know all too well that when these abuse-related interpersonal patterns
get triggered, it may be impossible to manage unresolved childhood
feelings constructively. Then, you may struggle or argue with your
boss, win some battles but lose the war, and move from job to job, not
realizing that the real struggle is with someone from the past, with
issues related to unresolved abuse.

Sometimes coworkers can trigger unconscious pockets of feeling
you have about siblings, cousins, or childhood friends. If this happens,
you may find that you feel annoyed with a coworker, agitated for
reasons you can't quite explain, competitive and threatened that the
other person will take away something you want, or fearful of being
hurt by this person. If *then* is mistaken for *now,* you might have no
idea that you a reexperiencing feelings from childhood about one of
your siblings or another relative with whom you have unresolved
issues.

As with all your present-day relationships, one of the benefits of
becoming aware of your triggers at work is that they can become
bridges to the pockets of time where parts of you are locked in the
past. As you explore the quality of work relationships, allow yourself
to be curious about how you may be reliving patterns from childhood

or bringing into conscious awareness how interpersonal relationships felt to you when you were young.

I'd like to make one additional point about handling yourself in your professional life. Please be certain that you protect the privacy of your childhood story when you are in any kind of work situation. Often, these non-intimate situations, including many social settings, are not truly safe enough to warrant disclosure of details related to what you went through as a child or how your early experiences may affect you in the present.

Remember, your safety is more in your hands now than ever before. You have a right to choose when, where, and with whom you share your story. Allow yourself to take the time to choose, and then choose with care. Those who are close to you, people you have brought into your life since you started healing, are likely to respect what you have experienced and what you are doing now to heal yourself. Even with these people, though, allow yourself to listen to your feelings. When a situation feels abusive or uncomfortable, check it out. Don't assume that everything you feel is simply a reflection of the past. You have a right to learn the difference between then and now, including when situations in the present need to be changed.

In the next chapter, we'll explore how the therapy process can become another safe place where you can share your history, learn how to distinguish between then and now, and find an essential guiding presence and support in your journey of healing.

12

What about My Therapist? In Fact, What about Therapy?

Healing from childhood abuse is usually too difficult to do alone. On a wall in my office, I have a lithograph called "self-analysis." It shows two masks looking at one another. When we attempt to heal our own psychological wounds, to look at the ways we adapted unconsciously to childhood hurts, often we see only what we already know about ourselves. There's no ready access to the "real face" that reveals what hurts too much to know consciously or reflects too much shame to accept easily.

Basically, then, it's too hard, as a rule, to be our own guide through the maze of childhood hurts. When we try to do it alone, we're likely to get lost in, gloss over, or overlook entirely some important awarenesses that were too painful to face when we were young. Also, what was too overwhelming to deal with in childhood can feel like more than we can handle alone as an adult.

While support groups can provide a lot of help, usually it will be necessary to seek out the help of a trained professional as you move along in your healing journey. In this chapter I'd like to share some of the benefits of engaging in a therapy relationship with someone who has been trained specifically to treat abuse survivors. I'd also like to point out some situations you may want to avoid, as well as some of the elements that are an essential part of safe therapy.

What If I'm Scared of Therapy?

Most of us are scared when we first go into therapy. It's a unique kind of relationship where you ask yourself to share personal and private events, pieces of your inner life, and feelings with someone you don't know very well. For adults who were abused as children, the process is complicated by the fact that authority figures from childhood may have been the very people who hurt you. This can make it hard for some people to feel comfortable being in a relationship where the flow of information is primarily one-sided, where the personal revelations go mainly in one direction, *to* the therapist. Also, there have been many stories in the media in recent years about therapists who aren't trustworthy and who have engaged in abusive behaviors with clients, the very people who most need to learn how to trust.

Also, *it's scary to change*. As much as you may want to be free of the pain of a hurtful childhood, sometimes it can feel even worse to enter the unfamiliar world of change. It can feel too uncertain to imagine being different from how you've always known yourself to be. Who can say who you will become or how you will be as a person when you have gone further along with the process? What changes may occur in your relationships as you learn more about yourself and develop new ways of coping with your present-day life? This is a challenge each of us must face: can I be brave enough to allow myself to move forward without a preview, a guarantee, of who I will become and how I will be as a person?

As you consider the possibility of beginning therapy, one of the first things to know is that you have a right to feel reasonably safe with your therapist. I say "reasonably safe" because there may be parts of you that don't feel safe with anyone, anytime. It needs to be okay to go ahead with your healing process, even though certain parts may be convinced that your therapist will prove to be like all the rest of the people who have hurt you.

For adults who were abused as children, an added complication in therapy comes from the fact that, throughout most of the process, certain parts of the client may continue to be convinced that the therapist cannot be trusted. Because this is a real possibility, both you and your therapist need to be willing to talk about these feelings, to check in regularly to see how these parts are doing, and to be willing to confront and deal with anything that happens in the therapy that doesn't feel good to you or to your therapist.

In fact, a lot of healing takes place as a result of the ongoing shifts and feelings that arise within the therapy relationship itself. Being able to talk openly about your negative feelings without being attacked may be a completely new experience, and listening to what you say when you have negative feelings about your therapist can reveal how you felt about important people who were in your life when you were a child. The same applies to positive feelings. Everything that happens in the relationship becomes a means for listening to the story of your childhood, and you deserve to be in therapy with someone who can help you understand that story.

Choosing a Therapist

The specific approach a therapist uses is less important than who the therapist is as a person, except that therapists who work with adults abused as children need special training in this area of practice. Theories and techniques of psychotherapy abound, and all have something valuable to offer to the process of healing. What really has an impact, though, is the comfort with which individual therapists live within themselves as people, their capacity to maintain a sense of internal equilibrium and equanimity in the face of the suffering of others, and the integrity with which they approach their commitment to help others heal.

Also, while credentials are important, they aren't everything. For example, a psychiatrist or psychologist isn't automatically more skilled in working with abuse survivors than a clinical social worker, a marriage and family therapist, or a mental health counselor. What *is* important is that your therapist has received training in dealing with people who were abused as children. It's also helpful if the therapist is involved in consulting relationships with other therapists. This means that your therapist occasionally, or regularly, takes his or her cases to other professionals for input. If your therapist asks you for permission to present your material to another professional, it's a sign that he or she is willing to continue increasing his or her level of expertise.

It may be difficult to find names of therapists in your area. If you can't find a referral from someone who has had a good therapy experience with a specific therapist, there are several places you can turn to for help. For example, you can call your local rape crisis line, or abuse hotline, and ask for referrals to trained therapists. You can also ask people who are members of abuse support groups for therapists they've heard about who are doing good work. You can call national or local professional organizations and ask them for the names of skilled therapists in your area.[1] In addition, professionals who have written books on recovering from childhood hurts may be a source of referrals.

Interviewing Therapists

Getting a therapist's name is just the first step. Then you need to call, make contact, and find out some specific information. First, you need to know the therapist's fee and insurance arrangements, if any. Also, it's important to know the therapist's training and professional background, especially as it relates to working with childhood abuse and other issues related to family and interpersonal difficulties. Many therapists will suggest an initial consultation session, where you can gather information and get a feel for how you work together. While most therapists charge for their time in a consultation, some offer this as a free service.

During the consultation session or the first session if you've decided to go ahead and engage the services of a particular therapist, you may want to learn the ground rules for that particular therapist. Some of these include: the therapist's policy if you miss a session; how telephone contact may be handled; whether or not the therapist travels and will miss sessions from time to time; when and how the therapist wants to be paid; and other "nuts and bolts" issues.

As an informed consumer, you need to gather information from prospective therapists about their biases and prior experience with abuse survivors. Don't expect to gather a great deal of personal information from your therapist, though. While it may seem strange that this person will know so much about you while you know so little about him or her, it's best to have a sense of what this person is like without knowing too much. You don't want to contaminate your healing process with concerns about your therapist.

Therapy is a professional helping relationship, not a friendship. While it may be tempting, and feel safer, to want to make your therapist a friend, allow yourself to talk about these feelings rather than act on them. Also, allow yourself to respect the treatment boundary that defines you as client and your therapist as informed, trained guide. This doesn't mean that your therapist knows more about you that you do yourself. Instead, it means you can expect that your therapist is there to help you explore and move through your healing process with a certain expertise that can make the journey safer and more reliable. Also, you can expect, because this is not a friendship, that you won't have to take care of your therapist. Your therapist is there for *you*.

For abuse survivors, this aspect of the relationship may be a completely new experience. You may have developed a powerful internal radar to try to anticipate your abuser's moods; now you may find yourself focusing this same radar on your therapist. You may also feel more in control when *you* are doing the giving. Receiving attention from your therapist may be fraught with fear and anger, as it was when you were a child. For these reasons, you may find yourself struggling with the boundaries that make treatment safe and effective. These struggles become more "grist for the mill" in your healing journey and allow you to explore the effects of early interpersonal experiences more consciously.

Boundary Issues in Therapy

If you came from a dysfunctional family or were abused as a child by people you should have been able to trust, learning about boundaries is an important part of your healing. I can't repeat it often enough: when children are hurt by the people they must depend on, they lose a sense of ownership over their own wishes, bodies, and needs. They may have grown up in an environment that was chaotic, where there was no privacy, and where the children in the home were force to witness or engage in violence. For others, the childhood environment may have been neglectful, with no sense of anyone to bump up against and learn about where "self" ends and "other" begins. Instead of learning who *they* are and what *they* want, traumatized children have learned to pay attention to what others want. They may also have learned how not to respect the boundaries of others and may, as adults, intrude on the privacy, or overlook the needs, of others.

A boundary issue that often is upsetting to abuse survivors involves therapists' limiting the amount of contact they are willing to have outside the therapy hour, including telephone calls. One of the primary feelings that characterize certain inner child parts of abuse survivors, which we explored earlier, is the urgent wish to be rescued and protected. For this reason, you may feel a desperate need to have the therapist be there for you each and every time you want to be reassured. It may be hard for you to tolerate it when your therapist says, "I can't talk to you from home whenever you want or I'll burn out and not be able to be there for you over the full course of our work together." Also, if your therapist is available to you without any reasonable limits, you may actually come to believe that you must be rescued. If this belief is reinforced, you may lose an important opportunity to reaffirm that you now live in the present, as your adult self, and have the right to discover your own internal ability to deal with your distress.

When therapists place limits on contact outside the session, on session times (so that even when you may want to keep going they have to end), or on the number of sessions per week, part of you may feel rejected. You may even feel like leaving therapy because you don't want to work with someone who is so "rigid." The truth is, though, that it is safer for clients when therapists set reasonable limits that honor their own needs, as well. If a therapist goes beyond what he or she is capable of doing comfortably, problems result. For example, therapists who have pushed themselves too far at one time or another report that they began to show up late for sessions or forgot some meetings altogether. Or they found that they would allow telephone contact at certain times but not at others, with little predictability about when they would be able to handle extra contact and when they wouldn't.

I remember a phone call I got a couple of years ago, from a woman was looking for a therapist to treat her multiple personalities. One of the questions she asked me was whether or not I allowed clients to call me at home. When I said, "No," she became angry and wanted to know why. She also wanted to know if that were my policy only for multiples and not for other clients. I explained that I don't give out my home number to any clients, because I need to know that there are times and places where I can take care of myself without interruption. She decided that she didn't want to come in for a consultation, because one of her requirements was to have a therapist who would be available to her whenever she wanted contact. If you feel this way, too, I urge you to work with the *feeling* of having such a deep need for ongoing contact with your therapist. Exploring the feeling can open the door to important healing awarenesses. To *act* on the feeling, by demanding that the therapist be available at any time, robs you of the discovery that you may be stronger than you realize, or that you can develop a capacity to deal with your feelings that you may never have imagined would be possible for you.

In fact, it is often in the struggle over limits and boundaries that adults who were hurt as children find and resolve important conflicts that arose in childhood relationships with abusers. When your therapist is trained to allow you to explore your feelings and wishes around wanting "more," the struggle is definitely worth the effort.

In my experience with clients, the importance of reliable boundaries has been demonstrated many times. I, too, am healing from childhood hurts and can offer some guidance to others in their journey. In that way, we are fully equal. During the therapy process, though, as a guide I am in a different position from the one they are in as an explorer of their past hurts. They need me to hold a point of view they don't have as yet. They need me to listen with an ear they are just developing for themselves. If we both enter the relationship as equals in every way, there won't be anyone holding the rudder when the going gets rough. And so, although I share a good bit about myself with clients, it is always within the context where I am the therapist and they are the client. I don't become a friend, even though I respect and care deeply for each person I see. I expect the same shift in relationship when I go to my own therapist. Even though we are both professionals, I don't need her as a friend or colleague. I need a reliable guide who can stay focused in her role as therapist, someone I can trust not to get caught up in my childhood issues.

And so, consistent, realistic limits and boundaries create a safe treatment setting for you to do the hard work of recovering from childhood hurts. This quality is one of the most important elements to look for in a therapeutic relationship. It helps to prevent reenactments of early childhood interactions with others, which is what we'll talk about next. You have a right to trust that your therapist has dealt with limit-setting in a constructive, thoughtful way, and that your wishes, demands, and needs won't overwhelm or drive away the very person you need to depend on to hold the line as therapy deepens and issues surface with greater immediacy.

Another boundary problem comes up with what is called dual relationships. Dual relationships arise when the therapist enters into more than one role with a client. Examples of dual relationships are when the therapist becomes a friend, lover (which is an illegal form of sexual abuse), business partner, mentor, or participates in a barter arrangement where services are exchanged between therapist and client.[2] Many difficulties can arise when therapists enter into dual relationships with clients. All too often, these kinds of relationships end up exploiting the client, either intentionally or unintentionally, and often replay, rather than resolve, hurtful experiences the client had with important people from childhood. It is precisely because of the inherently un-equal quality of the therapy relationship that dual relationships are strongly discouraged by most professional organizations. As tempting as it may be to allow the therapy relationship to become more than a therapist-client arrangement, please allow yourself the fullness of a safe healing process by saying "no" to to this kind of boundary blurring.

The Therapy Relationship as a Map to the Past

And so, my bias is that, whatever approach a particular therapist may take to the healing process, the relationship between client and thera-pist is primary.[3] It is within the interactions between these two people that childhood patterns, ways of thinking and feeling, and unconscious expectations and fears may emerge into the light of day. If you are willing to express even your most irrational thoughts and feelings about your therapist—and, as I mentioned earlier, if your therapist is well enough trained to handle these communications without becom-ing defensive or attacking you—an amazing process becomes possible. These communications become bridges to the past, revealing a way to become conscious of childhood experiences and expectations that may have never before been given a voice. They may have been expressed unconsciously in relationship after relationship, but with a competent and well-trained therapist these patterns can now be revealed and resolved.

While there are many helpful and effective approaches to therapy that deal specifically with the effects of childhood abuse, there arc certain approaches that are more appropriate than others. For example, some psychotherapy approaches are supportive in nature and don't engage in a close inspection of the interactions between therapist and client. These supportive approaches have a great deal to offer and can be quite helpful in dealing with day-to-day issues and with learning how to be more competent in your adult life.

What may be lacking in these approaches, though, is an ongoing focus on the *interactions* between client and therapist as they unfold in the consulting room. On the other hand, in psychodynamically based psychotherapy, which does spend a good deal of time exploring what is happening between therapist and client, deeper relationship issues are anticipated, brought to the surface, accepted, and worked through. In recent years, many therapists have discovered that, while they may be fully competent and accomplished as professionals, when it comes to helping abuse survivors move beyond interpersonal patterns learned during abuse, they need to become skilled in dealing with interpersonal issues that surface during treatment.[4]

When it is safe for you to recognize and give a voice to the responses you may have about your therapist, and when your therapist is free to comment on what he or she notices about how you engage the relationship, you gain an opportunity to map the world of your childhood in ways that may never have been available to you before. For example, let's imagine that you are someone who grew up in a violently abusive home. One of the biggest challenges for you, in terms of experiencing a relationship that is qualitatively different from anything you learned as a child, may be just to sit in the room with your therapist and discover that you can be honest without being attacked. You may not even know how afraid you are of expressing yourself until you discover that you are angry at your therapist and don't seem able to verbalize your feelings. As you explore what is stopping you from saying how you feel, you may discover how terrified you are of being hurt—and perhaps even more terrified of being abandoned. You may discover that, without having realized it before, you are convinced your therapist will throw you out of therapy if you disagree with, or become angry about, something the therapist has said or done.

Perhaps you have been burdened with deep and painful shame throughout your life, but have never known what to do to make it better. With a well-trained and compassionate therapist, you can allow that shame to come into the room and "speak for itself." You and your therapist can become witnesses to how difficult it was for you as a child—and how painful it still is—to feel the shame and fear that come to the surface when there is a possibility that someone will see you as you really are.

This process of allowing yourself to experience a full array of feelings with the therapist involves engaging what is called "the transference": unresolved issues from the past are "transferred" onto, or experienced as part of, current relationships. The helpful thing about consciously, and actively, engaging the transference with your therapist is that you can explore and work through difficult interpersonal experiences and feelings from the past within a context of safety and knowledgeable expertise. How much more healing this is than acting out unresolved feelings yet another time!

Also, if you are an abuse survivor, it may be difficult for you to deal with being disappointed. Since therapists are only human, they, too, are bound to disappoint you at some point in your therapy. As with all other issues from childhood that show up in adult life, disappointments are extremely valuable to explore in the therapy relationship. In an open and caring environment, the two of you can be curious about how you have dealt with this difficult feeling previously and observe your unfolding response in the here and now of the therapy session: you can experience, right here in this moment, how the past continues to play itself out in present-day relationships. Because the feelings are directed at the therapist right now, today, the whole process comes alive and learning is possible.

To Reparent or Not to Reparent

There is a wish in most of us to get what we didn't have in childhood, regardless of our age today. Often, this shows up in therapy as a wish to be taken care of, to be loved and nurtured by our therapist as we never were by our earlier caretakers. When therapies specifically oriented to abuse survivors began to emerge more than a decade ago, some therapists experimented with giving their clients nurturing experiences that had been missing in childhood. Many approaches were explored in an effort to ease the pain and heal the wounds that arose from a traumatic childhood. Among the strategies tried were: giving gifts; arranging special times together outside regularly scheduled sessions to go to the zoo or shopping; cuddling; and sometimes even offering a bottle to a hungry child part. While it may have been soothing to be cared for in these ways, many of these efforts ended disastrously.[5]

In hindsight, it appears that these efforts tended to fail because clients were seeking strength and healing from external sources. For this reason, clients were unable to discover for themselves that they now had an adult self present who could learn new ways of self-care—or at least the *potential* to develop an adult self—within the context of therapy. Because the therapists could never be good enough to make up for the terrible hurts from childhood, there were inevitable disappointments when they failed to meet what clients perceived as important needs.[6] No matter how hard the therapists tried, they couldn't change what had happened, they couldn't make the bad feelings go away, and they couldn't measure up to the deep need to be saved that their clients carried inside.

Because of these past experiences, many therapists today draw limits around the kinds of activities, contact, and interactions they will engage in with clients.[7] For example, your therapist may be willing to hold your hand or to hug you if you are going through a difficult time. This is a healthy, normal, and compassionate response from one human being to another. Many therapists, though, won't agree to allow you to sit in their laps because an inner child asks to be cuddled and reassured. They also are not likely to agree to make telephone calls on your behalf because you're scared to do an adult task. Most therapists *will* help you learn how to do these important things for yourself, which is essential for increasing your mastery in the present.

And so, rather than acting on your wishes to be reparented, you can offer yourself an additional healing opportunity if you are willing to give voice to these wishes and explore them in the context of your therapy relationship. As you do this, you can begin to learn new ways to meet your own needs, even as you deal with the grief and distress of knowing that the past is what it was: painful and difficult, filled with mixed feelings, hurtful experiences and challenges no child should have had to encounter. You have a right to discover your inherent strength. It's easier to do that if you are given a chance to experiment with new and constructive experiences of self-care, while receiving support from someone who wants to help you succeed.

It Hurts to Need Someone So Much

Many therapists have begun increasingly to focus on what are called issues of *attachment*. For young children, one of the primary experiences that makes the world safe enough to engage as a full self is early connection with parental figures who are reliable, available, and trustworthy. When caretakers are abusive, neglectful, or unpredictable in their emotional and physical responses to their children, it is impossible for these children to feel safe enough to explore their world effectively.

Every child needs what is called a *secure base*, which is what we develop when we feel securely attached with our caretakers.[8] When our world is safe in this way, then we can go beyond our caretakers, take a few steps into the unknown, and do so with the deep knowledge that our secure base will be there when we want to return.

Therapy provides the potential for you to rediscover a secure base within the relationship with your therapist. Over time, you have an opportunity to internalize, to take into your unconscious, the experience of reliable support that you deserved originally, as a child. Then, as your secure base develops, you can explore self-expression with a greater sense of certainty. What is important to know is that you need to be willing to engage the many deep feelings that come up as attachment issues are activated in therapy. For some adults traumatized as children, the therapist becomes the first person they have ever allowed inside, emotionally, the first person with whom they have dared to connect at a feeling level.

Some of the most difficult feelings for abuse survivors come up around the depth of need they feel for their therapists. For many survivors, it is humiliating and infuriating to be so desperate for connection. When you remember that this is how a child feels, and can recall that the therapy relationship is allowing you to tell the story of a wounded childhood, it becomes easier to tolerate these powerful feelings.

For others, even a hint of need or closeness to the therapist can send them running for cover. For example, it's not unusual for some of you who may have been deeply traumatized as children to react to kindness with anger or fear. Because you were hurt so cruelly by the people who were supposed to love you, a therapist's empathy, warmth, and caring may feel like a lie or a setup for abuse. If you've had this experience, it's helpful to allow yourself to talk about it. It's not unusual, and it makes a lot of sense when you look at it from an abused child's perspective.

It's in the area of attachment and connection that separations from the therapist can be so surprisingly difficult. For example, everything may be going along well in therapy when, for some reason or another, the therapist must miss a session. For example, your therapist may be going on vacation, attending a conference, or feeling ill, and so has to cancel or reschedule your sessions. When this happens, certain inner parts may find these separations hard to handle. For needy child parts, such a separation may feel like abandonment, and it can be deeply humiliating to have to express and explore these feelings. On the other hand, while some parts feel abandoned, others may feel abused. Some may be sad and frightened, and some may be furious. When the therapist returns, you might be surprised to experience just how much you don't care, how angry you are, how hard it is to feel connected again with your therapist, or how much you find yourself thinking about leaving therapy. It helps to know that when there have been wounds in attaching to important childhood caretakers, there are also wounds in your capacity to reattach after separations. By talking about and working through your feelings with your therapist, a new kind of inner strength develops. You discover that you can have these feelings, speak them, and learn to deal with them in new and constructive ways.

One painful fact is that these wounds around attachment and separation are inevitable when we are hurt as children, and their effects have a powerful impact on all our adult relationships. In therapy, they can be explored at the moment they are happening, even though it can feel awful to do so right there, in person.

What If I Still Don't Trust My Therapist Completely?

Trust is often the very last element that some parts of you will experience in the therapy relationship. It's important to accept this fact and to make room for mixed feelings throughout your therapy. There will be times when you are glad you're working with the therapist you have chosen. There may be other times when you wish you'd never met the person. Because of the processes of transference and projection (where unconscious feelings of your *own* seem to be coming from the therapist), there is a constant dance in therapy around making a conscious choice to risk talking about your feelings and to explore them within the interpersonal context of the therapy.

In fact, the therapy relationship can offer you a safe and excellent opportunity to learn how to experience and cope with mixed feelings. As we explored earlier, to many adults who were hurt as children it is an amazing discovery to find that you can be angry or disappointed with someone and have the relationship continue. As difficulties are worked through and the relationship is repaired, new learnings become possible that could not be experienced in an environment where the boundaries were not safe or violence was a possibility.

Recall, for a moment, my comments about *splitting* in Chapter 6: splitting happens when a child unconsciously creates two images of a parental figure—one that is all good and one that is all bad.[9] These internalized "working models"[10] of the parent are kept completely separate from one another. This is a useful coping mechanism because it would be too overwhelming, psychologically, to feel the love if you were simultaneously experiencing your terror of this person.

If you have used splitting to enable you to get through a difficult childhood, the experience with your therapist is likely to be similar. For example, there may be times when you feel that your therapist is the most wonderful person who ever lived. You may expect that your therapist knows everything about you, is aware of all the things that will make you better, and loves you in all the ways you want to be loved. This is the "good therapist." Then some event happens that upsets or disappoints you and you shift to the other side of the coin and experience the "bad therapist." Then you may feel that your therapist is incompetent, is deliberately trying to hurt you, wants to throw you out of therapy, or is an awful person.

As you put words to these feelings and explore how they remind you of past relationships, the split may begin to disappear. Within the moment-to-moment interactions with your therapist, you can develop what was denied you as a child: a total experience of a person you care about, which includes the good and the bad. As this occurs, mixed feelings become increasingly available. Along with mixed feelings comes an expanding array of potential responses, which is one of the characteristics of healthy adult functioning.

The Cognitive Aspect of Healing

When we are hurt as children, we have *cognitive*, as well as emotional, responses. Since abuse affects the way you think, an important part of therapy is to reframe and reinterpret how you view the world, yourself and your history.[11]

For example, if you were sexually abused as a child, you might have told yourself—with the only explanation available to your child's mind—that you were responsible for what happened to you. This thought, that you are the cause of abuse, may elicit feelings of shame, self-loathing, or guilt, to mention just a few of the self-defeating possibilities.

One of the ways therapists reframe this thought for survivors is to ask a grownup woman to explain how a three-year-old little girl could have had the kind of power she would need to elicit an abusive response from an adult. When there is sexual abuse, for example, the therapist might ask, "How does a little girl keep a big man from overpowering her physically?" As the client struggles to make sense of the question and to answer from the child's point of view, a process of reframing begins to occur. In time, there is a realization that the child could have done nothing to prevent what happened. Then it's possible to deal with the feelings associated with helplessness and profound vulnerability—and to realize that present-day abuse is not acceptable. Until the situation is viewed with an adult perspective and the child's cognitions are changed, it's hard to get to the feelings underneath.

And so, as your thoughts change, your feelings change as well.[12] For many adult survivors of abuse, the thoughts and beliefs that carry the greatest emotional power are those that were formed during childhood. Reflecting, as they do, a child's perspective and understanding of the world, they can create significant problems in present-day relationships.

But it's hard to do the cognitive work alone. It's like not being able to see the forest for the trees. With a trained therapist, you have an opportunity to become aware of distortions in your thinking—distortions that may be creating more distress in your life than you realize.

SPECIAL ISSUES FOR MULTIPLES

For multiples in therapy, there are a number of issues that require particular attention. One area that invites a special exploration is the many aspects of the relationship as they may arise within different parts of the self at any given time. A given interaction can seem just fine for certain parts, while other parts—deep inside—may be terrified, enraged, or ready to run away. When the therapist is skilled at including *all* the parts in the healing process and invites all the feelings to have a voice, then safety increases, new learning takes place around having an active role in the relationship, and the previously untold story of childhood has a greater chance of being shared.

In fact, it is essential for a therapist who works with multiples to develop a relationship with *every* part. Therapy doesn't go very far if there are parts inside that don't like the therapist, or don't want to be in therapy, or have no intention of cooperating, or are otherwise outside the therapeutic collaboration you have engaged.

Also, it is important for therapists who work with multiples to be sensitive to the small things that can send parts into terror responses or elicit rage from a protective part.[13] Also, time must be spent exploring the relationships between parts of the self in the client. A sort of "internal family therapy" is useful, to create a greater sense of collaboration and cooperation in moving through the healing process.

Again, this is an area where specialized training is required. It is important for therapists who discover they are working with a multiple to get supervision and increase their information and understanding of the special dynamics of therapy with this population. Also, it's important for therapists who discover a multiple in their practice to know that the solid clinical training and expertise they bring to any client relationship still applies when working with multiples. When therapists are competent and skilled, they only need to add some specific, additional training to their already developed expertise. It's not like starting over. Instead, it is taking what already works well and expanding it.

If you are a multiple, therapy can be a frightening proposition. The good thing to know is that with a trained therapist the prognosis for healing is good. It takes time, effort, and courage, but enough multiples have now gone through successful therapy for all of us to know that healing of even profound childhood trauma is possible.

Therapist Safety

Because of the lack of boundaries in homes where children are abused and the fact that abuse survivors often have witnessed a relationship between anger and violence, most therapists who specialize in this area have some ground rules to ensure everyone's safety.

A first basic rule is that neither a client nor any of the parts may threaten to hurt the therapist, the therapist's family, anyone connected with the therapist, or the therapist's possessions (i.e., office, home, car, and so on). As you might imagine, it would be impossible to sit in a room with someone you feared might attack you at any moment. It would be difficult to be an effective therapist if you constantly were distracted with concerns about being hurt. Also, it's impossible to have a viable relationship with someone who actively threatens you with violence. That's what children who were abused had to live with everyday.

Therapists generally ask clients to learn new ways to deal with aggressive or hostile feelings coming from parts that may not know how to handle anger or disappointment constructively and may want to strike out. Among other approaches, this new learning may include verbalizing feelings, writing, drawing, painting or sculpting, in place of action, to express these feelings. From the point of view of healing, the requirement that therapy be safe for both therapist and client is an important step in gaining mastery in day-to-day living. Knowing what to do with difficult and often overwhelming feelings is a major accomplishment for many adults who were traumatized as children.

A second common rule requires that the client take responsibility for ensuring his or her own safety if there is a chance that suicidal feelings might be acted out. For example, sometimes therapists ask clients to call them, a friend, or a relative if they can't keep themselves safe. Other therapists ask clients to take themselves to a local hospital emergency room if they feel they can't control the urge to kill themselves. Remember that suicidal feelings usually aren't about really wanting to die. Most often, suicide is viewed as a means to get away from the pain. It's difficult to work with clients who are in constant danger of killing themselves. What *is* possible is to learn to deal with the *feelings* of wanting to kill yourself. For most therapists, dealing with suicidal feelings is not a problem, since feeling this way is part of surviving abuse as a child. It's the constant threat of *acting* on the feelings that can disrupt the flow of healing in therapy.

Beyond these "rules," there may be requests and guidelines for therapy that reflect the individual therapist's biases and personal style.

Some therapists use contracts with clients that cover a range of issues, including agreements between parts of the self for lessening self-harm or commitments to undertake certain activities outside therapy sessions. Others ask clients to do work on their own between sessions, such as journal writing, poetry, art or some other way to sustain an ongoing awareness of the healing process. Still others may want their clients to participate in adjunctive activities, such as group therapy or body work.

The Process of Therapy

Regardless of the specific approach your therapist takes, there are certain common developments that occur as you move through therapy. What I'm going to describe here are generalizations; it's important to know that each therapy relationship and experience is unique. Your therapy may contain elements not mentioned anywhere in this book, or it may unfold in a way that neither you nor your therapist anticipated.

The beginning phase of therapy tends to focus on *developing a relationship* between you and your therapist, as well as on getting a full history and a feel for how you function in the present. Some abuse survivors want to move right into dealing with memories and trauma from the past, often because of an urgent wish to feel better. While this is completely understandable, most therapists have learned to slow down the work with trauma until later in the therapy. This is because it's important for you and your therapist to have a solid working relationship, and for you to have a sense of how your inner parts relate to each other, before you move more fully into reexperiencing your childhood trauma.

It's also important, in the early phases of treatment, to focus on strengthening your adult observer, as well as your ability to soothe yourself when the going gets rough. If you move into reliving childhood hurts too soon, or too fully, you may end up overwhelmed. Then, more, rather than less, time is needed to pull you back together before you can go further. Again, many therapists spend a good deal of time *slowing things down*, rather than speeding them up. It's important to respect whatever pace allows you to do your healing work while still handling your day-to-day life effectively.

Deep within your unconscious, a major development occurs, over time, as you and your therapist interact with one another. Assuming that your therapist is non-abusive, the relationship between you provides an opportunity to internalize a positive working model of someone who treats you with respect and empathy.[14] When we are abused as children, we internalize working models of people who have treated us badly. These become the seeds of future self-hate and self-harm.[15] When you have the opportunity to internalize the more positive working model of your therapist, you have a resource to draw on within yourself that increases self-respect and promotes self-care.

As the relationship with your therapist becomes more reliable, the hard work of reclaiming memories and working through trauma can absorb more of your attention. Throughout this difficult work, a process of continuing to explore and verbalize feelings about the therapy relationship continues. Strength builds as early wounds are revealed and processed. It's not just the remembering of past events that creates healing; it's the process of sharing and coming to terms with what you experienced and how it has affected you that brings true resolution. Many people have believed that the memory work is all that counts. It's not. It's just one part of a larger, more complex healing journey.

As therapy proceeds and draws to a close, you have an opportunity to learn something about autonomy that you may not have experienced in an abusive family. You may discover that your therapist truly and honestly celebrates your autonomy without abandoning you, becoming competitive, or demanding that you maintain a need for the therapist that you may have outgrown. To discover that you can move on to the next phase of your life without having to fight for it, and that you don't have to lose all contact with your therapist, can be a major, unexpected revelation to someone who was abused as a child.

While therapy is not a panacea for resolving the effects of abuse, when it is done well it offers a safe place in which to explore the story of your childhood and discover how it continues to affect relationships in the present. The therapeutic process then becomes a way to learn new modes of being in relationship with another human being that promote healthy autonomy, safety, and empathy for yourself and others.

What If I've Had a Bad Therapy Experience?

Unfortunately, many people have had experiences in therapy that they feel hurt more than helped. If this has happened to you, your bad therapy experience becomes another disappointing relationship that needs to be explored and resolved. While it may be hard to get back on the horse after falling off, you need to explore what went wrong with prior therapy relationships and to heal any wounds that may have been opened by them.

If you have had many therapists and feel you never really received any help, you might want to consider how these relationships may have replayed early childhood disappointments or other unresolved wounds. There's no reason to think that a new therapy relationship will be any different from the ones that didn't work *unless* you are willing to dig deeper and explore what your responses are telling you about what you experienced as a child.

It's true that some therapists are abusive and hurt their clients, but most are well-meaning people who disappoint clients from time to time. If you are fortunate enough to find someone with whom you can feel safe enough to move through the feelings that caused you to leave past therapies, you may discover that a whole new level of healing becomes possible.

Therapist's Challenges

Those of us who do therapy are constantly challenged to update our skills and stay connected with our own process of healing. It is our responsibility to be aware of how we respond to our clients, as well as to deal with how the material they bring into therapy affects us. Sometimes our work is overwhelming, and we need to seek out help for ourselves. Sometimes things are just fine; we need to know how to recognize when that is so. We need to check in with ourselves constantly and monitor how we are doing.

It's essential that therapists learn what their limits are and stick by them. If we ask more of ourselves than we are able to give comfortably, it hurts everyone. A characteristic of abusive families is that they tend to be closed off from the outside world. There is little new input, and secrets are held within the isolation of the cut-off family system.[16] If we are to have healing relationships within the therapy setting, the system needs to be open to receive constructive help and support from the outside.

For example, therapists have a variety of ways for increasing their expertise in the treatment of abuse survivors. Workshops and conferences offer training and information. Master therapists offer supervision and one-on-one training where issues can be explored in depth and therapist problems with setting limits or other treatment issues can be addressed and resolved.[17]

Healing Is More Possible Now Than Ever

Whether or not you have been in therapy before, it's important to know that there are resources available. In fact, each year our understanding of how to help gets better. Psychotherapy, body work, art and movement therapies, and spiritual approaches are increasingly effective in helping abuse survivors recover from the effects of a wounded childhood. The healing process takes courage, whether you begin alone or with someone to help guide you on your way. At least now, at this time in the evolution of psychotherapy, there is more help available than ever before.

The healing journey is a true adventure. It takes you into territory you may never have experienced before. Sometimes you may want to take the journey solo, going alone into areas of learning and recovery that constitute the next steps for you. At other times you probably will discover that there is no way you can go unsupported into feelings and early experiences that have not been processed fully. The important thing to know is that your healing is in your hands. It is your choice. It is your process. It unfolds in your present and is the foundation of your future.

*   *   *

I began this book with a dedication to a special person in my life, my aunt. She died in 1992, at the age of 76. She was a survivor of childhood sexual abuse, but no one knew what was wrong or how to help her for most of her life. Before she died, we had many long and important talks about why her life unfolded as it did. Her choices, difficulties, and challenges began to make more sense to her as she understood them in the context of childhood abuse. I wish there had been more help for her when she was younger, and I am immensely grateful that I was able to offer her some understanding before she died.

The shared journey we have taken in this book is for all the people who, like my aunt, have faced challenges that we therapists have begun to understand only recently. Together, we are traveling across a new terrain—participating in an exploration essential to the ultimate well-being of us all. Each new development in the understanding and treatment of abuse can bring both relief and gratitude that more people are being helped and healed from the effects of early trauma. As each survivor of childhood hurts heals from his or her past, the transmission of child abuse across generations can be slowed and, perhaps, stopped. What a profound gift we may give to the future if we take seriously the urgent need to stop abusing children, as well as our responsibility to offer healing to those who have been hurt already.

Notes

In the notes that follow for each of the chapters, you will find some that deal with general issues and self-help references and others that are more technical in nature. Those that are technical are primarily for therapists. As more survivors become aware of their early trauma, and as dissociative processes increasingly are acknowledged in mainstream mental health circles, more informed therapists will be called upon to provide appropriate psychotherapy for individuals who were abused as children. And so, in these notes I seek to share some of the information of which I am aware. As with every other avenue of knowledge and expertise, by the time this book is published new sources of information will have become available. If you, as a client, have heard of books, articles or conferences that deal with trauma and survivor issues, please know that it is helpful to pass along this information to your therapist and others who are involved with survivor issues. It is only through sharing what we learn that we further hone our ability to help ourselves and others heal from the effects of childhood trauma.

Chapter 1. Introduction
I KNOW I'VE BEEN HURT, BUT NOW WHAT?

1. Diagnostically, dissociation is defined in specific ways that distinguish degrees and kinds of dissociative processes. For example, in the *Diagnostic and Statistical Manual, Third Edition, Revised Edition, (DSM-III-R)*, which contains the standard diagnostic criteria used by mental health practitioners in the United States, *multiple personality disorder* (MPD) is defined as including the following elements:

> A. The existence within the person of two or more distinct personalities or personality states (each with its own relatively enduring pattern of perceiving, relating to, and thinking about the environment and self).
> B. At least two of these personalities or personality states recurrently take full control of the person's behavior." (p. 272)

A second major form of dissociation, not as severe as but similar to multiple personality is *dissociative disorder not otherwise specified* (DDNOS). The following description is included in *DSM-III-R:*

> (2) . . . cases in which there is more than one personality state capable of assuming executive control of the individual, but not more than one personality state is sufficiently distinct to meet the full criteria for MPD, or cases in which a second personality never assumes complete executive control. . . ." (p 277)

For a detailed description of multiple personality disorder, see *Multiple Personality Disorder: Diagnosis, Clinical Features, and Treatment,* by Colin A. Ross, pp. 81–84. Also, Frank W. Putnam's book, *Diagnosis and Treatment of Multiple Personality Disorder,* has an excellent section on "Confirming the Diagnosis," pp. 95–99.

2. I want to thank Christine Comstock for introducing me to this most useful phrase.

3. If you are interested in exploring some of the evidence that supports the idea of fluid memory, there are audiotapes available from the Eighth International Conference on Multiple Personality/Dissociative States, Special Emphasis: Memory: Association and Dissociation, Chicago, Illinois, November 1991. These tapes are available from Audio Transcripts Ltd., 335 South Patrick Street, Suite 220, Alexandria, Virginia 22314, 703-549-7334. Of particular interest, the following tapes report on recent research into the effects of additional information on memory:

"A Method for Studying the Malleability of Memory for Details of a Single Traumatic Event," by E. J. Frischholz and R. N. Haber.
"Memory Distortions," by E. Loftus.

4. The current debate focuses especially on the use of hypnosis to unearth memories that have been repressed or dissociated from conscious awareness. It is the intrusive and potentially retraumatizing quality of certain hypnotic procedures that may cause harm to trauma survivors. That hypnosis techniques can be tremendously helpful in healing is evidenced by many clients and therapists alike. In the following taped workshop, recorded at a major conference on the treatment of dissociative states, both sides of the issue are offered:

"Managing Abreactions in the Treatment of MPD," by J. Peterson. Fourth Annual Eastern Regional Conference on Abuse and Multiple Personality: Training in Treatment, Alexandria, Virginia, June 1992.

5. In the following tapes, examples are offered of different applications of hypnosis in working with abuse survivors. In the first, strategies for working hypnotically with memory material that has already become conscious are offered. In the second, hypnotic strategies for working with disruptive or distressing dissociative phenomena are described.

"Enhancing the Hospital Treatment of Dissociative Disorder Patients by Developing Nursing Expertise in the Application of Hypnotic Techniques without Formal Trance Induction," by R. P. Kluft. Eighth International Conference on Multiple Personality/Dissociative States, Special Emphasis: Memory: Association and Dissociation.
"Hypnotic Techniques Recommended to Assist in Associating the Dissociation in Abreactions," by J. Peterson. Paper presented at the Eighth International Conference on Multiple Personality/Dissociative States. These presentations are also available through Audio Transcripts.

6. One of the major tasks of healing from childhood trauma is to slow down the process enough to avoid retraumatization. When a survivor becomes overwhelmed because too much material is emerging too quickly, there is a greater chance that old, dissociative strategies will be used to cope with the experience. When this happens, often there is no therapeutic, healing gain, and the material will have to be dealt with again at a later time.

7. See *The Essential Jung*, compiled by A. Storr, pp. 18–19, 229.

8. Storr, pp. 68–71. Also, there are many books available that provide strategies for tapping into the creativity and healing potential carried within

the unconscious. For example, see *What We May Be: Techniques for Psychological and Spiritual Growth Through Psychosynthesis,* by P. Ferucci, and *You're in Charge: A Guide to Becoming Your Own Therapist,* by J. Rainwater.

9. Storr, pp. 68–71.

10. Actually, Jung believed that the collective unconscious is common to all humans—even, perhaps, to all animals. Op cit., p. 67.

11. The concept that what each of us accomplishes in terms of our own healing contributes to the collective good can be supported by much that has been discovered in quantum physics, and is an underlying premise in certain Eastern spiritual approaches. For example, see the following:

"In Indra's Net: Sarvodaya and Our Mutual Efforts for Peace," by J. Macy, in *The Path of Compassion: Writings on Socially Engaged Buddhism,* p. 178; *The Rebirth of Nature: The Greening of Science and God,* and *A New Science of Life: The Hypnothesis of Causative Formation,* by R. Sheldrake, pp. 115, 117; *Dialogues with Scientists and Sages: The Search for Unity,* by R. Weber, pp. 94, 183; and *The Quantum Self: Human Nature and Consciousness Defined by the New Physics,* by D. Zohar, p. 169.

Chapter 2. Dissociation and Childhood Hurts

1. There are numerous books available that address the concept of parts of the self." Some, to name just a very few, are:

Psychosynthesis: A Manual of Principles and Techniques, by R. Assagioli; *What We May Be,* by P. Ferucci; *Recreating Your Self,* by N. Napier; "Rescuing the Exiles," an article in *The Family Therapy Networker,* by R. Schwartz; *Embracing Our Selves: The Voice Dialogue Manual,* by H. Stone and S. Winkelman.

2. For some therapists, the use of the term "disorder" is a way of avoiding the *sociological* factors involved in pathologizing the outcome of child abuse. For this reason, I have chosen to omit the term *disorder* and to use, instead, "multiple personalities."

In a presentation called, "Conversation Hour: The Politics of Dissociation: A Feminist Perspective," at the Eighth International Conference on Multiple Personality/Dissociative States, Nancy Cole commented that the multiple personality *disorder* label, ". . . puts [people] in a category of disease rather than describing cultural pathology," and overlooks the fact that dissociative states often are a response to the ". . . impact of chronic fear and terror."

3. There are several psychological tests currently available that focus specifically on dissociative processes. The most comprehensive, and most recently developed, is the following:

SCID-D–Structured Clinical Interview for DSM-III-R Dissociative Disorders, published by the American Psychiatric Press, 1400 K Street, N.W., Washington, DC 20005, telephone 1-800-368-5777. For information about training workshops in administering the SCID-D, contact Marlene Steinberg, M.D., Yale School of Medicine, 100 Whitney Avenue, New Haven, CT 06510.

Two additional measures are:

DES–Dissociative Experiences Scale.
For information about this scale, contact Frank W. Putnam, M.D., National Institute of Mental Health, Bldg. 15K, 9000 Rockville Pike, Bethesda, MA 20892;
DDIS–Dissociative Disorders Interview Schedule.
For information about this interview schedule, contact Colin A. Ross, M.D., Charter Hospital of Dallas, 6800 Preston Road, Plano, TX 75024.

Also, for a discussion on the potential problems of misdiagnosing dissociation in clients, see "On the Misdiagnosis of Multiple Personality Disorder," by J. Chu.

4. Schreiber, F. R. (1974); Thigpen, C. H., and Cleckley, H. (1957).

5. Colin Ross, in his book, *Multiple Personality Disorder: Diagnosis, Clinical Features, and Treatment,* gives a moving description of the dynamic of the protective function of dissociation:

MPD is a little girl imagining that the abuse is happening to someone else. This is the core of the disorder, to which all other features are secondary. The imaging is so intense, subjectively compelling and adaptive, that the abused child experiences dissociated aspects of herself as other people. It is this core characteristic of MPD that makes it a treatable disorder, because the imagining can be unlearned, and the past confronted and mastered. (pp. 55–56)

6. See Bloch, pp. 27–32; Putnam, pp. 103–4; and Ross, pp. 108–20.

7. See Watkins and Watkins, "Ego States and Hidden Observers," and

"The Management of Malevolent Ego States in Multiple Personality Disorder." Also, see Bloch, pp. 9–11.

8. See Ferucci, p. 47, and Sliker, *Multiple Mind*, pp. 1–3, 63–64, 81–82, for example.

9. To read further about the subject of natural multiplicity, see Beahrs, *Unity and Multiplicity: Multilevel Consciousness of Self in Hypnosis, Psychiatric Disorder and Mental Health*, p. 36; Ornstein, *Multimind: A New Way of Looking at Human Behavior*, pp. 7–8, 9, 17, 144, 153, 191; and Richards, "Dissociation and Transformation."

10. See, for example, Bloch, pp. 27, 30; Braun, *Treatment of Multiple Personality Disorder*, pp. 18, 20; Putnam, p. 303; Ross, p. 81.

11. See, Putnam, p. 298 and Ross, p. 194.

For children, the outlook is even better. According to Ross,

> Childhood MPD seems to be treatable to long-term stable remission with short-term psychotherapy. This probably means permanent cure. *For this to happen, the abuse must stop.* In fact, it is unethical to try to treat childhood MPD in the face of ongoing abuse, because the treatment would rob the child of his or her way of coping. (p. 201, emphasis added).

See, also, Putnam, "The Treatment of Multiple Personality Disorder," in Braun, *Treatment of Multiple Personality Disorder*, pp. 183–4.

12. Richard P. Kluft, M.D., the acknowledged "master" in the treatment of multiple personalities, proposes his "Four-Factor Theory" in the development of multiplicity, as quoted in Ross, pp. 71–73. The four factors are:

> 1. Patients with MPD are extremely good at dissociation.
> 2. Patients with MPD have used dissociation to cope with severe childhood trauma.
> 3. The form and structure of MPD vary depending on the person's temperament and nonabuse experience.
> 4. The abuse didn't stop, and the victim did not receive enough consistent love and care to heal her wounds.

13. In *Childhood Antecedents of Multiple Personality*, Bennett Braun includes the possibility of a genetic predisposition to dissociation as one of the factors that leads to the development of multiple personalities. See, his article, "The Transgenerational Incidence of Dissociation and Multiple Personality Disorder: A Preliminary Report," pp. 127–150.

14. See Braun and Sachs, "The Development of Multiple Personality

Disorder: Predisposing, Precipitating and Perpetuating Factors." The "3-P's" presented are:

1. *Predisposing factors*, including an inborn capacity to dissociate, ". . . an excellent working memory, above-average intelligence, and creativity"; and " . . . inconsistent and unpredictable exposure to some form of traumatic abuse."
2. *Precipitating factors*, including ". . . some form of abuse that triggers defensive dissociative episodes."
3. *Perpetuating factors*, including personal (in terms of the individual's use of dissociative strategies to cope with abuse); interpersonal (involving the abused child's family dynamics); and situational (including ". . . direct exposure to traumatic events, as well as the more indirect effect of societal attitudes and pressures").

Also see Putnam, pp. 10, 52; Ross, p. 188; Braun, "Issues in the Psychotherapy of Multiple Personality Disorder," pp. 5–6; and Sachs, "The Adjunctive Role of Social Support Systems in the Treatment of Multiple Personality Disorder," p. 160.

15. There are many metaphors you can use to represent dissociative barriers, i.e., clarity of focus in a camera, vividness of colors (from vague to bright), dimness to brightness of light in a room, using a dimmer switch.

16. See Fink, "The Core Self: A Development Perspective on the Dissociative Disorders," and Bloch, p. 29.

17. The story of Marilyn Van Derbur was carried in many magazines, newspapers and on television. See, for example, *People Magazine*, June 10, 1991.

18. See Chase, *When Rabbit Howls*.

19. Involuntary dissociation can be dangerous, as well as distressing, for an adult multiple. See, for example, Kluft, "The Darker Side of Dissociation."

The whole issue of volition, and whether multiples should or should not seek to integrate as an essential part of their healing, represents an ongoing debate. The argument *for* integration posits that continuing involuntary dissociation places the survivor at greater risk for revictimization; i.e., (a) not seeing danger, because a part that may be aware of it cannot communicate across dissociative barriers; (b) acting inappropriately or destructively in interpersonal situations, as when a child or adolescent part reacts emotionally without the balancing effect of an adult's cognitive point of view; and (c) engaging in self-destructive behaviors, as when a part feels overwhelmed by stress and doesn't have the benefit of the soothing presence of parts that could be of help.

In "Dissociation and Subsequent Vulnerability: A Preliminary Study," Kluft describes some of the potentially negative effects of continuing dissociation in trauma survivors. He goes on to suggest that integration, by definition, implies that the individual has shifted from dissociative strategies to those that allow information to be taken in by the "whole self."

The other side of the debate proposes that the goal is to develop cooperation and collaboration among alters, without integration as a goal. See Bloch, pp. 71–73.

20. See, for example, Comstock, C. "The Inner Self Helper and Concepts of Inner Guidance: Historical Antecedents, Its Role within Dissociation, and Clinical Utilization," pp. 166–167, 171, 175. Also see, Torem, "Iatrogenic Factors in the Perpetuation of Splitting and Multiplicity," especially pp. 94–95.

21. Ross, C., and Anderson, G. "Treatment Techniques and Interventions," workshop presented at the Second Annual Eastern Regional Conference on Multiple Personality and Dissociation, and available from Audio Transcripts.

Chapter 3. Therapeutic Dissociation

1. Thanks to Pat Jobling for our many discussions of her use of techniques of creative dissociation in corporations.

2. *Adult observer* is my term for the psychological construct of an "observing ego." See Comstock, "The Inner Self Helper and Concepts of Inner Guidance," pp. 167–168.

Also see Ornstein, pp. 182–183, 185, on the "observation mind"; Sliker, pp. 14–15, 32, 77–78; and Stone and Winkelman, pp. 70–72, on the "aware ego."

3. See, for example, Ross, Norton, and Fraser, "Evidence against the Iatrogenesis of Multiple Personality Disorder"; and, Kluft, "Iatrogenic Creation of New Alter Personalities."

4. In *Multiple Mind*, Sliker talks about the benefits of getting to know your inner parts and how this allows you to *choose* change (see p. 32). Many books have been published that deal with contacting and getting to know subpersonalities. See, for example, books already referenced, i.e., Ferucci,

Rainwater, Sliker, Stone and Winkelman; also, Harris and Harris, *Staying OK*. Because of the many books that become available each month, it's always a good idea to go to your local bookstore and see what catches your attention.

5. Some multiples don't experience the presence of adult parts. If you have difficulty identifying an adult part, you may feel more comfortable thinking of this part of you as your "present-day observer." We'll explore this concept in more detail in Chapter 5.

6. Rossi and Cheek, in *Mind-Body Therapy*, describe a way to use the hands to "access creative resources," on pp. 38–41. They also discuss other "ideomotor" signaling techniques, including a pendulum, p. 17, and finger signals, p. 20.

7. See Storr, *The Essential Jung*, pp. 236, 329.

8. Carl Jung wrote extensively on the symbolic archetypes contained within the unconscious, archetypes that exert a powerful influence on both the collective and the individual. See, for example, Jung, *Man and His Symbols*, pp. 4–17, 377. Also see Achterberg, J. *Imagery in Healing*, which contains numerous stories of the effects of images on healing; Borysenko, *Minding the Body, Mending the Mind*, pp. 152–157; Epstein, *Healing Visualizations: Creating Health Through Imagery*; and Samuels, *Healing With the Mind's Eye*.

9. As with all exercises in the book, refer to *Recreating Your Self* for ways to go inside. See, especially, pp. 56–83. For now, simply close your eyes, allow your body to settle, take a gentle deep breath, and allow yourself to focus on whatever images or other awarenesses drift into your consciousness.

10. See Sliker's book for descriptions of how imagery/symbolic representations of subpersonalities change over time. Also, see Ferucci, pp. 117–142, who describes symbolic visualization exercises for communication with subpersonalities and increasing comfort via imagery.

11. Milton Erickson modeled an approach that assumes the wisdom of the unconscious and the capacity for unconscious processes to continue to operate once they are set in motion. Because there are so many books now available on Ericksonian approaches, I would ask you, if you are interested, to follow your instincts at your local bookstore and choose whichever Erickson book appeals to you.

12. See, for example, Beahrs, pp. 117–119; Bloch, pp. 55–57; Comstock, "The Inner Self Helper and Concepts of Inner Guidance"; and Napier, pp. 101–102.

13. See Ferucci, pp. 47–58; Harris and Harris, pp. 49–68; Sliker, especially pp. 36–77; Stone and Winkelman, pp. 47–81. Also see Ferucci and Rainwater, in general, and look at your local bookstore for additional resources.

14. For example, take a deep breath. As you exhale, close your eyes and allow your body to settle. Imagine you are in a beautiful field—somewhere where you can see a large, brightly-colored helium balloon tied down so it won't float away. Discover the rope that ties it. Find a place to sit down comfortably, take the rope in your hand, and pull the rope to release the balloon. Then, watch the balloon rise *slowly*, until it finally becomes a tiny speck of color up in the sky. As it becomes smaller, tell yourself you are going more comfortably into a self-hypnotic state. By the time the balloon disappears entirely, you can be at whatever level of trance you need for this time. Then, go on with whatever inner work you have planned. To bring yourself out, simply count, mentally, from one to three. On the count of three, allow your eyes to open spontaneously, your mind alert and focused in your present-day surroundings. Allow yourself to recognize that whatever healing process you have set in motion will continue, regardless of what activities you may engage after your inner work.

15. Thanks to Sidney Rosen, M.D., from whom I learned this technique.

16. There are many excellent books on stress reduction. A few to keep in mind are: Selye, *Stress Without Distress;* Stroebel, *QR: The Quieting Reflex;* and Schwartz, *Letting Go of Stress.*

Chapter 4. Identifying Triggers

1. We'll explore more about child parts in Chapter 8.

2. We'll look at this in more detail in Chapter 6.

3. An exercise for learning *how* to sit with feelings in on page 120 in Chapter 6.

4. Putnam describes a flashback on p. 177 of *Diagnosis and Treatment of Multiple Personality Disorder:* "The past and the present intermingle and follow each other in chronological confusion. Flashbacks, with their accompanying distortions of age and body image, send a patient hurtling backwards to relive trauma that seems more vivid now than when it actually occurred."

5. Throughout the book, I refer to "personalities" and "parts" interchangeably. When I work with dissociative clients, I tend to use "parts" as a means of reinforcing that we are working within *one* person's consciousness, even though it may have highly defined aspects.

Chapter 5. Healing with "Mindfulness"

1. There are *many* good books available on various forms of meditation, written in ways that make these practices available to Westerners. As a beginning point, look at: Goldstein and Kornfield, *Seeking the Heart of Wisdom: The Path of Insight Meditation;* Nhat Hanh, *The Miracle of Mindfulness: A Manual on Meditation;* and Levine, *Healing Into Life and Death.*

2. I refer people to books by Stephen Levine and Thich Nhat Hanh because their approaches have been applied to healing emotional wounds. Check at your local bookstore for any of the books written by either of these authors, and see which ones touch you.

3. See Thich Nhat Hanh's book, *Peace Is Every Step,* pp. 53–56.

4. See, for example, Thich Nhat Hanh's *Miracle of Mindfulness,* pp. 14–21. This is a hypnotic principle, as well. For example, see Hammond, *Handbook of Hypnotic Suggestions and Metaphors,* pp. 45–83.

5. For example, See Thich Nhat Hanh's *Miracle of Mindfulness,* pp. 14–21.

6. See, for example, Goldstein and Kornfield, and Daniel Goleman's *The Meditative Mind.* As is true with any self-help literature, allow yourself to find a bookstore that carries a good selection of the subject you want, in this case meditation, and then let your own wisdom direct you to the resources that are best for you at this point in time.

7. See Stephen Levine's "lovingkindness meditation" in *Guided Meditations, Explorations and Healings,* pp. 29–33.

8. See, again, *Guided Meditations, Explorations and Healings,* pp. 112–113.

Chapter 6. Containing and Sitting with Feelings

1. See *Recreating Your Self,* pp. 40–42.

2. See, for example, Loewenstein, "Somatoform disorders in victims of incest and child abuse"; and Ross, Fast, Anderson, Auty, and Todd, "Somatic Symptoms in Multiple Sclerosis and MPD."

3. See John Briere's book, *Therapy for Adults Molested as Children: Beyond Survival,* pp. 24–29, for a review of the kinds of acting-out behaviors engaged in by adult survivors of abuse.

4. See, for instance, Johnson, *Humanizing the Narcissistic Style,* p. 27; Masterson, *Psychotherapy of the Borderline Adult,* pp. 58, 61–63; and Rinsley, "An Object Relations View of Borderline Personality."

For some multiples, a similar phenomenon has more to do with *switching*, i.e., where different parts may have markedly different feelings about the same person. For example, a part that feels rage at the "monster Mommy" may be completely dissociated, while another part that has only positive feelings allows the child to experience the "good Mommy" without being overwhelmed by terror or anger.

5. We'll explore this further in Chapter 8.

6. To learn more about creating anchors, see, for instance, Bandler and Grinder, *Frogs into Princes: Neuro-linguistic Programming*, pp. 85–109; and Grinder and Bandler's *Trance-formations: Neuro-linguistic Programming and the Structure of Hypnosis*, pp. 61–63.

7. To get a sense of what the inner life of a person with multiple personalities feels like, including the urge to self-mutilate, see *Multiple Personality Disorder From the Inside Out*, edited by B. Cohen, E. Giller, and Lynn W. For a more clinical perspective, David Calof's presentation at the Fourth Annual Eastern Regional Conference on Abuse and Multiple Personality, entitled "Self-Injurious Behavior: Treatment Strategies," is available on tape from Audio Transcripts. Also see Coons, P., and Milstein, V., "Self-Mutilation Associated with Dissociative Disorders," which looks at the kinds of self-mutilation found in individuals with dissociative disorders.

Chapter 7. Disappointment and Despair

1. One of the essential tasks of healing from early abuse is dealing with the inevitable grief survivors feel about a lost childhood. The demand to be rescued is one way to fend off the impact of what has been irretrievably lost and must now be mourned. See Davies and Frawley, "Dissociative Processes and Transference-Countertransference Paradigms in the Psychoanalytically Oriented Treatment of Adult Survivors of Childhood Sexual Abuse."

2. It is important to realize, as well, that there may be times when you actually *have* chosen someone who has nothing to give. It's easier to identify this kind of situation, and have a clearer sense of what you want to do about it, once you have recognized and dealt with your unresolved childhood disappointments.

3. This exercise is adapted from one shown to me by Garrett Oppenheim, Ph.D.

4. There are times, however, when you need to pay attention to suicidal feelings, if you are at all afraid you may act on them. At these times, it's important to take whatever steps you need to keep yourself safe until you have shifted back into your present-day adult state of mind.

5. See Christine Courtois' book, *Healing the Incest Wound*, pp. 305–307.

Chapter 8. Dealing with Inner Child Parts

1. We humans seem to have an innate need to explain, or interpret, our experience so that it makes sense to us. See, for example, Michael Gazzaniga's book, *Mind Matters: How Mind and Brain Interact to Create Our Conscious Lives*, especially pp. 3, 11, 67, 71. On p. 99, Gazzaniga talks about how chemical changes in the body, creating anxiety, for instance, then cause us to seek an explanation for the anxiety. He says,

> The theories that the interpretive brain has generated to fit the felt state of mind are now stored as memories and as potential behavior patterns. They exist in conscious reality even though the stimulus that provoked their creation [an internal, chemical stimulus] has now been successfully treated.

Also see Cantor, "From Thought to Behavior: 'Having' and 'Doing' in the Study of Personality and Cognition"; and, Neisser, *Cognition and Reality: Principles and Implications of Cognitive Psychology*.

2. See p. 204 in Gazzaniga's *Mind Matters*.

3. If your goal is to prosecute abusers, there are certain things you need to keep in mind: (1) hypnotic evidence is not admissible in court, so that any memories you access during hypnosis cannot be used to build a case; (2) memories must be corroborated by additional sources, such as childhood medical records or eye witnesses.

4. Again, check at your local bookstore. There are *many* books available now that deal with visualization, guided imagery, and self-hypnosis.

5. The ongoing experience of trance in dissociated abuse survivors has been documented by many therapists. See, for example, Fraser, G. "The Dissociative Table Technique: A Strategy for Working with Ego States in Dissociative Disorders and Ego-State Therapy," pp. 205–206; Putnam, pp. 158–60; Ross, pp. 64–66; and Calof.

6. Review note 5, chapter 1. Also see Putnam, pp. 158–60, 170–172.

7. This doesn't mean that the psyche becomes a homogenized whole. Parts of the self continue to exist, but they become more harmonized, more in tune with the underlying urge towards wholeness. See, for example, Sliker, pp. 70–74.

8. Watkins developed the technique of the "affect bridge." For a description, see "The Affect Bridge: A Hypnoanalytic Technique"; and p. 179 of Hammond's *Handbook of Hypnotic Suggestions and Metaphors*.

9. A helpful strategy for dealing with wounded inner child parts is to learn how to talk to them, and to yourself, in healthier, more empowering ways. *How To Talk So Kids Will Listen and Listen So Kids Will Talk*, by Adele Faber and Elaine Mazlish, provides helpful information on how to talk to yourself in non-abusive, respectful ways.

10. See, for example, Gazzaniga, p. 204, where he says:

> Not only is our ability to recall greatly impaired when we are under stress; our memory for events experienced under stress is also undermined, since, as we have just noted, stress focuses the mind on particular activities. . . . Particular aspects of a fearful event become imprinted in the mind and sometimes haunt the victim for years. Other aspects of a fearful situation go completely unnoticed."

11. Past-life regression may or may not fit with your belief system. It doesn't seem to matter whether or not these memories are "real." Therapists who work with past-life regression report powerful healing experiences for their clients. See, for example, Moody, R. *Coming Back: A Psychiatrist Explores Past-life Journeys;* Oppenheim, *Who Were You Before You Were You? The Casebook of a Past-life Therapist;* and Woolger, *Other Lives, Other Selves: A Jungian Psychotherapist Discovers Past Lives.*

12. Thanks to Pat Jobling for discussions of this strategy, and for sharing her version, which she uses in corporations: If an executive is apprehensive about standing up and presenting, she has the person imagine walking in, hand-in-hand with the frightened child part. The child part, then, sits in the audience and watches the accomplished adult make the presentation—the fear is "out there," in the audience. The child's fear begins to diminish as he or she watches the adult perform competently. Because we tend often to draw on childhood strategies when we encounter stressful performance situations, this technique offers another way to break the habit of automatically reacting with fear.

Chapter 9. Shame and the Disowned Self

1. For example, see Fossum and Mason, *Facing Shame: Families in Recovery*, pp. 5–6; Lewis, *Shame: The Exposed Self*, pp. 121, 141–142. Donald Nathanson, in his book, *Shame and Pride: Affect, Sex and the Birth of the Self*, states that guilt is "... shame which is triggered along with *fear*" (p. 248, emphasis added).

2. See, for example, the introduction to Chapter 10, "Owning Your Dark Side," of *Meeting the Shadow: The Hidden Power of the Dark Side of Human Nature*, edited by J. Abrams and C. Zweig. Also see Stone and Winkelman, pp. 27–46, as well as Wilber's comments in *Meeting the Shadow*, p. 274, "Taking Responsibility for Your Shadow."

3. See Storr, *The Essential Jung*, pp. 87–92.

4. In his book, *Shame: The Exposed Self*, Lewis addresses the important difference between globalizing and focusing on the specific, and the role this dynamic plays in our experience of shame. See, for example, pp. 72–74 and pp. 103–108.

5. Nathanson, in *Shame and pride*, talks about learning from mistakes. He says, "... the entire system of learning by trial and error will be limited by shame," (p. 173) because, apparently, the potential for shame affect accompanies *any* new learning situation.

6. See *Recreating Your Self*, pp. 166–172.

7. For a thorough exploration of projection and its interpersonal effects, see Halpern and Halpern, *Projections: Our World of Imaginary Relationships*. They define projection as, "... *the blurred perception of another person that arises because we are seeing an aspect of ourselves rather than the other*" (p. 10, italics in original).

8. In *The Call For the Master*, Durckheim describes a process of slowly awakening internally to positive aspects of the self and capabilities, which are initially experienced as external and as residing in the teacher. Also see Halpern and Halpern, pp. 33, 36; Miller, "Finding the Shadow in Daily Life," p. 40.

9. See Davies and Frawley, p. 19, about how hope leads inevitably to despair.

10. For example, see Stern, *Diary of a Baby*, pp. 60–71, especially pp. 69–71, for a description of this kind of interaction between a mother and her baby.

11. In addition, Nathanson adds the concept of "shame affect," in his

book *Shame and Pride*. In essence, shame is presented as a natural and inevitable physiological, affective response that occurs from infancy and throughout life. Its biological purpose is to direct attention from some activity that is interesting or enjoyable but that has been interrupted. It is only as we grow up and gather experience that *meaning* is attached to shame— meaning that may leave us feeling devalued and devastated. *It is with the meaning of shame that we deal in our healing journeys.* As the meaning changes and is reframed, the power of shame to disable us emotionally lessens.

Chapter 10. Your Future Self

1. See *Recreating Your Self*, pp. 24–25.

2. See *Recreating Your Self*, pp. 110–131.

3. An understanding of the successive emergence of future selves has deepened as I have lived with this dynamic process over time. It has been my experience that, as time passes and new developments are integrated into ongoing awareness, the future self becomes an integrated aspect of the present-day self, naturally and automatically. When this happens, a new future self comes into view and the process of development continues. It is my assumption that future selves will continue to emerge throughout life, inevitably, just as today inevitably becomes tomorrow.

4. See Jeanne Achterberg's book, *Imagery in Healing*, for numerous examples of how the imagery process may affect physical states. Also, look again at note 8, chapter 3, especially the books by Achterberg, Epstein, and Samuels.

5. See Markus and Nurius, "Possible Selves," especially pp. 958–960.

6. A reminder: As I mentioned in Chapter 5, there are times when the mere fact of relaxing may cause some initial anxiety. When you remember that this is normal, it can be easier to allow it to flow on through your awareness without clamping down around it. There's no need to *do* anything about it—just be curious and observe whatever your responses may be to going inside.

7. See Michael Lewis' book on shame for a discussion of the development and pitfalls of "globalizing," especially pp. 103–108.

8. The center seems to encompass an *observer* aspect of consciousness. See, for example, Sliker, p. 77; also see pp. 40, 77–82, 87, 90, 180–181, for definitions of the Center. See, also, Comstock's comments on the observer function and the "innermost core," on p. 167 of her article, "The Inner Self

Helper and Concepts of Inner Guidance." Also see John Sanford's book, *Evil: The Shadow Side of Reality*, pp. 7 and 31.

Of particular interest, in relation to the future self, see p. 78 of *Multiple Mind*, where Sliker talks about the need, at times, to create an "external center, a model who acts as a center. . . ." The future self may fill this role, as you internalize the more balanced, aware perspective of this wiser part of you.

9. I also introduce clients to the concept of a "healing center," an internal source of wisdom and guidance—as well as waves of comfort, ease and healing—that remains within the unconscious. This aspect of internal wisdom may be called upon to intervene with dreams, feelings of comfort, or any kind of awareness that may further the healing process and ease the way.

10. See Sliker, p. 34, for a description of the higher self as an ever-present guidance center.

11. See Putnam, pp. 202–204, and Beahrs, pp. 117–119. Also see Comstock's article on inner self helpers, cited above; Bloch, pp. 55–57; and Adams, M. A., "Internal Self Helpers of Persons With Multiple Personality Disorder," *Dissociation*, 11(3), pp. 138–143.

12. There are many books available that focus on accessing inner guidance in the form of guides and helpers—human, animal, spiritual, and otherwise. As with all issues that involve discovering what techniques and concepts work best for you, recommendations from friends and a visit to your local bookstore provide good starts.

Chapter 11. What about the People in My Life?

1. Review Chapter 4, on Identifying Triggers, for ways to become more familiar with what specific things trigger you in the most powerful ways.

2. See, for example, Putnam, pp. 268–269; and Ross pp. 294–296. Also see Bader and Pearson, *In Quest of the Mythical Mate*.

3. *The Dance of Anger*, by Harriet Goldhor Lerner, discusses these dynamics of overfunctioning and underfunctioning. See, for example, pp. 45–66.

4. Both Putnam and Ross address the potential for abusive patterns to repeat themselves in the adult relationships of survivors. See, also, Sachs, "The Adjunctive Role of Social Support Systems in the Treatment of Multiple Personality Disorder," especially pp. 162 and 167. Other, less technical

books include *Outgrowing the Pain*, by Eliana Gil, especially p. 6, and *After the Tears*, by Jane Middleton-Moz and Laurie Dwinell, p. 65.

5. Harville Hendrix, in *Getting the Love You Want: A Guide for Couples*, addresses how to move through the first phases of romantic love and, then, deepen into more mature intimacy. Also by Harville Hendrix, see *Keeping the Love You Find: A Guide For Singles*, p. 220. In *Struggle for Intimacy*, Janet Woititz describes the qualities of a healthy relationship; see pp. 19–22. Also see *Escape From Intimacy*, by Schaef, which describes romance addiction on pp. 46–74.

6. See Eliana Gil's book, *Outgrowing the Pain Together*, which focuses especially on how spouses and partners can better deal with the difficult intimacy issues that are present in relationships with abuse survivors. In *Escape From Intimacy*, Schaef describes the elements found in healthy relationships on pp. 138–142. Also see Aaron Beck's book, *Love Is Never Enough: How Couples Can Overcome Misunderstandings, Resolve Conflicts and Solve Relationship Problems*, for a self-help, cognitively oriented approach to healthier relationships. You may also find that couples therapy can provide a helpful forum within which you can discover new ways of interacting.

7. Even for non-multiples, there are many ways that abusive behaviors may be passed along to children. See, for example, Alice Miller's *For Your Own Good*, pp. 3–4, 16–17, and 58.

8. See *Multiple Personality Disorder from the Inside Out*, edited by Cohen, Giller, and Lynn W., for stories, written by multiples, that describe the variety of ways survivors experience the dissociative process they developed as abused children.

9. In *Allies in Healing*, Laura Davis provides many examples of the struggles partners and friends have in dealing with the issues involved in healing from sexual abuse. She also offers stories of how people successfully overcame these struggles.

10. See *Multiple Personality Disorder from the Inside Out*, especially Chapter 8. When "telling" involves disclosing the abuse to family members, it is important to know that timing and preparation are all important. See Yvonne Dolan's book, *Resolving Sexual Abuse*, pp. 59–71. Also see Eliana Gil's book, *Outgrowing the Pain: A Book for and about Adults Abused as Children*.

11. Again, there are many new books available on how to handle intimacy issues, including conflict and anger, in relationships. One of the classics is *The Inner Enemy*, by G. Bach and L. Torbet. Also see, Bach and Deutsch,

Pairing: How to Achieve Genuine Intimacy, especially pp. 153–161.

12. Wendy Maltz, in *The Sexual Healing Journey,* discusses celibacy, as well as the entire range of issues faced by couples where one or both partners are sexual abuse survivors; see pp. 193–200.

13. Again, new books are coming on the market every month that have to do with healing from sexual abuse. Three that are rapidly becoming classics are: *Allies in Healing,* by Davis; *Courage to Heal,* by Bass and Davis; and *The Sexual Healing Journey,* by Maltz.

Chapter 12. What about My Therapist?

1. For example, the International Society for the Study of Multiple Personality and Dissociation, 5700 Old Orchard Road, First Floor, Skokie, IL 60077-1057, telephone (708) 966-4322, has a listing of member therapists throughout the United States and abroad who treat abuse survivors.

2. Some forms of barter relationship are allowed by certain professional organizations, as when clients have a product of a certain, identifiable value that can be traded for an equal value of treatment.

3. Therapists who treat survivors of abuse must be comfortable in the presence of the intense feelings and interpersonal issues that come up in this form of therapy. Two of the best books available for therapists on the treatment of abuse survivors are Briere's *Therapy for Adults Molested as Children: Beyond Survival,* and Courtois' *Healing the Incest Wound.*

4. See, for example, Bloch, pp. 50–51. In his article, "Ten Traps for Therapists in the Treatment of Trauma Survivors," James Chu describes some of the elements therapists need to be aware of so they can avoid being overwhelmed by the demands of working with abuse survivors.

In "Multiple Personality Disorder as an Attachment Disorder," Peter Barach addresses some of the underlying interpersonal issues therapists need to identify in their work with survivors. Christine Comstock, in "Countertransference and the Suicidal Multiple Personality Disorder Patient," addresses the difficult, but essential focus on the interpersonal dynamics of transference and countertransference within the treatment setting.

5. In the August 1992 issue of *Changes* magazine, Andrew Meacham reviewed the controversy over reparenting approaches in his article, "Call Me Mom." Also see Putnam's book, p. 193, on how reparenting must occur from

within the multiple. See Gabbard's article, "Commentaries on 'Dissociative Processes and Transference-Countertransference Paradigms in the Psychoanalytically Oriented Treatment of Adult Survivors of Childhood Sexual Abuse,' " especially p. 32. See, also, Kluft, "Today's Therapeutic Pluralism." In *Unity and Multiplicity*, Beahrs discusses how to encourage clients to take responsibility, as well as how "therapist's parental inclinations" can create additional problems (pp. 137–139).

6. Again, see Gabbard's article, cited above. The issue of setting reliable limits and boundaries in the therapy of abuse survivors cannot be overemphasized. Without them, the therapy cannot be the safe "container" it needs to be. Without them, the therapist may become overwhelmed and act out in ways that further complicate an already challenging experience. This is especially true when therapists attempt to meet the escalating demands of clients, instead of learning to work *with* these feelings. See, for example, Comstock's article on transference and countertransference, referenced above, especially p. 29. Also see Comstock's article on the inner self helper, pp. 172–173, where she discusses possible responses survivors may have to the idea of "listening inside" and "taking active responsibility for their own progress." See, as well, Kluft's article, "The Rehabilitation of Therapists Overwhelmed by Their Work with MPD Patients," *Dissociation*, II(4), pp. 243–249, especially pp. 244 and 248.

7. Books available to therapists provide fundamental information about setting limits—and the benefits of doing so. See, for example, Putnam, pp. 167–169, and Courtois, p. 201. Ross, p. 211, says that, "An organism that cannot establish boundaries and set limits will quickly die . . . limit setting is not an optional aspect of therapy. The only questions are what limits, and how rigid are they?" See, also, pp. 211–213.

An important source of comfort, support and nurture can be found in survivor groups run by competent and trained psychotherapists. A therapist-run group often feels safer for survivors, as someone is present who can set limits, when needed, and help the group struggle with difficult issues that may arise.

8. See Bowlby, *A Secure Base*.

9. See Manfield, *Split Self, Split Object: Understanding and Treating Borderline, Narcissistic and Schizoid Disorders*, pp. 80–81. See also Note 4, Chapter 6.

10. See Bowlby, pp. 129–130, for a discussion of the development of "working models" of important people in the child's life.

11. See Fine, "Thoughts on the Cognitive Perceptual Substrates of Multiple Personality Disorder."

12. See Ross, pp. 260–266, where he discusses the cognitive issues common to abuse survivors. There are a number of good books available on the subject of cognitive therapy. The following are just a few: Beck, *Cognitive Therapy and the Emotional Disorders;* Beck and Emery, *Anxiety Disorders and Phobias: A Cognitive Perspective;* Beck, Rush, Shaw, and Emery, *Cognitive Therapy of Depression.* These books provide an in-depth description of the theory and techniques of cognitive therapy for the general psychotherapy population. For information that relates cognitive therapy to dissociative abuse survivors, see the Audio Transcripts catalog, available from Audio Transcripts Ltd., 335 South Patrick Street, Suite 220, Alexandria, Virginia 22314, 703-549-7334, for many presentations and workshops that address this important issue.

13. See *Recreating Your Self,* pp. 87–101.

14. See Bowlby, pp. 138–140.

15. See Miller, *For Your Own Good,* pp. 160–161.

16. See Fossum and Mason, pp. 22–24 and 60–61.

17. Peer supervision and study groups also give professionals an opportunity to increase their expertise and, especially, share the fears, concerns, and vulnerabilities that are inevitably triggered when working with survivors. Professional meetings such as the following are particularly helpful for gathering information and developing an increased sense of competency: The International Society for the Study of Multiple Personality and Dissociation holds an annual conference, each November, in Chicago. For information, write to The International Society for the Study of Multiple Personality and Dissociation, 5700 Old Orchard Road, First Floor, Skokie, IL 60077–1057. Another particularly helpful annual conference is the Eastern Regional Conference on Abuse and Multiple Personality: Training in Treatment, held in the Washington area each June. For information, contact the Center for Abuse Recovery and Empowerment, The Psychiatric Institute of Washington, Washington, DC.

References

Abrams, J., & Zweig, C. (1991). Owning your dark side. In J. Abrams & C. Zweig (Eds.). *Meeting the shadow: The hidden power of the dark side of human nature.* Los Angeles: Tarcher.

Achterberg, J. (1985). *Imagery in healing.* Boston: Shambhala.

Adams, M. (1989). Internal self helpers of persons with multiple personality disorder. *Dissociation,* II(3), 138–143.

American Psychiatric Association. (1987). *Diagnostic and statistical manual of mental disorders, Third ed., rev.* Washington, DC: American Psychiatric Association.

Assagioli, R. (1965). *Psychosynthesis: A manual of principles and techniques.* New York: Viking.

Bach, G. R., & Deutsch, R. M. (1978). *Pairing: How to achieve genuine intimacy.* New York: Avon.

Bach, G., & Torbet, L. (1983). *The inner enemy: How to fight fair with yourself.* New York: Berkeley Books.

Bader, E., & Pearson, J. (1988). *In quest of the mythical mate: A developmental approach to diagnosis and treatment in couples therapy.* New York: Brunner/ Mazel.

Bandler, J., & Grinder, J. (1979). *Frogs into princes: Neuro-linguistic programming.* Moab, UT: Real People Press.

Barach, P. M. M. (1991) Multiple personality disorder as attachment disorder. *Dissociation, IV*(3), 117–123.

Bass, E., & Davis, L. (1988) *Courage to heal.* New York: Harper & Row.

Beahrs, J. O. (1982). *Unity and multiplicity: Multilevel consciousness of self in hypnosis, psychiatric disorder and mental health.* New York: Brunner/Mazel.

Beck, A. T. (1976). *Cognitive therapy and the emotional disorders.* New York: Basic Books.

Beck, A. T. (1988). *Love is never enough: How couples can overcome misunderstandings, resolve conflicts and solve relationship problems.* New York: Harper & Row.

Beck, A. T., & Emery, G. (1985). *Anxiety disorders and phobias: A cognitive perspective.* New York: Basic Books.

Beck, A. T., Rush, A. J., Shaw, B. F., & Emery, G. (1979). *Cognitive therapy of depression.* New York: Guilford.

Bloch, J. P. (1991). *Assessment and treatment of multiple personality and dissociative disorders.* Sarasota, FL: Professional Resource Press.

Borysenko, J. (1987). *Minding the body, mending the mind.* Reading, MA: Addison Wesley.

Bowlby, J. (1988). *A secure base.* New York: Basic Books.

Braun, B. G. (1985). The transgenerational incidence of dissociation and multiple personality disorder: A preliminary report. In R. P. Kluft (Ed.), *Childhood antecedents of multiple personality disorder.* Washington, DC: American Psychiatric Press, Inc.

Braun, B. G. (1986a). *Treatment of multiple personality disorder.* Washington, DC: American Psychiatric Press, Inc.

Braun, B. G. (1986b). Issues in the psychotherapy of multiple personality disorder. In B. G. Braun (Ed.), *Treatment of multiple personality disorder.* Washington, DC: American Psychiatric Press, Inc.

Braun, B. G., & Sachs, R. G. (1985) The development of multiple personality disorder: Predisposing, precipitating and perpetuating factors. In R. P. Kluft (Ed.), *Childhood antecedents of multiple personality disorder.* Washington, DC: American Psychiatric Press, Inc.

Briere, J. (1989). *Therapy for adults molested as children: Beyond survival.* New York: Springer.

Calof, D. (1992). Self-injurious behavior: Treatment strategies. Workshop presented at Fourth Annual Eastern Regional Conference on Abuse and Multiple Personality: Training in Treatment, Alexandria, VA.

Cantor, N. (1990). From thought to behavior: "Having" and "doing" in the study of personality and cognition. *American Psychologist, 45*, 735–750.

Chase, T. (1990). *When rabbit howls.* New York: Jove.

Chu, J. (1988). Ten traps for therapists in the treatment of trauma survivors. *Dissociation, I*(4), 24–32.

Chu, J. (1991) On the misdiagnosis of multiple personality disorder. *Dissociation, IV*(4), 200–204.

Cohen, B. M., Giller, E., & Lynn W. (Eds.) (1991). *Multiple personality disorder from the inside out.* Baltimore, MD: Sidran.

Cole, N. (1991). The politics of dissociation: A feminist perspective. Conversation hour at Eighth International Conference on Multiple Personality/Dissociative States, Special Emphasis: Memory: Association and Dissociation, Chicago, IL.

Comstock, C. (1991a). Counter-transference and the suicidal multiple personality disorder patient. *Dissociation, IV*(1), 25–35.

Comstock, C. (1991b). The inner self helper and concepts of inner guidance: Historical antecedents, its role within dissociation, and clinical utilization. *Dissociation, IV*(3), 165–177.

Coons, P. M., & Milstein, V. (1990). Self-mutilation associated with dissociative disorders. *Dissociation, III*(2), 81–87.

Courtois, C. A. (1988). *Healing the incest wound.* New York: Norton.

Davies, J. M., & Frawley, M. G. (1992). Dissociative processes and transference-countertransference paradigms in the psychoanalytically oriented treatment of adult survivors of childhood sexual abuse. *Psychoanalytic Dialogues, 2*(1), 5–36.

Davis, L. (1991). *Allies in healing.* New York: HarperCollins.

Dolan, Y. M. (1991). *Resolving sexual abuse: Solution-focused therapy and Ericksonian approaches for adult survivors.* New York: Norton.

Durckheim, K. G. (1986). *The call for the master: The meaning of spiritual guidance on the way to the self.* New York: Dutton.

Epstein, G. (1989). *Healing visualizations: Creating health through imagery.* New York: Bantam.

Faber, A., & Mazlish, E. (1980). *How to talk so kids will listen and listen so kids will talk.* New York: Avon.

Ferucci, P. (1982). *What we may be: Techniques for psychological and spiritual grown through psychosynthesis.* Los Angeles: Tarcher.

Fine, C. (1988). Thoughts on the cognitive perceptual substrates of multiple personality disorder. *Dissociation, I*(4), 5–10.

Fink, D. (1988). The core self: A developmental perspective on the dissociative disorders. *Dissociation, II*(2), 43–47.

Fossum, M. A., & Mason, M. J. (1986). *Facing shame: Families in recovery*. New York: Norton.

Fraser, G. A. (1991). The dissociative table technique: A strategy for working with ego states in dissociative disorders and ego-state therapy. *Dissociation, IV*(4), 205–213.

Frischholz, E. J., & Haber, R. N. (1991). A method for studying the malleability of memory for details of a single traumatic event. Paper presented at Eighth International Conference on Multiple Personality/Dissociative States, Chicago, IL.

Gabbard, G. O. (1992). Commentaries on "Dissociative processes and transferenece-countertransference paradigms in the psychoanalytically oriented treatment of adult survivors of childhood sexual abuse." *Psychoanalytic Dialogues, 2*(1), 35–59.

Gazzaniga, M. S. (1988). *Mind matters: How mind and brain interact to create our conscious lives*. Boston: Houghton-Mifflin.

Gil, E. (1983). *Outgrowing the pain: A book for and about adults abused as children*. New York: Dell.

Gil, E. (1992). *Outgrowing the pain together: A book for spouses and partners of adults abused as children*. New York: Dell.

Goldstein, J., & Kornfield, J. (1987). *Seeking the heart of wisdom: The path of insight meditation*. Boston: Shambhala.

Goleman, D. (1988). *The meditative mind*. Los Angeles: Tarcher.

Grinder, J., & Bandler, J. (1981). *Trance-formations: Neuro-linguistic programming and the structure of hypnosis*. Moab, UT: Real People Press.

Halpern, J., & Halpern, I. (1983). *Projections: Our world of imaginary relationships*. New York: Seaview/Putnam.

Hammond, D. C. (Ed.) (1990). *Handbook of hypnotic suggestions and metaphors*. New York: Norton.

Harris, A. B., & Harris, T. A. (1985). *Staying OK*. New York: Harper & Row.

Hendrix, H. (1990). *Getting the love you want: A guide for couples*. New York: Harper & Row.

Hendrix, H. (1992). *Keeping the love you find: A guide for singles*. New York: Pocket.

Johnson, S. M. (1987). *Humanizing the narcissistic style*. New York: Norton.

Jung, C. G. (Ed.) (1968). *Man and his symbols*. New York: Dell.

Kluft, R. P. (1985). *Childhood antecedents of multiple personality disorder*. Washington, DC: American Psychiatric Press, Inc.

Kluft, R. P. (1988). Today's therapeutic pluralism. *Dissociation, I*(4), 1–2.

Kluft, R. P. (1989a). Iatrogenic creation of new alter personalities. *Dissociation, II*(2), 84.

Kluft, R. P. (1989b). The rehabilitation of therapists overwhelmed by their work with MPD patients. *Dissociation,* II(4), 243–249.

Kluft, R. P. (1990a). The darker side of dissociation. *Dissociation,* III, 125.

Kluft, R. P. (1990b). Dissociation and subsequent vulnerability: A preliminary study. *Dissociation, III,* 167–173.

Kluft, R. P. (1991). Enhancing the hospital treatment of dissociative disorder patients by developing nursing expertise in the application of hypnotic techniques without formal trance induction. Paper presented at Eighth International Conference on Multiple Personality/Dissociative States, Chicago, IL.

Lerner, H. G. (1985). *The dance of anger.* New York: Harper & Row.

Levine, S. (1987). *Healing into life and death.* Garden City, NJ: Anchor.

Levine, S. (1991). *Guided meditations, explorations and healings.* New York: Anchor.

Lewis, M. (1992). *Shame: The exposed self.* New York: Free Press.

Loftus, E. (1991). Memory distortions. Paper presented at Eighth International Conference on Multiple Personality/Dissociative States, Chicago, IL.

Loewenstein, R. J. (1990). Somatoform disorders in victims of incest and child abuse. In R. P. Kluft (Ed.), *Incest-related syndromes of adult psychopathology* (pp. 89–97). Washington, DC: American Psychiatric Press, Inc.

Macy, J. (1988). In Indra's net: Sarvodaya and our mutual efforts for peace. In F. Eppensteiner (Ed.), *The path of compassion: Writings on socially engaged Buddhism.* Berkeley, CA: Parallax Press.

Maltz, W. (1991). *The sexual healing journey: A guide for survivors of sexual abuse.* New York: HarperCollins.

Manfield, P. (1992). *Split self, split object: Understanding and treating borderline, narcissistic, and schizoid disorders.* Northvale, NJ: Aronson.

Markus, H., & Nurius, P. (1986). Possible selves. *American Psychologist, 41*(9), 954–969.

Masterson, J. F. (1976). *Psychotherapy of the borderline adult.* New York: Brunner/Mazel.

Meacham, A. (1992). Call me mom. *Changes, 7*(4), 57–63.

Middleton-Moz, J., & Dwinell, L. (1986). *After the tears: Reclaiming the personal losses of childhood.* Deerfield Beach, FL: Health Communications.

Miller, A. (1983). *For your own good: Hidden cruelty in child-rearing and the roots of violence.* New York: Farrar, Straus, Giroux.

Miller, W. A. (1991). Finding the shadow in daily life. In J. Abrams & C. Zweig (Eds.), *Meeting the shadow: The hidden power of the dark side of human nature* (pp. 38–44). Los Angeles: Tarcher.

Moody, R. (1990). *Coming back: A psychiatrist explores past-life journeys.* New York: Bantam.

Napier, N. J. (1990). *Recreating your self: Help for adult children of dysfunctional families*. New York: Norton.

Nathanson, D. L. (1992). *Shame and pride: Affect, sex and the birth of the self*. New York: Norton.

Neisser, U. (1976). *Cognition and reality: Principles and implications of cognitive psychology*. New York: Freeman.

Nhat Hanh, T. (1976). *The miracle of mindfulness: A manual on meditation* (Rev. ed.), Boston: Beacon.

Nhat Hanh, T. (1987). *Being peace*. Berkeley: Parallax.

Nhat Hanh, T. (1990). *Present moment, wonderful moment: Mindfulness verses for daily living*. Berkeley: Parallax.

Nhat Hanh, T. (1991). *Peace is every step: The path of mindfulness in everyday life*. New York: Bantam.

Oppenheim, G. (1990). *Who were you before you were you? The casebook of a past-life therapist*. New York: Carlton.

Ornstein, R. (1986). *Multimind: A new way of looking at human behavior*. New York: Doubleday.

Peterson, J. (1991). Hypnotic techniques recommended to assist in associating the dissociation in abreaction. Paper presented at Eighth International Conference on Multiple Personality/Dissociative States, Chicago, IL.

Peterson, J. (1992). Managing abreaction in the treatment of MPD. Workshop conducted at Fourth Annual Eastern Regional Conference on Abuse and Multiple Personality: Training in Treatment, Alexandria, VA.

Putnam, F. (1989). *Diagnosis and treatment of multiple personality disorder*. New York: Guilford.

Rainwater, J. (1979). *You're in charge: A guide to becoming your own therapist*. Los Angeles: Guild of Tutors Press.

Richards, D. (1990). Dissociation and transformation. *Journal of Humanistic Psychology, 30*(3), 54–83.

Rinsley, D. B. (1977). An object relations view of borderline personality. In P. Hartocollis (Ed.), *Borderline personality disorders*. New York: International Universities Press.

Ross, C. A. (1989). *Multiple personality disorder: Diagnosis, clinical features, and treatment*. New York: Wiley.

Ross, C. A., Norton, G. R., & Fraser, G. A. (1989). Evidence against the iatrogenesis of multiple personality disorder. *Dissociation, II*(2), 61–65.

Ross, C. A., Fast, E., Anderson, G., Auty, A., & Todd, J. (1990). Somatic symptoms in multiple sclerosis and MPD. *Dissociation, III*(2), 102–106.

Ross, C. A., & Anderson, F. (1990). Treatment techniques and interventions.

Workshop at Second Annual Eastern Regional Conference on Multiple Personality and Dissociation, Alexandria, VA.

Rossi, E., & Cheek, D. (1988). *Mind-body therapy*. New York: Norton.

Sachs, R. (1985). The adjunctive role of social support systems in the treatment of multiple personality disorder. In B. G. Braun (Ed.), *Treatment of multiple personality disorder*. Washington, DC: American Psychiatric Press, Inc.

Samuels, M. (1990). *Healing with the mind's eye*. New York: Summit.

Sanford, J. A. (1981). *Evil: The shadow side of reality*. New York: Crossroads.

Schaef, A. W. (1989). *Escape from intimacy: Untangling the "love" addictions: Sex, romance, relationships*. San Francisco: HarperCollins.

Schreiber, F. R. (1974). *Sybil*. New York: Warner.

Schwartz, J. (1982). *Letting go of stress*. New York: Pinnacle.

Schwartz, R. (1992). Rescuing the exiles. *Family Therapy Networker*, May/June, 33–37.

Selye, H. (1974). *Stress without distress*. New York: Signet.

Sheldrake, R. (1981). *A new science of life: The hypothesis of causative formation*. Los Angeles: Tarcher.

Sheldrake, R. (1991). *The rebirth of nature: The greening of science and God*. New York: Bantam.

Sliker, G. (1992). *Multiple mind: Healing the split in psyche and world*. Boston: Shambhala.

Stern, D. M. (1990). *Diary of a baby*. New York: Basic Books.

Stone, H., & Winkelman, S. (1989). *Embracing our selves: The voice dialogue manual*. San Rafael, CA: New World Library.

Storr, A. (1983). *The essential Jung*. Princeton, NJ: Princeton University Press.

Stroebel, C. F. (1982). *QR: The quieting reflex*. New York: Berkeley.

Thigpen, C. H., & Cleckley, H. (1957). *The three faces of Eve*. New York: McGraw-Hill.

Torem, M. (1989). Iatrogenic factors in the perpetuation of splitting and multiplicity. *Dissociation, II*(2), 92–98.

Van Derbur, M. (1991). *People Magazine*, June 10.

Watkins, J. G. (1971). The affect bridge: A hypnoanalytic technique. *International Journal of Clinical and Experimental Hypnosis, 19*, 21–27.

Watkins, J. G., & Watkins, H. H. (1979). Ego states and hidden observers. *Journal of Altered States of Consciousness, 5*, 3–18.

Watkins, J. G., & Watkins, H. H. (1988). The management of malevolent ego states in multiple personality disorder. *Dissociation, I*(1), 67–72.

Weber, R. (1986). *Dialogues with scientists and sages: The search for unity*. London: Routledge and Kegan Paul.

Wilber, K. (1991). Taking responsibility for your shadow. In J. Abrams & C. Zweig (Eds.), *Meeting the shadow: The hidden power of the dark side of human nature.* Los Angeles: Tarcher.

Woititz, J. (1985). *Struggle for intimacy.* Deerfield Beach, FL: Health Communications.

Woolger, R. J. (1988). *Other lives, other selves: A Jungian psychotherapist discovers past lives.* New York: Bantam.

Zohar, D. (1990). *The quantum self: Human nature and consciousness defined by the new physics.* New York: Morrow.

Index

For information about
prerecorded audiotapes, workshops and
professional training opportunities,
please write to:

Nancy J. Napier
Post Office Box 153
New York, New York 10024